Beyond Conformity or Rebellion

Beyond Conformity or Rebellion

Youth and Authority in America

Gary Schwartz

The University of Chicago Press
Chicago and London

GARY SCHWARTZ, an independent scholar, was formerly co-research director of the Institute for Juvenile Research. He is the author of *Sect Ideologies and Social Status*, also published by the University of Chicago Press, and of *Love and Commitment*.

Library of Congress Cataloging-in-Publication Data

Schwartz, Gary.
  Beyond conformity or rebellion.

  Bibliography: p.
  Includes index.
  1. Youth—United States. 2. Youth—Illinois.
  3. Intergenerational relations—United States.
  4. Intergenerational relations—Illinois. 5. Community.
  6. Authority. I. Title.
  HQ796.S4186 1987   305.2′35′0973   86-30801
  ISBN 0-226-74206-7

The University of Chicago Press, Chicago 60637
The University of Chicago Press, Ltd., London
© 1987 by The University of Chicago
All rights reserved. Published 1987
Printed in the United States of America

96 95 94 93 92 91 90 89 88 87   5 4 3 2 1

To the memory of Henry D. McKay

Contents

Preface

This book may be the last large-scale research report from the now defunct sociology department of the Institute for Juvenile Research. It may be too soon after the demise of the sociology department for those affected by it to assess the wisdom of those who decided that its time had come. This book, however, argues that the authority of the older generation ultimately rests on its ability to nurture the talents of the younger generation. As one of the "younger" beneficiaries of the intellectual vision of Clifford Shaw and Henry McKay, the leading figures of the sociology department, it would be unseemly not to comment briefly on the fate of the work of my forebearers.

James Bennett's *Oral History and Delinquency* (1981) provides an illuminating analysis of the development of this research on delinquency and youthful deviance. It is necessary only to add a few words about the circumstances surrounding the closing of the sociology department in order to give a final coda to this moment in the history of the social sciences.

The sociology department (later the research department) was part of the Institute for Juvenile Research, which was a free-standing child guidance clinic supported by the Department of Mental Health. However, the decisions of its administrators were deeply influenced by the department of psychiatry of a medical school with which it was presumably only tangentially affiliated through a training program for residents in psychiatry. As Bennett notes, the psychiatrists who controlled the funding of the sociology department were never comfortable with work that lacked medical legitimation. Ironically, it was a physician and psychiatrist, William Healy, who as the institute's first director noticed that his young patients' emotional difficulties could not be understood without knowledge about their social background. The idea that the cultural diversity of urban life was implicated in the ways in which young people got into trouble or behaved self-destructively supplied the impetus for the research associated with the Institute for Juvenile Research for more than forty years.

By the time the sociology department closed its doors, the life of the communities in which young people grow up were of interest to psychiatrists as bits of information contained in a patient's social history. The outlook of those who determined the fate of the sociology department had come full circle. They felt no need to look beyond the consulting room to understand the difficulties of the young people they were authorized to assist.

In retrospect, one is tempted to characterize the decision to close the sociology department as something less than a noble gesture. I prefer to think that it was a minor miracle that this kind of independent research tradition could have flourished for so long in spite of the vocational orientation of those who ultimately controlled its destiny.

This project required the cooperation of many people. It was generously supported by a grant from the Law Enforcement Assistance Administration (grant no. 77-JN-99-0055). Dr. James Howell was a very understanding grant monitor. He helped us through a difficult period of reorganization when one of the principal investigators left the project to take a job at a university. Emil Peluso and the late Joe Puntil made our efforts to establish research sites into an enlightening and pleasurable process. In addition, Puntil took the responsibility for the day-to-day administration of the grant.

For a number of years after the field data had been collected and provisionally organized, Ms. Fran Behan was the only person besides myself who was interested in bringing the project to completion. Without her encouragement and assistance, I might have given up the enterprise. Dr. Frank Rafferty, former director of the institute, was supportive of research on youth, in general, and of this project, in particular.

Dr. Michael Ducey was an active partner through the planning, fieldwork, and preliminary analysis of the data. Our discussions and even our disagreements had an invigorating effect upon the project. The role of the fieldworkers is evident in each chapter. We were fortunate to have recruited a talented group of people. Much of the substance of this book is based on the observations of Charles Michaelak, Paul Harder, Mal Lambert, Richard Vision, Ruth Horowitz, and Peter Langer. Drs. Horowitz and Langer used their field material for doctoral dissertations in sociology at the University of Chicago. Dr. Horowitz's dissertation was published as a monograph entitled *Honor and the American Dream* (1983).

My colleague and friend, Dr. Merten Krause, with whom I had the singular pleasure of serving as co–research director of the Institute for Juvenile Research, was the research director at the time when the LEAA study included a very detailed survey of youth. When the principal investigator on the survey side of the project left the institute, Dr. Krause, on his own initiative, took the responsibility for pulling together the data from a statewide sample into a comprehensive monograph. The result was an as yet unpublished study, "Delinquency and the Adolescent Predicament," which is theoretically imaginative and methodologically innovative.

Professors Peter Manning and Hanan Selvin were perceptive readers of an early draft of this manuscript. Professor Howard Becker also read part of an earlier draft of the manuscript and gave helpful advice. Professors James F. Short, Jr., and Robert J. Bursik, Jr., provided detailed critiques of the manuscript which greatly improved it. I am indebted to both of them for their criticism and suggestions. To my colleague and friend, Dr. Don Merten, I owe virtually everything I know about youth and much of what I know about life. Whatever merit this book may have is largely the result of what I have learned from conversations with him.

I would also like to thank Don Merten and Bob Bursik for allowing me to take time from our current project in order to work on the revisions of this manuscript. This slowed down our progress on an NIMH-funded longitudinal study of early adolescent development and deviance that has both an ethnographic and survey component. While the data for this study were collected while we were at the Institute for Juvenile Research, the sociology department closed before the material could be analyzed, and the work has continued under other institutional sponsorship. I am particularly grateful to Bob Bursik for showing me that the kind of insight into social reality that I once associated with qualitative research is also possessed by those who prefer quantitative methods. I regret not being able to show him that the reverse is also true. Finally, I would like to thank Ms. Katie Roebuck for typing this manuscript.

1

Introduction

Looking Back

Youth occupied center stage in American society in the late 1960s.[1] Although protests against unpopular wars and urban riots were not new features of the American political landscape, in the past youthful dissent generally came from the margins of society.[2] Beatnicks, Hell's Angels, and ghetto youth were familiar figures of rebellion against the mores of conventional society. What was new about the counterculture was that it recruited the most privileged sectors of the younger generation.[3] The spirit of opposition found its most forceful expression on college campuses and even touched high schools (see Libarle and Seligson 1970).

Many adults were shocked by the sight of college students spitting on the flag and taunting the police. This contempt for patriotism and authority was something most adults could not understand. It seemed like these students were throwing away their future in order to settle a grudge with an embattled president.

1. Gillis (1974) points out that since the industrial revolution working-class youth who are not in school are less responsive to adult direction than their more privileged counterparts. This does not mean that students have always been docile. Kett (1977) observes that college students in antebellum America often were rowdy and rebellious. He concludes that it was not until the invention of the concept of the adolescent as an immature person that adults perceived students as tractable.

2. The image of rebellious youth as a marginal person is developed in two studies of youthful resistance to being incorporated into conventional society. See Berger (1963b) and Matza (1961).

3. Spender (1969) points out that much of the student animus against the administration of Columbia University concerned the style in which official business was conducted. These students refused to accept a separation between personal values and public policies, and they demanded, in effect, an ethic of personal responsibility for institutional decisions. Flacks (1970) stresses the continuity between the liberal, middle-class family backgrounds of student activists and their humanistic orientation and ethical sensibilities.

Disturbances on college campuses were not confined to the war. Students challenged the right of universities to work hand in hand with government agencies and large corporations. They questioned the way in which institutions of higher learning were governed. Why, students asked, were university policies formulated without the consent of its largest constituency, the student body?

Some adults feared that youthful antinomianism would undermine the work ethic.[4] Young people were experimenting with altered states of consciousness and casual sex. They were joining communes, religious cults, and radical political movements, and, in general, turning their backs on the values of achievement, productivity, and success.[5] Commentators on the youth scene wondered whether this was a generation of well-educated misfits who would not hold jobs, rear families, or vote in elections.[6]

Of course, all of this is past history. After the campus rebellions subsided and students began to worry about their grades, the youth scene seemed to return to normal.[7] Drugs, blue jeans, rock and roll, and sexual precocity appeared to be all that remained of the cultural ferment of the 1960s. What was proclaimed as a youthful movement to liberate Americans from an overly materialistic culture seemed to have left the younger generation with somewhat greater freedom from the preoccupations of respectable, middle-class society.

Before concluding that the 1960s left youth culture essentially unchanged, we should examine how we ordinarily think about young people. We are accustomed to thinking about the relationship of youth to society in dichotomous terms. Either a youthful revolution is on the horizon, or young people are quietly going along with

4. This fear of affluent youth falling prey to a seductively hedonistic way of life is nicely captured in the title of Nicholas Von Hoffman's (1968) account of Haight-Ashbury, *We Are the People Our Parents Warned Us Against*. See Partridge (1973) for an ethnographic description of the "hippie ghetto."

5. See Roszak (1968) for an influential justification for turning away from the materialistic preoccupations of our society.

6. See Pitts (1971) for attack on what the author sees as the self-indulgence and self-deception of the counterculture, and Brown (1969) for a defense of hippies against the agencies of social control.

7. In an astute analysis of the hippie movement, Davis (1971) remarks that this youthful "enclave" is not likely to be locked in a continuous struggle with defenders of conventional norms. Nonconformist youth subcultures need not be either completely "for" or "against" the dominant culture. This book shows how much of the cultural innovation of the 1960s has been reworked into stable forms of adolescent sociability in the 1970s. While the freak culture of the 1970s could hardly subvert adult authority, it nevertheless created a social milieu in which young people experienced ways of relating to each other that are not always congruent with the values of youth-socializing institutions.

the program. This leaves young people with two options: overt rebellion, or passive conformity.

On reflection, however, this is rather simplistic. There is considerable room for maneuver between unyielding resistance and compliant acquiescence to authority. Youth, like all others, are capable of evading some rules, accommodating themselves to others, and subverting yet others when it suits their purposes.

Thinking of youth in terms of apocalyptic images of revolutionary upheaval obscures significant changes in youth culture. Except under special historical circumstances, youth do not have the political power, economic resources, or organizational knowledge to alter the institutional structure of society. This does not mean, however, that changes in youth culture have no bearing upon the viability of the larger culture. The ways in which young people organize their lives and give meaning to their activities reveals a great deal about the integrity of the culture's ideals and values.

What we will find in this study of high school–aged youth in the early 1970s is that the heritage of the 1960s influenced the succeeding generation. But what we will discover about youth culture in the 1970s will not live up to the expectations of either cultural radicals or conservatives.

For conservatives, the youth culture of the 1960s was a bad dream. From their point of view, this outburst of irrationality is better forgotten now that most young people realize that there is no realistic alternative to going to school and getting a job. For radicals, the youth culture of the 1960s was a golden age. They believe that young people will rise again to build a more humane society.

The actual situation of youth is more fluid and ambiguous than either the conservative or radical position would suggest. Youth are not ready to endorse conventional morals with the enthusiasm that would please cultural conservatives. On the other hand, most youth are not ready to abandon the idea of making out in a competitive society.

What is significant for the culture at large is going on within the youth culture. The ways in which young people define themselves in relation to their peers and adult authorities illuminates as much about the conflicts implicit in their parents' aspirations as it does about the meaning of youth culture identities and styles. Instead of thinking of youth as a force for conserving or changing societal institutions, we shall look at them as people who are working their way through tensions that exist in the environing culture.

It would be easy to misinterpret the contrast between youth who cast themselves in the role as actors in the political arena or as crit-

ics of burgeois culture (see Laqueur 1962) and youth whose experience rarely transcends the compass of their personal relationships
and private affairs. We think of the former as cosmopolitans who
are demonstrably responsive to the issues of the day that form the
experiential basis of a generational perspective (see Mannheim
1952). And, I believe, we tend to think of the latter as provincials
who, lacking a genuine historical consciousness, do not demand to
be heard unless the problems of the time directly touch their vital
interests. There is undoubtedly some truth to the notion that cosmopolitan youth are more visibly involved in the political struggles
and cultural debates of the day. However, the implication that cosmopolitan youth are active agents and provincial youth are passive
agents in the conservation or transformation of the common culture
misses the essential historical point.

It may well be true that the youth movements of the 1960s, as
social historians (see Starr 1985) claim, broadened participation in
the important social issues of the time such as civil rights and gave
new depth to traditional American commitment to cultural pluralism and ideological diversity. But it would be a mistake to overlook the reason why we think of the 1960s as a *cultural* watershed in
contemporary American history. Young people no longer accepted
the standard interpretations of the aesthetic, moral, interpersonal,
and gender categories which adults believed were the natural and
necessary foundation of a rational and orderly existence. In a sometimes perverse, sometimes playful manner, youth culture inverted
their meanings. It treated what adults thought of as ugly as beautiful, as crude as refined, as effeminate as manly, as erotic as mat-
ter-of-fact, etc.

One of the casualties of this process is the distinction between
provincials and cosmopolitans. It is no longer safe to assume that
the connotation of location near to the center of the national culture,
high status, and concern with important matters are uniformly associated with cosmopolitanism. Correlatively, we cannot assume that location at the periphery of the larger culture, low status, and concern
with inconsequential matters are associated with provincialism.

The youth culture of the 1960s, therefore, has undermined the
notion that the "best and the brightest" of the younger generation
would instinctively gravitate toward centers of cosmopolitan values
(e.g., large cities, elite universities). Orientations that stress the
local, rural, nonsophisticated, nonintellectual, and so on are given
equal cultural parity even by many youth who adopt a more conspic-
uously cosmopolitan mode of living. Thus, the principal theme of
this book—that youth culture must be understood in light of how

broader cultural issues are given specific meaning in the context of local events and institutions—should not be read as an argument for or against provincialism. Rather, this analysis should help us transcend the limits of these constructs and to see youthful involvements and activities as part of the process by which adults and young people jointly construct the moral and social fabric of the common culture.

Before trying to characterize youth culture in the 1970s, we must point out that any global characterization is bound to be somewhat misleading. In fact, one of the major points of this book is that the situation of high school–aged youth reflects the considerable diversity of the culture of local communities. Yet there is one change in youth culture that seems to transcend the varied situations of youth in different communities. This refers to the emergence of a new sort of cultural pluralism within the peer-group world. The hallmark of this change is what people call "freak culture" or the "hippy lifestyle."

In the past, youth culture revolved around the contrast between youth who accepted or rejected adult authority. The former listened respectfully to adult authorities or, at the very least, did not tell them to mind their own business. Young people who exemplified this posture were often called "socies" (see Schwartz and Merten 1967, 1968).[8] As Larkin (1979) remarks, the "jocks" and the cheerleaders, the student council crowd, the "brains," and the "quiet, ordinary students" are still very much in evidence.[9]

8. In a book that treats "socialites" and "greasers" as the two dominant youth styles, the Schwendingers (1985) hardly mention the "freak" identity although they certainly are not unaware of the influence of drugs in contemporary youth culture. They describe what they see as evidence of "socialite" duplicity and callousness as a strong disposition to engage in certain kinds of delinquency. While the "socialite" style does not preclude garden variety delinquency, the sort of moral opportunism and indifference that offends the Schwendingers ought not to be confused with behavior that violates the law. Although I think the description of the "socialite" suffers from ideological distortion, it is a mistake in principle to confuse immorality with crime. For a very different view of the socialite style, see Schwartz and Merten (1980).

9. While all of these youthful social identities differ from each other, they share the same commitment to living within the boundaries established by adult authority. By way of contrast, a refusal to defer to authority has led many British students of youth culture to emphasize the political significance of rebelliousness among working-class youth. Brake (1980) and Hall and Jefferson (1976) emphasize the connections between a sense of injustice among these youth and the symbolic content of youth culture. There is very little evidence of similar ideological developments in the United States. Not only is class-consciousness among working-class youth rare but, as Cusik (1973) notes, American high school students show little interest in others who are not directly involved in their own friendship networks.

Young people who cultivate the art of standing up to adult authority are also very much part of the youth scene. Youth who are known as "greasers" or "badasses" give teachers a hard time, intimidate less aggressive students, and occasionally confront the representatives of law and order.[10] It has not gone unnoticed that this sort of antagonism to adult authority is associated with these youths' position in the class structure of the community (see Hollingshead 1949) and their perceptions of the probable fate in the economic system (see Stinchcombe 1964).

What makes the "freak" or "hippy" different from either of these two traditional stances toward adult authority is that this style treats the issue of compliance with the rules with indifference. This book can be read as a description of a new sort of "deviance" within youth culture,[11] deviance that is not defined by persistent violations of the law as much as it is by disinterest in the "classic" image of success.

Deviance

It is almost impossible to discuss the notion of deviance without taking sides in the controversy about the ontological status of the

10. It is common to confuse what many adults experience as irrational truculence—a seemingly excessive readiness to engage in personal confrontations with peers—and a code of honor, moral autonomy, and loyalty to friends. For an extended analysis of this ethic and its roots in working-class culture, see Schwartz (1972).

11. The image surrounding deviance emphasizes situations in which there is conflict between those who define the behavior as illegal, inappropriate, or abnormal and those who would evade, resist, or avoid these potentially stigmatizing allegations. Thus, implicit in this conception of deviance is the notion that someone has done something that is wrong, indefensible, or, in its least conflictual form, mistaken (e.g., a child eating with its fingers at the dinner table). This work has been extended by Matza's (1964) concepts of "drift" in which the actor's sense of the exigencies of the situation frees him temporarily from the grip of the rules, and "ban" (1969) in which an actor experiences the coercive effect of the power of the state to set him beyond the bounds of propriety. This approach does not encompass nonconflictual modes of turning away from the rules and of neutralizing the moral power of the values that justify the rules. In other words, it is possible to obey the rules and still engage in deviance as long as the pattern of one's life and the meaning one give to one's activities and relationships symbolizes (i.e., is collectively interpreted as) disinterest in or disaffiliation from those beliefs and values that legitimate the rules. Students of religious movements are familiar with this sort of deviance in which the members of a group obey all of the rules and yet turn decisively away from the cultural orientations that justify these rules (See Schwartz 1970, chap. 1). If we were to characterize the form of deviance with which this book is primarily concerned, we would call it symbolic or cultural deviance, that is, deviance with respect to commitment to beliefs and values the larger society accepts as an authoritative model for everyday activities and relationships.

deviant act (see Gove 1975). As the issue is currently phrased, Does deviance exist in the eye of the beholder, or is it an objective property of a class of real events?[12] To say that it must be both will inflame passions on both sides of the debate. They seem to agree on one point. Either definitions of deviance are grounded in culturally and situationally variable notions of right and wrong, or there are certain acts that are universally and justifiably regarded as antithetical to any rational conception of social order.

The social constructionists examine the ways in which a person accepts, rejects, or evades negative assessments of his behavior which transgresses other peoples' sense of what is appropriate or proper. This has led to a rich sense of the intentionality of the deviant act. They show how a person's consciousness of his deviance arises out of how he interprets the significance others impute to behavior that initially may have had ambiguous or confused meanings for the actor (see Matza 1969).

The proponents of the objective view stress the irreversible material and moral consequences of deviant actions. They ground the concept of deviance in individual responsibility for one's actions. From this point of view, the social constructionist seems to overlook the fact that there is a difference between law-abiding and law-violative behavior. Moreover, the social constructionist does not give a coherent account of the difference between relatively minor acts of deviance and serious violations of the law (see Hirschi 1975).

It is odd that no one seems to have remarked that each of the contending parties rests its case on a presupposition associated with the position of its antagonist. The social constructionists argue for a strict social determination of the meaning of the deviant act whereas the objectivists champion the idea of a moral will that is not the creature of social constraints and pressures. The constructionists

---

12. Howard Becker's (1963:9, original emphasis) statement that *"social groups create deviance by making the rules whose infraction constitutes deviance, and by applying those rules to particular people and labeling them as outsiders. From this point of view, deviance is not a quality of the act the person commits, but rather a consequence of the application by others of rules and sanctions to an 'offender,'"* crystallized the debate about the nature of deviance. The suggestion that deviance is not an immanent property of an act identifiable by all normatively competent individuals seemed to go beyond the bounds of moderate cultural relativism. In the eyes of sociological objectivists, Becker was proposing the sort of infinite regress associated with the most extreme forms of subjectivism, that is, how the persons who witness an event interpret its meaning determines all of its sociologically relevant features. As they interpreted Becker, he was saying that, *whatever* meaning the sociologist or his informants give to an action or activity, there is no invariant, external, universal normative grid against which its local significance can be evaluated.

claim that in the final analysis the actor's perception of the probity of his conduct depends on the vagaries of the situation in which it occurs. Seen this way, the actor lacks the ability to make a judgment about the moral validity of his conduct that transcends his social milieu.

Objectivists resist the insinuation that intentionality can be divorced from a moral will that can recognize right and wrong and can act in terms of that knowledge. They believe that the reason we can hold people responsible for their behavior before the bar of law is that moral consciousness is an integral component of our nature as social beings. The ability to choose that which is right or wrong is in its very essence the power that enables us to create and maintain a viable social order.

In a discussion of similar issues, Hegel (1975:251) remarks that it is a "striking modern innovation to inquire continually about the motives of men's actions. . . . Nowadays we insist on looking into men's hearts and so we presuppose a gulf between the objectivity of actions and their inner side, the subjective motives." Hegel observes that there is a danger in thinking of crime as something that is distinguished by positive characteristics rather than as an act that negates the will of the other by refusing to recognize the universality of the law as right. The judgment that an act is deviant depends upon the subjective intentions of the actor (otherwise how could one distinguish between an accidental killing and murder?) and the real consequences of the deed itself. But, as we learned from the previous discussion, we need a third term that will mediate the opposition between subjective intentions and objective consequences.

Hegel speaks, I believe, of the universal law or norm which takes the intention and the objective properties of a deviant act into consideration by examining the circumstances that invariably shape the meaning (or sanction) associated with acts of this type. In order to grasp the universal significance of the act itself we must be able to recognize those particular features of the deed that allow us to classify it as belonging to this or that category of deviant behavior. This rather theoretical analysis is relevant because the concept of authority grounds the deviant act in a construct that serves in the Hegelian sense of a universal norm.

Authority resides in judgments of actions that take account of the bearing of particular circumstances on the intentions of the actors insofar as they are relevant to a shared image of what is fair, just, or reasonable.

It may seem that proposing authority qua fairness is a legalistic

approach to deviance. Once the concept of authority has the connotations of the arbitrary exercise of power removed, however, it
becomes apparent that those who claim the right to make authoritative judgments are sensitive to local conceptions of what is
equitable. Although Short and Strodbeck (1965:195) do not use the
term "authority," their description of black, inner-city delinquent
gangs shows that leaders make decisions in terms of a finely tuned
sense of what is reasonable to ask of others under unpredictable
circumstances:

> Leaders we have observed are cautious not to exercise lead-
> ership arbitrarily, and often overtly disavow that they lead the
> gangs. The percentage of total activities that are formally orga-
> nized is low, and leaders are, in general, very careful to obtain
> clearance from other high status group members before staking
> their prestige on a given course of action. . . . Among conflict
> gangs the leaders are known to have the capacity to function
> aggressively against other members when necessary to main-
> tain their dominance, but the overwhelming preponderance of
> their actions is co-ordinating and nurturant.

Six Communities

In this book we will compare youth groups in six communities[13]
located in a midwestern agricultural and industrial state: Ribley is a
small town in the economically depressed, coal-mining region of the
state; Patusa is a small town in the rich agricultural belt of the state;

13. The names of these communities as well as of all persons, groups, and institutions (such as names of schools) are pseudonyms. There is a vast literature on the
definition of the community. Various authors emphasize ecological and territorial
criteria, residential propinquity and social interaction, common institutions, shared
economic and political interests, shared goals and values, and even similar perceptions of physical and geographic boundaries (see Hunter 1974). König (1968) notes
that, while functional specialization, social conflicts, and economic stratification are
evident in community life, it is possible to conceive of the local community as the
"totality" of all social relationships that arise out of common habitation. This form of
social life, although it is bounded and, in part, determined by larger social units such
as the state, has its own individuality. He says that "although it is true that the
community is typical of a more comprehensive culture (i.e., microcosm in the appropriate macrocosm) it is at the same time a specific microculture with its own individuality and its own traditions" (p. 48). He observes that the sense of the community
as "home" creates a symbolically coherent entity in its members' minds. Gusfield
(1975) puts a similar emphasis on the sense of belonging. For the purposes of this
book, we can say that community is the place young people recognize as "home" and
where their relationships with one another and with adults is informed by the meanings they give to their involvements in local institutions.

Parsons Park is an urban, ethnic working-class community; Cambridge is a suburban working-class community; 32d Street is a Mexican inner-city community; Glenbar is an affluent suburban community.

In passing, we should note that we did not select these communities on the basis of the usual sort of variations in the demographic characteristics of localities. To our knowledge, there is no empirical analysis of the relationships between cultural features of local communities and demographic variables. Thus, there is no way in advance of actually studying a particular community that one could predict how the age distribution of the local population, for example, would affect community culture.

We chose communities on the basis of general features such as location (urban, suburban, rural), class composition (working and middle class), and ethnic composition (Eastern European and Mexican American). This selection hardly exhausts the universe of potentially significant differences between local communities. On the other hand, there is nothing about the culture of the communities described in this book that might lead one to conclude that they are fundamentally different from similar types of communities elsewhere.

The culture of the local community defines both the degree to which particular communities are comparable and the nature of the comparisons between them. Each of the comparisons deals with two communities whose cultures reflect different resolutions of similar issues. Ribley and Patusa are small towns where the issue is whether troublesome youth are protected by or extruded from the community. Parsons Park and Cambridge are working-class communities where the issue is between loyalty to local traditions and social mobility. Glenbar is an affluent suburb, and 32d Street is a relatively poor inner-city neighborhood. Yet the issue for this unlikely pair of communities is not essentially dissimilar. In both communities, there is a powerful tension between the reality of the American dream of success and investment in the expressive satisfactions of peer group sociability.

This book pays attention to an aspect of American life that is often ignored by problem-specific studies of communities. Local communities, as novelists have long realized, tend to develop distinctive moral climates. The ways in which local groups and institutions handle the problems of everyday life are guided by community traditions, that is, by norms and values that make sense in light of what is going on in the community.

What This Study Is Not

Before discussing the concept of community culture, we must digress. There is an element of the conventional format of a social science research report notable by its absence in this book. Although there is a discussion in the Appendix of some of the problems we encountered in the fieldwork, we provide no methodological rationale for the scientific validity of the data presented in this study.

The reason for this omission is that many of the social sciences are closer to history than to a nomothetic science like physics. In fact, I would argue that ethnography is a branch of history, although a rather special one. Histories differ from other genre in the field of human studies because they tell a story. As Hayden White (1973, 1978) points out, narrative is the sine qua non of history. A history is comprised of a cast of characters and a plot. Something must happen to someone. That event, in turn, must affect other persons as they experience its repercussions as their lives unfold over time.

Most readers of ethnography would admit that this genre has an analogous form. The plots of ethnographies rarely are linear. Yet their dramatic effect is created by the reader's engagement in the everyday lives of human beings whose actions have consequences for other people. Institutions and groups are not static abstractions in ethnographic studies. They impose a teleology on what otherwise might seem like a formless series of fortunate and unfortunate occurrences. Because they pursue their own interests, institutions and groups often limit the actions of the main cast of characters. Not unlike the chorus in a Greek tragedy, they remind the actor that his destiny is never something that is entirely of his own making.

Unlike other narrative forms, ethnographic plots do not revolve around how things "turn out" for the characters who engage our interest. Only in exceptional cases can an ethnography be said to culminate in a denoument which can be characterized in terms we apply to individual lives, for example, as tragic. Ethnographic plots lead us to make qualitative judgments about the character of an entire social world. It is not so much a particular state of affairs that moves us in ethnography such as the death or incarceration of a sympathetic character. Rather, it is these sorts of events that enable us to conceive of how it would be to think and feel if the issues that command the deepest sense of our being somehow were transposed to another plane of existence.

It is customary in methodological discussions to link the problem of how one derives the data to the question of what one is trying to explain. This induces us to conceive of the phenomena as the material substratum from which one uncovers empirical regularities. These recurrent and homogeneous events form the factual basis against which predictions derived from deductively generated hypotheses can be tested. By their very nature as historically constituted phenomena, ethnographic data do not fit this mold. However, one should not infer that ethnographic explanations are simply ad hoc.

White's (1973) suggestion that different kinds of historical analysis are rooted in incommensurable figures will help us understand the nature of ethnographic explanation. As a very general poetic device, these figures selectively organize the raw material of innumerable (and practically inexhaustible) human events into intelligible patterns of discourse and action. In ethnography as well, the author's choice of an organizing image determines what kind of explanation of relationships between events the reader will encounter.

We need to contrast only two of the figures White discusses to reveal the kind of explanation that one can expect to find in this book. And, equally important, the distinction between these two figures will disclose what sort of ethnography this book is not.

White (1973:35) refers to the first as the figure of metonomy. It casts human events and relationships in a part-to-part context where the primary intent of the figure is to reduce "one of the parts to the status of an aspect or function of the other." Incidentally, thinking of how casual relationships are given symbolic form in historical studies does not imply that notions of causation are themselves merely figures of speech. Nor does the idea of metonomy as such discriminate, as Collingwood (1972) points out, between the principal ways in which this concept can be deployed: as something that is produced by the deliberate decision of an agent, as something whose prevention or production is thought to nullify or produce the "cause" associated with this state of affairs, as something whose existence is the necessary consequence (in the sense of logical implication) of something else such that if the latter exists so will the former.

In the social sciences, metonomy is the idiom of causal explanation in all three of the above senses. Looked at in these terms, one might ask whether the phenomena under consideration in this book—the nature of community culture and authority, relations between youth and adults, and patterns of deviance—can be explained as the product of certain casual forces or agents. For example, one might identify social structure, the economic situation of the region, the local mechanisms of social control, and so on as candidates for this sort of explanation. While it would be perfectly legitimate to explain the data in these terms, this is what this ethnography is not.

White points out that synechdoche treats distinctions between parts and the whole as provisional because the part, in a representative sense, is the whole. It exemplifies those qualities and discloses those relationships that makes the whole apprehensible. White (1973:34) says that "with synechdoche . . . a phenomenon can be characterized by using the part to symbolize some *quality* presumed to inhere in the totality," and he observes that the microcosm/macrocosm contrast is the organizing principle of this figure.

Thus, the kind of explanation the reader will encounter in this book should draw seemingly disparate things together. Of course, studies of the relationship of youth groups to authority cannot completely constitute the totality of the life of a community. But there is an advantage to the selective nature of this approach. It intensifies our perceptions of certain features of community that otherwise would go unnoticed. And most important, this account should let one see the whole without losing sight of the significance of the parts.

Community Culture

This book examines the relationship between the styles and identities of youth groups in particular communities and the norms that shape the policies of youth-serving institutions. This is a book about the relationship between youth and authority. Here we think of authority as more than the power to enforce the rules. Authority also involves the values that legitimate the rules both in the eyes of those who make and who obey them. Thus, the book focuses on the ways in which youth groups accept, ignore, redefine, or reject the rules of local institutions. That is, why youth feel that is reasonable or unreasonable, fair or inequitable or stupid or smart to go along with authority.

The ways in which local authorities selectively define, interpret, and apply the rules reflect that community's conception of what is good, desirable, or necessary for youth. The values that support the policies of youth-serving institutions and the norms that are enforced by local authorities refer to what we call community culture. Admittedly, this is a selective view of the culture of local communities.

The reason for drawing these boundaries around the notion of community culture is, in part, methodological and, in part, theoretical. In this book, the reader understands the meaning of youth contacts with local institutions largely through the experience of young people. The fieldwork on which these studies are based was done primarily within the confines of the peer-group world. Therefore, the fieldworker learned to see local events from the youth's perspective. A study of youth from the perspective of teachers, policemen, ministers, youth workers, and other adult authorities undoubtedly would yield a quite different picture of community culture. One could study the normative structure of local institutions, for example, by examining the school principal's interaction with the school board or the youth officer's involvements with city officials. However, there is little information about the political culture of local institutions in this book that does not bear directly on the nature of the relationship between youth and authority.

At the theoretical level, the notion of community culture runs against the grain of current sociological images of how the social diversity of American life affects primary group relationships. Americans are physically mobile; people rarely spend their entire lives in one place. Local communities are stratified by race, class, and ethnicity. Conflict and disagreement are as likely as harmony and consensus. Finally, communities are sometimes little more than a collection of residential and other functionally differentiated geographical areas.

It is easy to conclude that communities play a relatively peripheral role in shaping social relationships that constitute the core of a person's sense of self. Work, religion, politics, and similar concerns that go to the heart of a person's conception of his identity often transcend the confines of community.[14]

The writing of the "new Chicago school" takes this stance toward the significance of community in a pluralistic and urbanized society. When Janowitz (1961) speaks of the "community of limited liability," the image is of the contractual and contingent character of people's involvement in the local community. In fact, community is defined by the instrumental nature of its functions rather than by the significance of the ideas and values that inform the operations of local institutions.

The thesis that there is very little in the way of moral integration in the life of modern communities runs through the work of Suttles (1972). He argues that community is a creature of precisely those

14. The idea that the autonomy of the local community is being progressively eroded by larger forms of social and economic organization and is losing its capacity to shape social relationships is prominent in the work of Roland Warren (1972).

needs that cannot be met by larger and more efficient forms of economic organization and public administration. Consequently, the meaning of community is restricted to how well it, for example, satisfies its members' desire for safety in public spaces.

We have no quarrel with this conception of community except to say that it does not apply to the situation of young people. Regardless of how minimally the culture of the local community may affect the lives of adults, the policies of local institutions have a substantial impact on young people. We tend to forget that young people rarely choose where they will grow up. The local community is the place where most of them go to school, form friendships, find things to do in their spare time, and, more generally, explore ways of defining themselves in relation to the world outside of their families.

As far as local institutions are concerned, young people are a captive audience. Of course, they can transfer schools, drop out, leave home, or otherwise escape a punishing or inhospitable environment. But, for the most part, young peoples' contact with authority outside of the family comes through their relationship to local institutions. In this context, young people learn that how they are treated is intimately connected to the kind of person authorities see them as being.

It is misleading to describe this process as if it occurs primarily between individuals and representatives of authority. Relationships between youth and local institutions are mediated by a powerful form of primary group affiliation—the peer group. It is in the company of others who a young person sees as being in much the same situation as oneself that the peer group becomes something more than a source of friendship and emotional support outside of the home. It is the means by which a young person can express his feelings about where he fits into the institutional life of the community.

The idea of community culture recognizes that social differentiation in the larger society influences how local institutions deal with youth groups. The policies of local institutions are fashioned with an eye toward the meaning of a person's or group's status in the larger society. Nowhere, for example, is being lower class and black perceived by local authorities as prestigious. Yet, by the same token, no societal status is a completely reliable guide to how a young person will be treated by local authorities.

The meaning of these distinctions between categories of persons in the larger society is partially transformed by the culture of local communities. Local concerns and traditions shape the way in which authorities perceive and respond to different kinds of youth groups. Looked at somewhat differently, the policies of local institutions selectively emphasize certain values and norms of the larger society. The issue for local authorities is not whether how they implement these values and norms is consistent with general cultural mandates. Rather, local authorities are sensitive to whether their institutions fit harmoniously into the local culture.

The concept of community culture is analogous to variations on a musical theme. We are not thinking of simple melodic transformations on a stable harmonic structure. Instead, we imagine something like polyphony where the counterpoint between local concerns and traditions and societal norms and values creates a sense of inner tension and richness. The way in which this cultural material is developed and resolved in the institutional life of the local community incorporates and reflects the normative and structural conflicts within the larger society. Community culture rests, therefore, on a precarious dialectic with the larger society. Changes in local priorities or national ideologies can alter the configuration of cultural elements that identify the culture of local communities.

Youth Subcultures

At first glance, the concept of a subculture does not seem problematic. In common usage, subcultures refer to groups of people who are out of step with the larger society. Yinger (1960:628) says that subcultures are distinguished by "norms that set a group apart from, not those that integrate a group with, the total society."

This concept of a subculture assumes that the larger society has a coherent set of norms and, moreover, that these norms shape the policies of societal institutions. Viewed this way, the meaning of societal norms is unambiguous. Institutional authorities agree about what they ought to do and why these things are worth doing. The problem is finding the best means to these consensually validated ends.

This conception of subcultures rests upon a fairly simplistic image of the culture of the larger society. There is little evidence that shows that presumably common values either mean the same thing to different groups of people (see Miller 1969), or that groups who agree about the meaning of these values pursue them in compatible ways. Nor is there any basis for assuming that such values such as economic success have a direct, unequivocal bearing on the norms of diverse institutions. Educators, for example, may say that school ought to prepare young people to make a living. But there is enormous variability in the way this vague objective is translated into practice.

Finally, this image of the larger society overlooks the fact that the groups who define and enforce societal norms are usually more responsive to the interests of their own constituencies than they are to general cultural directives. It is true that institutional authorities invoke societal norms and values to explain and defend their policies. Commencement Day addresses attest to that. But the rules that govern how people go about their business are framed with less abstruse considerations in mind. There is considerable room for the interpretation of the meaning of societal norms, and there is no single, unambiguous standard for evaluating whether specific institutional practices conform to these norms.

Yinger's definition does not stipulate that subcultures must oppose societal norms. Yet the picture here is of subcultures as a force that moves people toward the margins of mainstream culture (see Schwartz 1972). We use the concept of a subculture in a more catholic fashion. It encompasses the cultural differences which distinguish the groups and strata that comprise a pluralistic society. Using the term this way, one can speak as legitimately of the subculture of investment bankers as of inner-city delinquents.

There has been considerable confusion about what makes the attitudes and activities of youth subcultural. Part of the problem lies in a failure to discriminate between the social structural origins of a subculture and the cultural significance of its styles and identities. The other source of difficulty comes from thinking of a subculture as a group defined by certain membership criteria.

As Miller (1971) points out, subcultures are formed when age, class, race, and similar social structural factors create easily recognizable statuses in the larger society. People who occupy such statuses often have common interests, activities, and experiences. According to Miller (1971:114), this status "serve(s) as a basis for identification and allegiance." Subcultural traditions that are handed from generation to generation account for many of the behavioral differences between socially distinct segments of the larger society.

Although Miller explains how subcultures are formed, social structural theories tell us little about the content of subcultural traditions. Why do certain styles and identities characterize a particular subculture? What meaning do these styles and identities have for the persons who adopt them? How are they elaborated and changed by the people who participate in a subculture? These questions shift the emphasis to the specifically cultural aspect of the concept of a subculture.

Subcultures are cultural phenomena in the sense that they arise out of the way in which people give symbolic significance to shared experiences, activities, and interests. Yet subcultures are more than a shared interpretation of a common situation. Subcultures are symbolic modes of relating to others (i.e., styles of dress, demeanor, and speech) and of representing the self (i.e., one's identity) which have definite moral and aesthetic meanings. Subcultures, therefore, revolve around the symbolic meaning of stylized presentations of self and around the meaning that these performances have for a person's image of what makes him or her a distinctive kind of human being. In his discussion of life-styles in an urban ghetto, Rainwater (1970:381) captures the symbolic importance of stylized representations of self: "[I]n the development of the dramatic self, the whole emphasis is on *qualities*, on what a person *is* by virtue of his actions rather than what he *does*."

We can see now why subcultures are not groups to which a person belongs. One can be immersed in, committed to, or intrigued by a subculture. One adopts the styles and identities associated with a subculture, or one does not.

This is not to say, however, that subcultures exist without group interaction. It is obvious that subcultures can flourish only when the symbolic representations of one's identity are understood and appreciated by others. Nor should the concept of a subculture imply that participation is equivalent to an all-absorbing passion. Experimentation with subcultural styles and identities can be a passing fancy. The importance of a subcultural identity depends upon the extent to which one feels that this way of relating to others symbolizes qualities one values most about oneself.

The concept of a youth subculture is both broader and narrower than the cliques, interest groups, and friendship networks that comprise the peer group world of a particular community. It is broader because youth from different communities can exemplify the same style. It is narrower because these styles are highly selective and lack the richness of group life in a particular community.

Many observers have noticed that youth culture seems to be a minority group phenomenon. The majority of young people in a community do not appear to be heavily invested one way or the other in subcultural styles and identities. Although this is true in general, it is equally true that young people who are invested in youth culture styles and identities stand out from the crowd in the eyes of their peers. Whether the adherents of a particular style are admired or feared, they are usually regarded as taking a stand on issues that concern most of the young people in the community. This does not mean that they have definite ideas about such issues as the fairness of academic tracking in school. Rather, they present themselves as the *kind of persons* who can be expected, for example, not to back away from a personal insult or allow themselves to be pushed around by the school principal. Youth culture, therefore, occupies the symbolic center of peer group life. The adherents of a youthful style dramatize those feelings about adult authority that make a difference in the lives of many young people.

We might think of youth culture as analogous to amusement park mirrors that distort one's image (see Coleman 1961). Looking at one's reflection one laughs because one knows that the ridiculous picture one sees is only an artificial effect of the mirror. All the same, for an instance, there is a glimpse of the truth that those things we hold as sacred about ourselves can look absurd when viewed from a radically different perspective. So, too, youth culture styles and identities take their materials from the adult world. Youth culture rarely creates new cultural forms or values. The ways in which young people interpret the values, beliefs, and concerns of the adult world sheds light on the conflict between what Americans want for their children and how they actually live their lives. Youth culture reflects the tension between what adults prefer to believe about themselves and how they actually go about preparing young people to take their place in society. What we, as adults, see in the youth culture tells us things we would prefer not to know about ourselves.

Instrumental Concerns and Expressive Values

Sociological writing about youth culture has, by and large, focused on the meaning of the expressive aspects of peer group activities.[15] In what was perhaps the first sociological essay on the subject, Parsons (1954) defined youth culture in terms of "hedonistic" and "irresponsible" behavior. He suggested that what adults see as youthful irrationality is merely a temporary reaction to the pressure of doing well in school and finding a place in adult society.

---

15. The expressive aspect of peer group activities refers to those things young people do together which do not have clearly defined practical ends. This covers a great deal of territory: all the way from "hanging around in the park getting stoned" to spending hours on the phone with a friend talking about who has a "crush" on whom. Sociologists, on the whole, have been more attentive to expressive activities that either offend adult sensibilities (e.g., youthful behavior at rock concerts) or cause problems (e.g., youthful vandalism) than in the everyday pleasures and pains of peer group sociability (e.g., not being able to find a date for the class prom).

In subsequent work, Parsons (1961, 1963) and Eisenstadt (1956) depict youth culture as a way of easing a young person's movement from the security of family life to the rigorous competition of the occupational system.

Sociological analysis, in this instance, reproduces the cultural categories in which our society thinks about the aims of socialization. The entire socialization process is conceived, implemented, and judged in terms of a single, overriding instrumental value. As far as the role of adolescents in the larger society is concerned, acquiring the knowledge and skills necessary to take their place in the labor force is the principal goal of the socialization process. Whatever educators may say about moral development, civic responsibilities, or creative growth, the plain truth is that our culture puts a premium on those abilities and talents that integrate young people into the economy.

This concern with the practical results of socialization is deeply ingrained in sociological interpretations of youth culture. Coleman's (1961) study of high school youth culture is a case in point. He identified peer-oriented value complexes which endorse popularity, sports, personal appearance, and similar expressive concerns. Coleman argued that the importance young people give to these values creates an irrational element in the socialization process. In his opinion, it is obvious that the aim of schooling is to improve a young person's intellectual skills, and it is equally obvious that academic performance is linked to success or failure in later life.

For Coleman, the rationality of the socialization process depends upon its instrumental significance. This is, in effect, the official ideology of adult authorities: youth ought to put greater emphasis on hard work and academic achievement than on good times and popularity. Coleman's analysis does not imply, as some critics (Berger 1963a) would have it, that young people ought to be concerned with the life of the mind—a value not shared by most of their parents. The point is that youth ought to be thinking first and foremost about developing marketable skills (Coleman, et al. 1971).

We now can understand why the older generation views expressive peer group activities as irrational forms of behavior. Looked at in terms of an instrumental standard of value, expressive modes of conduct do not serve as means to useful ends.[16] Usefulness, in its technical, economic, or material sense, is the

16. Parsons and Shils (1951) have developed the most systematic theoretical basis for the distinction between instrumental and expressive values. He treats the instrumental as equivalent to an ends/means schema where the schema is grounded in cognitive criteria, that is, criteria that are rational in the ordinary sense of the word

measure of instrumental value. The playful, adventurous, sensuous, impractical, and quixotic qualities of many peer group activities obviously do not enhance the values of academic achievement and economic productivity.

However, there is one notable exception to the generally negative adult impression of adolescent expressive behavior. When expressive activities can be harnessed to values that promote instrumental aims, they are encouraged and supported by adult authorities. Athletics are a good example. Sports promote the values of discipline, hard work, competition, and rigorous standards of achievement. Athletics, according to adult authorities, are excellent training grounds for later life because they infuse pleasurable expressive activity with powerful instrumental meanings.

The question of what expressive behavior means cannot be separated from the question of what youth culture styles and identities mean to their youthful exponents.[17] These styles and identities have little, if any, pragmatic value in the larger society. The pleasure young people get from how they present themselves to peers comes from the satisfaction of perfecting this symbolic representation of self and from the approval peers bestow on these stylized performances.

Thus, adolescent styles and identities are appreciated for the ways in which they give form and meaning to certain youthful experiences, activities, and relationships. Expressive values integrate young people's feelings about those things they value about them-

---

(see p. 90). Parsons separates what he calls the evaluative from the expressive: the former being moral and the latter aesthetic values. In this book, the distinction between instrumental and expressive has somewhat different meaning. The moral and aesthetic properties of social relationships and activities constitute the expressive component of peer group life. The instrumental concerns the technical control of human activities for practical ends whereas the expressive concerns the intrinsic qualities of human sociability as such. In everyday life, we identify the instrumental because it has some tangible "pay-off" whereas the expressive either "looks and feels good" or is seen as inherently right and proper. This distinction draws from the Frankfort school of sociology, especially Horkheimer (1947).

17. The concept of a social identity emphasizes the importance of the identification of oneself and others in terms of broad social categories in an interactive situation. See George McCall and J. L. Simmons (1966) for a discussion of the relationship between the categorical and personally expressive aspects of social identities. Helen Lynd (1958) points out that the identities one chooses and the way one plays them out in social life are revelatory of the self and that the feelings of shame and embarrassment are at the heart of this process. It is particularly noteworthy that feelings of shame and embarrassment underlay so much of adolescent social experience and give the process of trying to adopt or reject a particular social identity such powerful expressive meanings.

selves and their perceptions of the qualities that make relations with others pleasurable. Expressive values are communicated by symbols and actions that have aesthetic (e.g., a particular style of rock music) or moral (e.g., not "ratting" on friends to authority) meanings. These symbols and actions are expressive because they say something *to* an audience of peers *about* the *kind* of person who appropriates these symbols or performs these deeds.[18]

For adolescents, expressive values are embodied in certain ways of doing things together which do not have utilitarian meanings, for example, smoking pot or looking for a fight. These patterns of conduct enable young people to understand the symbolic significance of intangible moral qualities. In other words, actual forms of behavior represent such personal characteristics as courage, loyalty, daring, and so on. And these modes of behavior are interpreted as signs of an individual's character (e.g., this person is able to take great risks in dangerous situations) and as an indication of the moral qualitites associated with a youth culture identity (e.g., badasses are really fearless). Consequently, from a young person's perspective, it is what makes a style and identity attractive or ugly or admirable or contemptible that makes a difference in that person's evaluation of his or her peer's conduct.

Perhaps most important from our point of view is that expressive values, as they are embodied in distinctive styles of behavior, become emblematic of a young person's solidarity with others like himself or herself. Youth culture identities enable a young person to say, in effect, "I am indeed this rather than that kind of person."

There is no hard and fast line between a youthful style and identity. The concept of style accents the idea of performance. It is what a person does and how he or she does it that makes a difference in this context. Yet the modes of speech, behavior, and appearance that distinguish a youthful style are also intimately connected to a young person's image of a particular identity. The way in which a person acts exemplifies the virtues or vices young people associate with this identity. Thus, as young people enact what they feel are convincing realizations of a particular style, they also give material form to a conception of self.

The concept of identity stresses the way in which the self is apprehended through one's perceptions of how others see and evaluate one's behavior in relation to them. In other words, we know "who"

18. Following Parsons and Shils (1951), it is the orientation to the *qualities* of the other person that delineates the expressive significance of an act or symbol. But, as we noted previously, that meaning is amplified by the fact that these symbols and acts are embued with moral connotations.

we are in social contexts largely through monitoring the reactions of others to the way we present ourselves to this audience. This notion of a youthful identity may sound abstract and elusive. But young people have little trouble discerning youth culture identities because there are terms for many of them, for example, "badass" or "rah, rah." Young people who share an identity also tend to have similar attitudes toward a host of issues and concerns: friendship, dating, sex, sports, school, work, authority, music, drugs, and personal honor.

We should note that these attitudes refer to feelings and opinions that are expressed in public or peer group contexts. For example, no self respecting "badass" would say in the company of peers that he loves school and always does what the teachers tell him to do. Of course, his private attitudes may be more complex than this or even at variance with the sorts of things he says in front of his friends. But the point is that what a young person says in the company of peers projects a persona the audience recognizes as being compatible with their sense of who they are.

We should also remember that these identities, even for young people who are devoted to them, are partial and situated identities. They rarely encompass a young person's relation with the world at large. Young people who present themselves as this or that kind of person in the company of peers may project a very different identity when talking with the minister of their church or visiting relatives. Similarly, these identities are, by and large, restricted to a young person's participation in the peer group world. As a young person moves out of a particular adolescent social circle, he may simply drop the identity favored by his peers. Finally, these identities do not entail commitments to specific adult careers.

Authority and Tradition

To this point, we have discussed authority in general terms. We must define this concept more precisely because there are two divergent interpretations of the nature of this phenomenon.

Gadamer (1975:245) speaks of the necessity for the intellectual "rehabilitation of authority and tradition." The Enlightenment thought that authority was responsible for what it saw as humanity's passive acceptance of the will of a superior power. Because it persuaded humanity that it had privileged access to the truth, authority was, according to the Enlightenment, an impediment to rational criticism of established institutions.

Weber is the most prominent exponent of what we shall call the "realistic" interpretation of authority. His most recent translators (1978) translate authority as "domination" in order to underscore its affinity to power. Weber was responsive to the Enlightenment critique. He had no illusions about the power of authority to limit the consideration of alternative policies and affirm the orthodoxy of those who are in power. Yet he saw authority as a crucial aspect of the maintainance of the social order. Authority gives corporate groups the capacity to mobilize resources necessary for collective enterprises. As a legitimate form of power, it appeals to values and interests that form the basis for Weber's well-known classification of the grounds upon which subordinates accept the commands of superordinates (i.e., rational/legal, traditional, and charismatic).

As a "realist," Horkheimer (1972) asserts that authority is based upon the threat the state employs to keep its members from behaving disruptively. The presence of an alien will in the consciousness of those subject to authority is its distinguishing feature. One submits to authority, according to Horkheimer, because one does not have the moral or psychological strength to disregard it. Authority is the ultimate mystification of social hierarchy. People who are subject to authority feel incapable of making decisions because they fear or stand in awe of a power they believe has greater insight into the forces that shape their destiny.

Sennett (1980), who falls into the "realist" camp, wonders why people delude themselves about maintaining their autonomy when they are seduced by authority's promise to take care of them. The terms for this arrangement are set by the superordinate party in the relationship. Like others who take a "realistic" stance toward authority, Sennett believes that we cannot live a dignified life with or without it. The best one can do is to avoid the self-deception that comes from becoming dependent upon a power which, in our pretensions to autonomy, we claim not to need.

In a neo-Weberian analysis, Lukes (1978) argues that there is a crucial connection between the acceptance of authority and willingness to suspend one's judgment. According to Lukes, one believes authority in the unusual sense that, while one is receptive to the reasons authority gives for its decisions or commands, one somehow suspends one's further interest in the matter. One (Lukes 1978:639) "refrain(s) from examining what one is being told to do or believe" because one tacitly accepts a "second-order" reason that stipulates one will not subject that order or proposition to critical scrutiny. For Lukes (1978:639), authority is "not to have to offer reasons, but to be obeyed or believed because one has a recognized claim to be."

Note that there is some equivocation in this statement. Lukes claims that authority does not "have to" offer reasons. But this implies that authority does offer reasons under some unspecified circumstances. Lukes is trying to account for what he, along with others aligned with the "realist" position, perceive as its paradoxical nature.

The content of what authority says to those who listen to it is the apparent source of its ability to move its adherents to action. In other words, people who accept authority say that the reasons authority gives for the course of action it urges its followers to pursue are the sine qua non for their adherence to it. And yet authority seems to create a spirit of what "realists" see as uncritical obedience.

Lukes says almost nothing about what happens when the judgment of authority is manifestly wrong. That is, everyone agrees that it was wrong, and yet there is no crisis of authority. On the face of it, this would seem to strengthen the argument that there is an element of nonrational assent, of an uncritical willingness to go along with the putatively superior wisdom of authority. What is significant to those who recognize authority is their assessment of the overall pattern of its judgment in light of the unforseen contingencies that make the outcome of any action or project difficult to predict. People obey authority, not because they do not weigh and evaluate its decisions but because they are usually willing to give authority the benefit of the doubt in instances where most people realize that it is difficult to know the best course of action. Thus, they gauge their assessment to its performance in the long run.

It is hard to devise an apt label for the position that this book follows. Perhaps the communal interpretation of authority might be adequate. Lukes refers to the idea of standing "outside custom and tradition in order to apply critical standards" to authority. The communal interpretation believes that one must stand within one's own tradition in order to understand authority.

The distinctive feature of authority, according to Carl Friedrich (1958:40), is its "capacity for reasoned elaboration." However, without saying why this potentiality for giving reasons is not invariably employed, we end up in the same equivocal position as the realists. In this respect, Hannah Arendt's (1958) discussion is helpful even though her definition of authority is so stringent that no modern instance could meet its requirements. Like Gadamer, Arendt believes that authority is grounded in and validated by tradition. Neither an expression of the coercive aspect of power nor of free discussion and dispassionate analysis, authority arises out of what Arendt calls the experience of foundation, which she links to the

Roman polity. That experience is so infused with ultimate value and sacred meaning that it creates a template for all future decisions and judgments. Foundation is immanent in a sense of connectedness to the source of one's being and identity. Those who are open to this experience accept the pronouncements of authority because it puts into words those feelings that make the present a moment in the re-creation of a glorious past.

I do not suggest that one must postulate a fixed and inflexible historical referent for this concept. Instead, authority crystallizes a sense of the purchase of the past upon the present. The judgments of authority animate norms and values that are ordinarily on the periphery of a person's consciousness of his everyday involvements. There is a sustaining and orienting force to authority which, in a society like ours, is difficult to identify because we believe that we are free from the "dead hand" of tradition.

Gadamer (1975:248) says that authority is not based "on the subjection and abdication of reason, but on recognition and knowledge—knowledge, namely, that the other is superior to oneself in judgment and insight and that for this reason his judgment takes precedence, i.e., it has priority over one's own." Thinkers who are influenced by the Enlightenment critique overlook this point because they assume that a reasoned judgment must adhere to the form of discursive logic. That is, the intuition of particulars is irrelevant to the demonstration of one's point.

Yves Simon (1980:20) observes that authority resides in judgments that discern the significance of the particular. Authority is sensitive to the local, contingent, and traditional aspects of social life:

> But it should also be remarked that the more a law is universal, natural and impersonal, the more it has the character of a law, whereas the distinctive features of authority are more intensely present in the particular and contingent law than in the universal and necessary one, in the decree than in the law, in the decree regulating matters strictly determined with regard to here and now than in the decree concerned with somewhat general cases, and in the command marked by the personality of a leader than in an anonymous and impersonal ordinance.

In the way we are using the term, authority has much more to do with communal relationships than affairs of state. It is a civic rather than a societal construct. As Simon mentions, relations-based universal and impersonal principles such as contract do not invoke the sense of commonality that gives authority its special significance.

An authority is someone who knows what ought to be done in view of the peculiarities of a situation and who has a good sense of how things will turn out if they are done in the manner prescribed by this judgment. Insofar as it helps us see what is fair or just, authority discloses the rational, though not logically demonstrable, aspect of practical judgment which deals with "historically-conditioned, absolutely concrete; individual, and possibly unprecedented and unrenewable circumstances" (Simon 1980:36). Finally, Simon says that authority is a constituent of tradition because it embodies what a community feels is valuable or worthwhile about its past regardless of whether that experience is intelligible in terms of universal laws.

Authority and Intergenerational Relations

Our society tends to assume that intergenerational relations are ancillary to familial relationships. The nature of the relationship between parents and children is thought to determine largely how a young person responds to adults in general. Outside of functionally defined contexts, we think of contacts with nonfamilial adults as relatively inconsequential. Adults are important to the extent that they have specific knowledge to transmit to youth; otherwise they are shadowy figures who fill in the background.

During adolescence, the importance of contacts between adults and youth transcends the specific task in which they are jointly engaged or the formal rationale for their association. A young person's contact with adult authority figures outside the home reveals how the community regards such a young person. While family certainly has a great deal to do with the sort of identity a young person can realistically claim in the wider community, parents do not have the symbolic power to affirm or negate that persona.

In order to acquire a proper perspective on intergenerational relations, we need only to examine a situation where more than perfunctory contacts between youth and nonfamilial adults is rare. Rivera and Short (1967) remark that useful information is missing from the contact black gang youth have with local adults. However, what is absent from contacts between these youth and adults goes beyond the sort of vocational orientation that would have practical value in the labor market. It points to the vital component of intergenerational relationships—support and guidance—which underwrites respect for the authority of the older generation. Black gang youth are deprived of the kind of ordinary assistance from adults that other youth take for granted.

For "realists," who believe that authority is manifestation of power, intergenerational relations are instructive because the sanctions adults can use to get young people to recognize their authority have a limited usefulness. Adolescents do not often do what they are told to do solely because they fear that authority will use its power against them. They listen to adults who they at least provisionally grant some right to tell them what to do.

The right to exercise authority is predicated on the fact that adolescents realize that they are dependent upon people who are familiar with the ways of the world. Benne (1971) states that authority arises out of a "web of interdependence." A person in a dependent position grants obedience to those who can give him the direction and guidance he needs. This does not mean, however, that young people blindly accept the judgment of any adult who claims to know how to make the right decisions. Authority must not only justify its judgment in the eyes of those subject to it. It also must be able to make its decisions relevant to the values and aspirations of those young people who identify with the individuals to whom this judgment applies.

We will deal with the legitimacy of authority at greater length in the next section. For the moment, we need to emphasize the significance of the feelings of mutual respect between the generations. In a society where there is a relative paucity of ritualized forms for bringing the generations together, authority must communicate a good deal about what the older generation really values. If authority understands that the younger generation inevitably will see the world in somewhat different terms, then sense of linkage between successive generations will endure. The task of authority, then, is to mediate between the generations. It must create a basis for mutual recognition despite the real differences in their receptivity to the new and, to the older generation, unsettling possibilities of a society that worships change.

Authority and Socialization

Eckstein and Gurr (1975) distinguish between the power of authority to command and the grounds upon which authority is seen as legitimate by those subject to it.[19] Scharr (1970) remarks that au-

19. Eckstein and Gurr (1975:198) state that "the bases of legitimacy are values which govern perceptions that authority patterns are rightly constituted and therefore worthy, that is, of actions that tend to keep the patterns in existence and functioning effective." The reason for this stress on the legitimacy of authority is that some observers of the youth movements of the late 1960s saw the rise of youthful

thority must justify its power to determine what is right and wrong by articulating a vision of the ends its rules facilitate.[20] Authority, in this sense, tells those subject to it what goals are worth striving for and how they must act in order to reach them. In Scharr's words, the legitimacy of authority is based on a meaningful "account of reality," which is implicit in the rules it enforces.

In our terms, this means legitimate authority must be reasonable as well as rational. To be reasonable, authority must be exercised in ways that respect the dignity of those subject to it. To be rational, authority must be a means to those ends that are meaningful to persons subject to it.[21] It is important to note that these two features of the perceived legitimacy of authority vary independently of one another. On some occasions, authority can be experienced as rational but not reasonable, and vice versa. Of course, it can be experienced as neither rational nor reasonable.

For adults, the legitimacy of those who exercise authority over youth depends primarily upon the degree to which their policies incorporate the value of instrumental rationality. Young people rarely directly challenge the legitimacy of instrumental rationality. As countless observers have remarked, American youth, from the most affluent to the most deprived, want to get a job and make money.

The reason why authority is such a tender issue for some youth is

---

rebelliousness as a symptom of the instability of conventional forms of authority. Frank Musgrove (1974) remarks that the classic forms of authority outlined by Weber had little legitimacy in the eyes of youth who were turning their backs on the values of conventional society. One of the themes of this book is that young people do not need to openly challenge adult authority in order to cast doubt on its legitimacy. It is the moral dimension of the expressive properties of peer group activities that conveys a sense of youths' disenchantment with adult values. Rather than directly attack the validity of adult values, the more common response is to deflate the claims of adult authority by acting in ways that implicitly deny its *moral relevance* to their situation.

20. Scharr (1970) argues that perceptions of the intrinsic worth of basic cultural values is as much a part of the legitimacy of authority as perceptions of the equity with which rules are administered. In other words, people must feel that persons in authority are leading them in the right direction and that the reasons that justify the use of authority must reflect principles that command the respect of those subject to authority. When people feel that the goals which authority announces as the justification for its power are confused, worthless, or contradictory, then authority is undermined.

21. To put this another way, authority must be seen as efficacious by those subject to it. For example, school authorities often tell young people that if they obey the rules and do their work, then they will be rewarded with a decent job. If young people believe that this is not true, then the rational basis of authority is weakened.

that the policies of local institutions often violate their sense of personal worth and disrupt peer group solidarities.[22] When local institutions negate young peoples' feelings about what makes them worthy of respect or make it impossible for young people to associate freely with each other, conditions are ripe for challenges to authority. The issue is what youth experience as the unreasonableness of authority.

For young people, reasonableness involves whether what a person is told to do makes sense in terms of his or her conception of who he or she is and what he or she is capable of doing.[23] This refers to the various ways in which adult authorities deal with young people on a routine basis. Thus, reasonableness concerns whether youth feel that authorities who tell them what to do are willing to support them to accomplish these things. For example, a young person who is told by the principal that she must improve her grades but who feels that her teachers do not care whether she comes to class is likely to regard the principal's edict as unreasonable. Moreover, young people are aware of the fact that authorities tend to treat them as certain types or categories of persons rather than as individuals. To develop the example above, being labeled an "unmotivated student" or a "slow learner" certainly affects the amount of attention a young person will get from teachers. It is not unrealistic to suppose that young people who believe their teachers to be disin-

22. To put this somewhat differently, there are two modalities of authority that many youth experience as illegitimate. The first is authority that intentionally puts them in a humiliating position. The feeling of shame and embarrassment is experienced as intolerable because adult authorities have no "right" to treat them this way. This perception probably varies with the degree to which adult authority is seen as personal or impersonal. Youth make more allowance for authorities who treat them personally and probably are more willing to suffer embarrassment at the hands of authority who they feel care about them as individual persons. The second modality concerns what youth experience as an arbitrary intrusion into their own affairs or as excessive coercion. Adults often have very different ideas than youth about what sorts of behaviors or activities the former can legitimately regulate and control. The struggle here often takes the form of "you can't tell me how to run my life" or "we like doing things this way because it feels right and proper to us." The issue underlying these conflicts sometimes revolves around the message, as youth experience it, that they are too immature or unreliable to manage their own affairs. Youth often accept the legitimacy of adult authority but reject the way it is implemented as too coercive. For example, a young man may accept the coach's right to "chew him out" when he makes a mistake but may reject a slap as excessively coercive.

23. For example, it is one thing for the school principal to tell a young person that his behavior in class must improve and quite another to find ways that will accomplish this goal. To many young people the commands of authority are mystifying, not because the ends authority seeks are unintelligible but because for a person in his situation there does not seem to be a viable way to achieve them.

terested in them will feel that it is unreasonable to be asked to take the academic side of school seriously.

Reasonableness also involves young peoples' perceptions of the justice with which authority administers the rewards and sanctions at its disposal. Youth are sensitive to the fact that conformity to the rules often goes unrewarded. They also know that how one breaks the rules is often more important than the fact of breaking them. Finally, youth are not blind to the selective biases of authority when it comes to enforcing the rules. It is common knowledge that authorities feel that some youth deserve a break when they get into trouble and that other youth do not.

Reasonableness involves more than whether disciplinary measures for the same offense are administered in an evenhanded fashion. It most particularly concerns whether the way youth are admonished or punished demeans, humiliates, or embarrasses them. Their personal dignity is at stake. The issue is not the fairness of the rules or the equity of the penalty for breaking them. It is the youth's feeling that he or she has been officially determined to be a less than complete, incompetent, or damaged human being. The experience is one of a diminished sense of self, of being cast in the role of someone who is incapable of doing those things that identify "normal" members of the community.

As far as youth groups are concerned, reasonableness often involves their feelings about whether their niche in an institution such as the school is comfortable or uncomfortable. The experience here is feeling unwelcome or unwanted or that the authorities will extrude them at the first opportunity. Authority is unreasonable when it encroaches on the social space youth groups mark out for themselves. Being run out of a park by the police for "loitering" is a good example. Finally, authority is experienced as unreasonable when it does not respect the right of youth groups to govern their own affairs but rather imposes arbitrary standards of proper behavior. Dress codes in school are an example.

It is somewhat misleading to talk about youths' perceptions of the legitimacy of authority if we mean that they clearly see the issue as one of justice. It is more accurate to say that they experience the legitimacy of the demands made upon them but do not articulate the grounds upon which they judge them as good or bad, right or wrong. Rather, youthful styles and identities are informed by a general stance toward authority. This is more of an affective response to authority than a thoughtful critique of its legitimacy. Adult authorities, however, pick up this mood that is conveyed by youthful styles, even if they are unaware of the identity on which it is based.

Adult authorities will say that some youth can be counted on to be belligerent whatever one says or does to them.

As a way of summarizing the relationships between rationality and reasonableness, we will state them in three propositions about youthful attitudes toward authority: (*a*) To the degree that youth experience authority as rational and reasonable, they will accept adult images of work, achievement, and propriety. There is no conflict between the things adults want youth to do and how they get them to do these things. (*b*) However, if youth experience authority as rational but not as reasonable, then they will adopt a strategic attitude toward the rules. They will obey the rules when they think it is smart or profitable to do so. But they will not do so because they think the rules are fair. (*c*) If youth experience authority as neither rational nor reasonable, then they will obey the rules only when they are constrained to do so or when the costs of breaking them are prohibitive. Under these circumstances, the rules are seen as, at best, irrelevant to their lives and, at worst, a form of victimization by persons who are more powerful than themselves.

Part I

Small-Town Life

PATUSA IS A little more prosperous and larger than Ribley. Otherwise, on the surface, these communities look pretty much alike. Their civic life revolves around the symbol of small-town unity, high school basketball. Community institutions are pervaded by an awareness of class differences without enforcing a particular class interest. There is a democratic flavor to the inward-looking quality of small-town life.

However, if one looks closer at these two communities in terms of theoretical framework outlined in the previous chapter, we see that they are mirror opposites of one another. At the normative level, Patusa stresses order and security, Ribley freedom and personal expressiveness. Patusa subscribes to an ethic of control whereas Ribley is committed to an ethic of personal understanding. Ribley draws what Kai Erikson (1966) calls the moral boundaries of the community by throwing a protective shield around its young people whereas Patusa draws its moral boundaries along the lines of permissible public behavior for young people. In Patusa, membership in the community is not an automatic benefit of simply growing up there and knowing other people on a personal basis. In Ribley, tolerance for others is a natural concommitant of living together. In Patusa, living together harmoniously entails constant vigilance against threatening outside influences and internal disturbances.

This normative contrast is embodied in the policies of local institutions. In Patusa, any form of expressive behavior that goes beyond very narrow bounds is seen as a potential insult to authority. The nearly automatic reaction of authority is to clamp down on youthful offenders before, in their opinion, the problem gets out of control. It is for this reason that relatively minor issues seem to become major violations of the rules in Patusa. It is not the specific violation of the rule that matters so much to authority as the state of mind of the young person who intentionally breaks it in a public setting. If authority is satisfied that this deviant act was simply a slip that a youth is willing to rectify by proper behavior in the future, then the punishment is not harsh. But, whatever the offense, if a young person looks like someone who will purposely try to get away with whatever he or she can, their extrusion from the school is a likely response.

In Ribley, authorities are willing to tolerate expressive youthful behavior that goes beyond the rules. Authority is reluctant to label any youthful violation as a sign of irreversible deviance. Authority in Ribley assumes that no matter how dangerous or destructive a youthful act may seem, it can be contained and neutralized by the caring concern of the community. Extrusion into the formal legal system is seen as the absolute last resort: something that breaks the moral bonds between the generations and disrupts the solidarity of the community as a whole. This nuturant attitude toward youth is simply one side of the community's view of authority as a means of drawing young people into the protective circle of those who understand their personal backgrounds and problems.

This contrast between community cultures is replicated by the differences between youth styles and identities in these two towns. In Patusa, distinctive youthful styles and identities are notable by their absence. The empty shell of the identities of freaks and greasers exists in Patusa. But they are devoid of much content. On the other hand, youth styles and identities in Ribley are much richer though they are not sharply opposed to one another. There is considerable continuity within the youth world of Ribley whereas peer groups are highly fragmented in Patusa. Young people are allowed to engage in a good deal of expressive behavior in public without adult resistance, and, consequently, there is a soft edge to youth styles in Ribley.

Ribley values reasonableness. Justice is played out in terms of what seems appropriate in particular circumstances. The idea that authority ought to ignore the individual in order to make enforcement of the rules uniform is repugnant to the culture of Ribley. What matters in Ribley is the sense of the dignity of each person. It is only when a person intentionally and repeatedly does not respect the norm of mutual tolerance that the community reacts punitively.

Authority, in Patusa, is cast in what seems like a rational mold. Rules are enforced in a manner that is consistent with the goals of local institutions. When one looks beneath the surface, however, authority is less concerned with the instrumental efficacy of the rules than with its power to contain and suppress any form of youthful expressiveness that would disrupt the equanimity of adults. What matters here is conveying the message that it is costly if one steps out of line in a way that draws public attention to one's conduct. The basic thrust of authority is to let young people know that the first item of business is knowing how to stay out of trouble.

2

Ribley

Community Setting

The square in the center of Ribley brings together most of the retail stores and the county's historic courthouse surrounded by shade trees and park benches. Almost everybody passes through here every day.

Ribley has no "better part of town." There are two dilapidated sections inherited from its past. Bone Yard Woods in the southeast corner and West Ribley across the interstate on the west owe their existence to the coal mining boom of the twenties. They remain— tar paper shacks, cluttered yards, abandoned railroad equipment— as a reminder of past failures. John Cass, a Ribley attorney, explains why Ribley has no aristocracy:

> We have some old prominent families here, but I can't recall any families being the big land owner. Quite a bit of this had to do with the coal industry. Some local people did have investments in the mines, but to a large extent mines were promoted and developed by people from outside the area. As the mines became defunct, this killed off a great deal of the local entrepreneurial class.

The failure of the mines was only one of Ribley's disappointments. The first settlers came up from their farmed-out ridges in Kentucky and Tennessee. Ribley was incorporated as the seat of Borden County in 1831. The new land was promising, but farming customs of the day rapidly depleted the land's agricultural potential. Then the railroads came to the area, filling it with new immigrants. Eventually the main lines passed the area by. It never became a major regional center of transportation and commerce.

Coal was discovered in 1896. The county's population went from 26,000 in 1910 to 57,000 in 1930. Ribley peaked at 10,000, but nearby

Westwood peaked at 24,000. Ribley is now 7,000, Westwood 9,000. This was the era of greatest prosperity but also the one of union-management struggles, mine disasters, and the final blow: The Great Depression. Coal mining is still the main industry of Borden County. The jobs pay well, offer excellent fringe benefits, and grant solid respectability, but are limited in number.

Social Outlook

As a perceptive observer of the local scene, John Cass describes Ribley's values:

A lot of people do not have a sense of competition, and they aren't concerned with keeping up with the Jones. I think they're resigned to the fact that we are a depressed area. In fact, it's even kind of desirable not to make a big splash. We feel that we're all common men. We're here together, and it's not appropriate for somebody to stick his head above the crowd.

When Cass says "we're all common men," he is not referring to an abstract sort of egalitarianism that views social differences between the classes with distrust. Rather, he is pointing to the feeling that snobbery based on wealth, education, and influence is out of place in Ribley, though, of course, those differences exist here. He implies, moreover, that conspicuous consumption is seen as something more than bad taste in a town like Ribley where even middle-class families live modestly by urban standards. He is saying that there is a feeling of solidarity, of being "here together," that arises out of a sense of having a shared past that places real limits on what they can expect to accomplish in the future.

Not everyone, of course, is completely satisfied with the town's modest aspirations. Yet even Jim Shaw, town councilman who criticizes the do-nothing attitude of the city council, is against "making Ribley completely over and changing it from top to bottom." This accent on stability as opposed to growth is widely shared, with one striking exception. When it comes to high school basketball, Ribley aspires to greatness.

State basketball competition is divided into two divisions. Class A teams are drawn from schools with up to 749 students. Class AA teams include schools with 750 or more students. Ribley High School usually has approximately 750 students and takes care to insure that there are at least 750 students enrolled when the official count is taken. Although the smallest school in its conference, it has won the conference championship six out of seven years prior to 1972.

Hutchkins' Grill looks unpretentious but is a meeting place for children and adults. The front window displays last year's conference championship basketball trophy, which stays at the Grill until it is permanently enshrined in the high school lobby. Inside, there is an astounding array of pictures on the walls: larger-than-life portraits of past basketball greats, three-foot by four-foot pictures of Ribley's basketball teams over the years.

John Arbogast of the high school faculty understands Ribley's obsession with basketball:

> They'd probably ride me out of town on a rail if they knew how I felt. I believe in a good sports program. But I think any time you win consistently, it's because you are giving somewhere else. What you do is you set up a dynasty that starts way down in the second grade, and this is what has happened. I don't blame the people, because it's the only thing they've got. This is their Metropolitan Opera.

Police and Youth in Ribley

In this small world of shared biographies, the foreign, powerful cop and the dangerously unknown troublemaker never confront each other. Young people refer to individual police officers by first name. The youth officer describes the low-key tenor of law enforcement:

> Most of my juveniles come from homes where they've never really had a break in life. You've got to keep showing these kids that you're interested in them, and that you're one to give them a break in life. Most crimes are solved. Everybody knows everyone else. When a kid breaks into a gas station or a pharmacy and gets away with it, he will usually brag about it to some of his friends. In a small town the police know that there are only a small percentage of guys who would burglarize. So they go around asking questions and sooner or later you find someone who knows something and you locate your suspect.

A local lawyer points out that the law stays out of the "private affairs" of people, even when those affairs would be considered serious crimes elsewhere:

> Lower-class people who hurt each other by shooting, stabbing, or hitting each other are not especially prosecuted for it. One

fellow was shot with a shotgun and his assailant was charged with disturbing the peace. Another man was shot between the eyes with a pistol but didn't die, and his assailant was charged with some very minor offense. As long as people don't die, it would be considered a very minor infraction.

Among the working-class youth, this tolerance for "wild" behavior is recognized in the saying, "In Ribley, you can get away with murder." Every so often, Ribley pays a price for its indulgence. A state trooper was killed in a head-on collision with an intoxicated teenager. The body of a local youth was found floating in Lake Ribley one morning. But there is no public outcry at these rare excesses; the underlying refrain is, "These things will happen."

Everybody in Ribley knows three police personalities: Chief Earl Kraemer, Elmer Hardy (his assistant), and Benny Frazier. On one occasion, word reached the teenagers of Ribley that Kraemer was going to quit his job and take a better-paying job with the security force of one of the coal mines. The youth of the town were immediately galvanized into action. By the time school was over, they had passed the word around and marched across Main Street to the courthouse 200 strong to demonstrate against Kraemer's resignation. This is the only youth demonstration anyone in Ribley can remember.

The half-serious, half-humorous nature of this incident reveals a fundamental attribute of authority in Ribley. Because reasonableness is an integral part of authority, in general, there is a personal side to authority that is hard to disguise in even the most formal court of law. In some measure, a judicial decision is stamped by the "personality" of the judge because the way the judge takes the particulars of the case into consideration is not something that can be completely determined in advance by rules of procedure. In Ribley, the culture of the community brings the personal dimension of authority into bold relief.

As we shall see, there is a quiet "conspiracy" in Ribley to grant adults only as much authority as the community feels is consistent with the personal judgment of the official who exercises it. The faith Ribley places in the judgment of individual officials is not determined by their job qualifications. It is demonstrated by their ability to read behind the lines when it comes to dealing with youth. An official in Ribley should not confuse the "seriousness" of youthful behavior with the provocative way some young people approach their elders.

Looked at from a slightly different angle, law enforcement officers in Ribley are expected not to exacerbate situations where there is a possibility of an open show of antagonism on the part of youth. Thus, authority must keep a delicate balance between overly indulgent paternalism and rigid moralism. In the following tale, we can see how the way in which adults make their presence felt teaches youth a good deal about how the exercise of authority discloses personal strengths and weaknesses. In other words, it is impossible to hide one's stature as a moral being behind the mask of one's official role in Ribley.

Finally, we will discover that the negation of authority does not invariably result in disdain or hostility. Ridicule rather than anger is the more appropriate response in Ribley to exaggerated displays of authority. This temporary breach of the tacit understandings that make the flow of social life so even occurs against the background of a taken-for-granted feeling of connectedness between youth and their elders.

Benny Frazier's presence on the police force is reputed to be due to his uncle's political influence. He carries a gun but is not allowed to have it loaded. Instead, he is permitted to carry one bullet in his shirt pocket in case of dire emergency. A young man tells a classic Benny Frazier story:

> Did I tell you about the time Benny Frazier threw me in jail, or at least threatened to? I was up at the Country Eats for a hamburger. It was pouring down rain and Benny says to me, "If you've got a car, leave, and if you're walking, walk out of here." I asked, "What for?" He said, "You do as I say." I said, "What's the charge?" He grabbed me by the arm and put me in his car. He wanted my name but I wouldn't give it to him because he hadn't given me my rights. So, he took me to the jail. So I told Elmer the story, and he goes, "Yeah, well, Benny. He don't know much anyway." And then Elmer told me to leave.

What is interesting about the two preceding incidents is that they show how finely peoples' evaluation of authority are graded in Ribley. Although Elmer Hardy had a reputation for being harder and less fatherly with youth than Chief Kraemer, he could not present himself as a reputable authority figure if he took the situation in the restaurant seriously. Bringing someone to jail because they gave a police officer a little "lip" would be cause for more than a little laughter at Hutchkin's Grill. No self-respecting authority figure, no matter how much he would prefer, like Hardy, to have youth defer to his official status, would make an issue out of something as trivial as thumbing one's nose at authority. Supporting Frazier in this instance would not only endorse his poor judgment but establish a policy of intolerance toward symbolic gestures that harmed no one, save the feelings of those who did not have enough sense to overlook them.

While youth were concerned that Hardy might replace Kraemer and therefore demonstrated in support of the police chief, the young man recognizes the appropriateness of Hardy's response to this situation. He expresses no bitterness about being "falsely arrested." Quite the contrary, he leaves the jail after having exchanged mutual assurances that they understood the personal deficiencies that disqualified Frazier as a creditable authority figure in Ribley. And it goes without saying that in this town turning every less-than-gratifying contact with youth into a real struggle for dominance and control completely violates its spirit of tolerance and mutual accommodation.

In Ribley youthful deviance is treated as "serious" if its consequences are patently destructive (e.g., killing someone in a car crash) or if the person who commits an illegal act (e.g., stealing) is known as someone who is resistant to persuasion. The first impulse of authority figures is to caution and counsel young people who get into trouble. The local police are very reluctant to send young people through the court system unless they are convinced that they are deaf to "fatherly advice." That authority figures define permissible behavior in terms of what Ribley is willing to tolerate is evident in the remarks of the police officer to boys picked up for fighting in a nearby town: "If you get into trouble here, we can take care of it, but if you do it out of town, there's nothing we can do."

The Drug Problem

In 1973, about ninety people met over growing concern about the presence of drugs in the community. The tone for this program was set by two speeches at the second meeting of the Concerned Citizens. Mr. Clancy, a football coach at the high school, said:

> When this came along, the first thing I realized is that Ribley is my hometown, and I'm proud of it, and I want to take part in it. There is a drug problem here. There's no use hiding it. I think we should try to help these kids. If we find somebody that needs help, yes, we should give the information to a doctor or to law enforcement if the person is going to hurt themselves.

It is hard to get the emotional flavor of the coach's speech by reading his words. Yet the affective connotations of what he said on this occasion reveals Ribley's attitude toward youthful deviance. Ribley values all of its young people, good kids and troublesome youth alike. Because the family background and personal history of each young person is woven into the fabric of everyday life in Ribley, the town sees them as "our" kids.

This nurturant and protective attitude toward young people makes it almost impossible for the town to treat young people who get into trouble impersonally, that is, as drug addicts. Thus, the normative boundaries of this community normalize youthful deviance rather than expelling and segregating categories of youthful offenders. The frightening and alien qualities of drugs are defused by the almost maternal response of the wife of the county sheriff at the meeting:

> I think that the thing that parents need to understand is to keep their own cool and not make the child feel like a nothing, but really see him or her as a person and then try to go on from there. I just can't see these people jumping all over and getting all excited. I know it's a terrible thing, but you've got to deal with it and there's no use to lose your head because that child has made a mistake.

Church Youth Programs

There are twenty-three churches in Ribley and its immediate vicinity, and another dozen or so in rural areas of Borden County. With one exception, all church youth programs are low-key and traditional. Teenagers gather at the church for Bible discussion and Ping-Pong, go on occasional outings together, take part in Sunday services with adults. Each church attends to its own youth. There are no specially designed programs for the unattached. The one exception to this pattern is the program of the Church of God. It has a flamboyant outreach program which uses mass-market oriented public relations techniques: give-aways, contests, promotional circus events. This kind of program has increased the size of the congregation, but it also has attracted unattached adults and preteens more than teenagers.

There are no coffee shops, rock bands, or professionally guided therapy sessions. The youth programs of Ribley's churches discuss the Bible, sing about Jesus, and give many teenagers more personal adult attention than they would get from a comparable institution in an urban setting. The fieldworker describes a special youth program:

> Went over to the Church of God to view an interchurch youth presentation of *Natural High,* which is a musical dialogue of sorts on the theme that it is better to be high on God than on drugs. Because most of Ribley's youth belong to the youth groups of their respective church, these interchurch presentations are popular as they give many of the kids the chance to get together with their friends who belong to other churches. About forty kids, male and female, participated. The quality of the music was good, and the performers were really excited and spirited. Following the singing, there was a chance for personal testimonies. One girl became so emotionally involved that she started crying and could barely finish her testimony. I recognized this girl as a junior in high school who drags Main in a red Barracuda, and I felt sure that in spite of her testimony she would continue to drag Main in her queen-of-the-road fashion.

There are two inconspicuous aspects of this scene that tell us a good deal about the culture of Ribley. These young people are quite unself-conscious about their enthusiastic endorsement of a public and unreserved sort of goodness. Their contemporaries in many other communities could not imitate this performance without giving these sentiments a disingenuous twist. This spontaneous disregard of trying to appear sophisticated among one's peers is rare in the aftermath of the 1960s but fits into the cultural style of Ribley.

The other noteworthy aspect of this event is the easy juxtaposition of two modes of being that would be experienced as antithetical by most youth in urban communities. As we shall see, "dragging Main" is the prototpyical sign of adolescent freedom from adult strictures in Ribley. And yet a girl who is devoted to this activity feels no contradiction when she gets up at the service in front of her peers and rededicates her life to Christ. The symbolic opposition between these activities goes unnoticed in Ribley because its culture is committed to the reconciliation of differences through mutual acceptance.

Ribley High School

Mr. Rigdon, the acting principal of Ribley High, accepted the job for one year while the school board searched for a permanent principal. The school board chose him because of the widespread respect for him in the community, especially among faculty and students. Rigdon was very candid about the dynamics of community control:

> Mostly what the community wants from the school is a good basketball team. So, for many administrators a good basketball team is a panacea for all their problems. Usually there's not too much pressure on the school until something goes wrong and then only when it's from that one part of the community . . . of course you have to realize that those students who are going to college are from the better families, and the better families control the community. So basically it is a college prep type thing.

Thus, community control means the leadership of middle-class families. This does not mean that school issues are drawn along tightly defined class lines. There is a great deal of overlap and consensus, although Rigdon is aware of real differences in prestige and power when families want something done for their child. The school, however, tries not to make working- and lower-class youth feel uncomfortable, and also has classes in agriculture and shop facilities.

The Faculty

There are forty-one certified personnel on the staff of Ribley High School. Mrs. Moore is an old-fashioned teacher.

> Jeannie has American History with Mrs. Moore, a short fiftyish woman whom the kids frequently joke about because she is always smiling and "just loves" to have students smile and wave at her. She has the reputation of being an easy teacher to "brown up" to. This you do by smiling at her, joining her History Club, and pretending you're very interested in history.

At first glance, Mrs. Moore strikes one as an anachronism, a throwback to the time when busywork and inanities were the standard repetoire of many high school teachers. Many students see "through" Mrs. Moore but are not in the least offended by someone who accepts surface conventionalities and empty pleasantries as the essence of social reality. Mrs. Moore goes through the day without experiencing any of the discontent or disdain that she would in a suburban high school in a community like Glenbar. Because she is an ineffective but not destructive or malicious teacher she falls within Ribley's ethos of live and let live. The only penalty she pays is that she is not taken very seriously by most students. But rather than look past her, most students engage in a mock ballet of "refined" gestures in which the lack of substance in their relationship reveals itself to those who are aware of what is happening.

Mrs. Parker, the American Problems teacher, is also old-fashioned, but as one student points out, ". . . but at least she's better than Mrs. Moore; she's not a racist."

> Mrs. Parker is a tall slender sixty-year-old woman with glasses—the old-fashioned type with long dresses. Holden told me about one time they were talking about tariffs on foreign goods and he told Mrs. Parker that he never heard of anybody paying a tariff on any Turkish hash. Mrs. Parker said she always makes hers from scratch and doesn't buy the ready-made kind.

Putting a joke over about drugs on a very naive teacher is only the ostensible point of this story. What is not said is that in Ribley youth can gently mock the older generation without dismissing them as responsible, and, ultimately, acceptable persons. Heard in an urban classroom, Holden's remarks would be interpreted as a sign of his contempt for Mrs. Parker's ignorance of the basic facts of life. But in Ribley the accent is on Holden's amusement over Mrs. Parker's otherworldliness. Yet her being out of touch with the currents of the time does not remove her as a legitimate representative of authority in the eyes of most young people in Ribley. Equally important, this little incident shows that as long as one deflates the supposed superiority of one's elders without malice there are no accusations of disrespect from the older generation. In fact, in Ribley these sorts of encounters seem to increase rather than reduce the younger generation's tolerance of adults who cannot help them fashion a coherent response to the world into which their lives are moving.

Mrs. Cass is a teacher who acts as a broker between the younger generation and the more conservative elements of the faculty. A student describes how she handles delicate situations:

> I went up to Mrs. Cass's room. She was talking to Miss Reed, who said to me, "You arrived at the right time, there's a crisis going on." Miss Reed said that J. B. asked her this morning if she would be the sponsor of the Hi Y Club, an all-male club. Evidently the present male sponsor of the club was not doing anything, and he had suggested that since Miss Reed is always stating how women should have equal opportunities, that J. B. ask Miss Reed to be the sponsor. Miss Reed was furious and was half-way thinking of taking the position just to show the

male chauvinists, such as the present male sponsor and the coaches who are always putting down women's lib. Mrs. Cass was sympathetic, but advised Miss Reed not to take the job because it might not look good for a young single teacher to be sponsor of an all-boys club, besides the breaking of a tradition. Miss Reed rationalized that she already had numerous extracurricular activities and said she would probably not take it.

The normative principle operative in this incident is not simply respect for tradition or not upsetting one's colleagues. In Ribley, the notion of not creating a fuss over the small stresses and strains of everyday life involves tolerance for the idiosyncracies of others. J. B., in the incident above, was provoking both Miss Reed and the male teachers. He was hoping that a few sparks might emerge out of a clash between the champion of women's rights and the sexual conservatism of male teachers. Sensing this, Mrs. Cass invoked the basic cultural norm of the town. She said that everyone has a point: Mrs. Cass for espousing her values, J. B. for wanting to press the issue, and the male teachers for wanting to continue things as they have done in the past. Mrs. Cass did not say that Miss Reed was impolitic for making her somewhat "radical" views on sexual equality public knowledge. Rather, in Ribley, the implicit assumption is that there is enough room for everyone to express their personal values. The local norm, however, is that no one will push their own position so far that it threatens the values of others and leads to open conflict.

We can see how the culture of the town can assimilate youthful deviance without becoming either blind to dangerous or self-destructive behavior or, on the other hand, unduly harsh and restrictive. Ribley affords enough normative space for people to live in ways that are comfortable for them without infringing directly upon the cherished values of others. This normative flexibility rests, however, upon the assumption that the apparent deviance of others from consensual norms is not particularly threatening because that deviance is both easily contained by persuasion and is easily understood in light of a person's family background and personal history. Without this sort of intimate familiarity with the biography of people who live in the town, it is hard to see how such tolerance for youthful deviance would become part of the institutional culture of Ribley. One must not forget that what makes this tolerance something more than "benign neglect" of troublesome behavior is that adult authorities communicate a sense of caring to many of the young people they encounter on a routine basis.

The ethnographer describes a teacher who, despite her apparent similarities to Mrs. Parker and Mrs. Moore, is culturally out of place in Ribley:

> Mrs. Jones is a tall, slender person who carries herself in a slow, almost fragile manner. She is very soft-spoken and extremely polite. Most of the kids take advantage of her nonaggressive style by talking aloud, running around, disrupting the class. ("It's Mary's birthday today. Can we sing Happy Birthday?"—three or four kids start singing.) Rather than yell at or threaten them, she tries to shame them by pointing out that "this behavior is very unbecoming of seniors" or "what would the principal think of this class if he should pass by?"
>
> J. B. spoke highly of Mrs. Jones, commenting that "she is too smart for us dumb kids" and that she should be teaching college instead of high school. Many kids have already dropped her English class apparently because she is so hard. Kerrie told me that she doesn't have her class but that some kids said they didn't like her because she is "too snobbish."

The rather unruly behavior of the students in this class should not be seen merely as an indication of Ribley's tolerance for youthful high jinks. The students' rowdiness is a protest, albeit a mild one, against Mrs. Jones's violation of one of the tenets of the local culture. In effect, she is trying to impose, though in a gentle and ineffective way, a cultural identity on these students that is alien to their backgrounds and aspirations. She fails in the first requisite of life in Ribley. That is, she is unable to recognize the personal identity of the other person because she is committed to an abstract image of the sort of human being she would like her students to become.

The students do not reject cosmopolitan aspirations or even academic ambitions out of hand. Students like J. B. are respected because of their stated desire to strike out in the world beyond Ribley. But it is quite another matter for a teacher like Mrs. Jones to assume that she can hold up the standards of high intellectual achievement as the norm and expect students to compliantly accept the gross distortion of their sense of who they are. In essence, Mrs. Jones does not see that tolerance in Ribley implies that everyone is allowed to find their own level. Consequently, when someone in authority pushes young people to move in directions where their natural inclinations would not lead them, they are resisted, although without much animus.

While it is more appropriate for a coach to indulge in gross humor than an English teacher, the relaxed tenor of this classroom is more in keeping with the normative orientation of the town. The ethnographer remarks:

> The Family Living class is taught by Mr. Fahey, the crew-cut, ex-marine baseball coach. Discussions are usually filled with a number of kids shouting out their opinions in a random way, and there seems to be an effort by the teacher and some students to turn serious topics into exchanges or joking remarks. There was a discussion about how some people fear showing their nude body in front of their spouse, and Holden quipped, "I sort of dig nude bodies." The coach asked Holden: "All bodies or just certain bodies?" Then he added, "You've probably heard the old saying that if you turn the body upside down, girls all look alike." This elicited a paroxysm of laughter—more intense the more the guys thought about it.

Coach Fahey's encouragement of locker-room *grosseries* in class, however, is about the limit of his tolerance for youthful disregard for conventional proprieties:

> In between classes I witnessed Mr. Fahey yanking the hair of a long-haired youth who happened to step in front of him as a group of people were going through a door. As he pulled his hair—taking him back a step or two—he said, "Don't ever let me see you do that again." The boy was somewhat bewildered and said, "What did I do?" The coach said, "You stepped right in front of me. You better learn some respect or you'll really be in trouble." The coach walked on. I watched the boy's face change from an expression of bewilderment to one of hate, contempt, and disgust.

This incident tells us a number of things about Ribley. It would be wrong to assume that because Ribley values tolerance and accommodation that it is immune to the ideological conflicts in the larger culture. Nor is the town able to put a protective cultural barrier around itself in order to ward off the anxieties and suspicions that have lead some theorists to infer that generational tensions are the sign of an oedipal situation. While the coach may be a callous man, he is not ordinarily brutal. His impulsiveness and his unfocused anger in this instance result from a gap, so to speak, in his ordinary consciousness of contacts with young people. Unable to consciously recognize the threat he experiences from cultural symbols that appear to demean everything he has worked to create for himself, he strikes out at the most convenient object. And it is impossible for him to articulate what it is that he is protecting because it is so implicit in his taken-for-granted consciousness of himself. That is, he exemplifies a certain fusion of masculinity, social respectability, and dedication to social conventions with a dash or two of "old boy" rowdiness. He experiences himself in a diffuse way as being shunted aside as irrelevant or ridiculous by long-haired (i.e., "hippie") youth. The irony, of course, is that Ribley is one place where the local "hippies" would probably accept the coach more or less on his own terms.

Counselors

The Guidance Department of Ribley High administers the tracking system. Mrs. Clark, a counselor, observes:

> In English we track on the basis of academic achievement. They take an eighth-grade placement test. Based on the test results, the eighth-grade teacher makes a recommendation. Now this is a flexible placement and is called AB English. This is definitely our brighter students. I have a girl who came into our office. We've been working with her since she's been in the school. She's very, very bright, in the top 10 percent of her class academically. Every year we have tried to get her into this program, but this girl has such a poor self-image that she says the kids are nice to me, the teacher is nice to me, and the work isn't too hard, and she was in a class with popular kids, but she still won't stay.

There is one false note here, and it is not a reflection of the internal logic of the culture of Ribley. Note that an otherwise compassionate counselor points to this girl's "poor self-image" as a principal cause of her inability to realize her potential. This is the idiom of any number of professional, "therapeutic" ideologies that individualize failure. This doctrine suggests that there is an internal flaw or personal deficiency for her apparent passivity in the face of genuine encouragement and support to better herself. This ideology not only blames the victim but, more important, absolutizes the values of the dominant cultural strata in the large society. Perhaps this girl's refusal to "move up" is a statement of loyalty to her friends and family. It may take greater courage to stick with people who are seen by representatives of the larger culture as "losers" than to pursue success on terms dictated by those with whom one feels no cultural affinity.

Mrs. Clark goes on to say that it bothers her to talk about "social classes." Yet she says that economic pressures combined with a lack of self-confidence makes it hard for lower-class youth to participate in extracurricular activities. One might be tempted to say that the culture of Ribley downplays the realities of class: that people in authority minimize the importance of class in the lives of youth at the very time that they admit its influence on institutions such as the school. What makes class-related issues relatively unvolatile in Ribley is that persons in authority do not ordinarily use their power to embarrass or belittle poor youth. In the case of the bright, lower-class girl who would not move into a higher track, Mrs. Clark went out of her way to smooth the transition if the girl was willing to take the social risk such a move implied. That this girl was not comfortable being with higher-class youth tells us something about the continuing influence of class upon academic aspirations and peer group association. But in Ribley there was no social penalty—no humiliation for failing to move up and no disgrace for staying put—attached to this girl's decision.

Student Experience: Discipline

At lunchtime, many Ribley students eat in the school cafeteria, a bare, dingy room in the basement. Each noon hour, the principal—Mr. Rigdon—works his way down the line with a cigar box, making change, chatting and joking with the students. This seems to be a custom associated with the office of principal, for when Rigdon was away, Mr. Parelli performed this task. Although the high school often has this pleasantly informal atmosphere, some members of the faculty and administration remind students that tolerance is not the same thing as permissiveness:

> During lunch hour I went to the main office where basketball tickets are sold by Mr. Parelli, the superintendent. Several students were waiting in line when I arrived. Parelli walked up and asked the first lad what he wanted. He was a short-haired, innocent-looking youth. The boy said, "I want three basketball tickets." As the youth pulled two crumpled dollars from the pocket of his pressed Levi's, Parelli reached under the counter for the tickets and muttered, "The kids don't have any respect. They don't know how to say 'Sir' anymore. And for basketball yet." The youth promptly added a quick "Sir," and Parelli replied, "That's better."

On the face of it, very little seems to happen in this incident. The acting principal's feelings are ruffled because he is not recognized as someone worth a modicum of public deference, and after letting his irritation show, the youth makes the appropriate compensatory gesture. However, there is more to it than that. Authority lets youth do things as a matter of course that would be seen as intolerable violations of public order at most high schools. Students will hang out of the window in English class and shout encouragement to students working on homecoming floats, or working-class boys look forward to minor fights in shop class as a way of breaking up the monotony of the day. And yet Parelli seems extraordinarily sensitive to an act that can hardly be considered a challenge to his authority, as disruptive or as intentionally disrespectful.

Parelli had a legitimate point to make with respect to the culture of Ribley. The solidarity of the generations does not arise out of peerlike camaraderie that obscures differences between young and old. Quite the contrary, intergenerational relationships are grounded in a certain amount of formality and distance because these qualities allow both parties to see the differences in experience and judgment that account for their elders' authority. Thus, once the young person makes a gesture that restores the feeling of respect, the situation can revert to one of easy familiarity.

In the following incident, Norm got kicked out of school for calling a teacher a "bitch." Norm was relatively new to Ribley, which made it difficult for the principal to decide whether this was an isolated outburst or a sign that Norm did not understand how conflicts with authority figures were handled in Ribley. Rigdon, who was known for his disinterest in discipline, acted forcefully in this case because he wanted to emphasize something that was taken for granted by the other students. They could come into his office and say whatever they wanted to say about teachers, within reason of course. If he could do something to ameliorate the situation he would. But under no circumstances would he take the side of a student who cast a teacher in a demeaning light.

Rigdon talked to our fieldworker about how difficult school must be for lower-class students because they get the short end of the stick, both in terms of what they are taught and how their parents are regarded by the school board. Given this sensitivity to the "underdog," one might assume that he would bend over backward to give Norm a break. But in Ribley tolerance has its rules, and the primary one is not backing others into a corner. Norm, in effect, forced the teacher to demand punishment since he left no room for negotiation and compromise—the basic instruments of the culture of Ribley. The fieldworker describes the situation:

Norm was kicked out of school for ten days. One day last week he was in the girls' gym during lunch hour, and there was a GAA meeting going on. The girls' gym teacher told Norm to get off the mats he was standing on, and the teacher accused Norm of calling her a bitch, refusing to get off. She told Mr. Rigdon about it. He called Norm into his office and had him tell what happened. There was some conflict between Norm's version and the teacher's, but Rigdon sided totally with the teacher.

Pete, a lower-class youth who gets into his share of trouble, illustrates the more usual response from authority. Pete's outward deportment is similar to Norm's: brash and rough. But Pete, unlike Norm, has been in Ribley all his life. Rigdon said of him with a smile, "I wish all my problems were with kids like him." Pete sometimes walks into Rigdon's office, sits down in his chair and puts his feet up on the desk. When he gets into an argument with a teacher, he may receive a reprimand but Rigdon is sure of Pete's respect for authority.

This is an instructive contrast in another regard. Ribley makes room for youth to demonstrate their independence vis-à-vis the older generation. For many working-class youth this means specifically not doing what they are told and, at times, even going out of their way to show that they cannot be ordered about. There is a subtle distinction, however, between being asked to do something that might seem unreasonable (such as getting off the gym mats) and being pushed aside as someone who is not worthy of serious consideration as a person. Though it is impossible to know this for certain, Norm tended to confuse the two. He responded as if he was being demeaned by the teacher when she was probably trying to tell him, though rather unskillfully, that he was in the wrong place at the wrong time.

Norm did not understand Rigdon's interpretation of the culture. As Rigdon sees it, adults have the "right" occasionally to tell youth to do nonsensical things (such as getting off the gym mats) simply because they have a certain priority in deciding how things will be run. However, he grants youth the equal "right" to evade these commands if they can. Pete, who is hardly a model student, comes to see Rigdon because he understands that as long as he does not show excessive hostility he can pretty much say what he wants to about authority figures. In other words, Rigdon does not demand that youth credit the pronouncements of authority as correct or substantive if they think that they are silly or pointless. This gives everyone who understands the rules great latitude while minimizing the opportunities for bitter confrontations.

The Peer Group World

The adolescents of Ribley live in a world imbued with familiarity. It is made up of familiar friends, familiar haunts, familiar routines, and even familiar enemies and evils. It is this apprehension of the whole that makes Ribley a comfortable place. Ribley's teenagers are divided into groups and cliques which do not have much intimate contact with one another. But, in going their separate ways, each group seems to know where all the others are. Thus the relationships that comprise the peer world—including conflicts, injustices, accommodations—are stable and reliable ones.

Dragging Main

The fieldworker first thought it must be a wedding. One adult described it as "just a dumb ol' thing the kids do around here." Not everybody goes to basketball games, not everybody even goes to school, but everybody drags Main. One of his first times out on Main Street, the fieldworker was with a group of working-class girls:

> Cindy and Chasty came over and wanted to know if I wanted to drag Main with them. As the five of us pulled away, I was amazed at the level of excitement that came over the girls. Driving up and down Main Street produced an intense involvement, a sort of "we've been waiting for this all day" feeling. They paid a lot of attention to noticing who was out with who. Cindy would hang out the window and yell to the people standing by their cars in the supermarket parking lot. Chasty said kids will put fifty or sixty miles on their car in one night of draggin' Main. The girls wanted to get beer. I asked if kids always drink while dragging Main. Chasty said, "You pull over almost any car that has kids in it, and somewhere in that car you'll find an ice chest loaded with beer."

The fieldworker describes an evening when he watched the cars pass by from the supermarket parking lot:

> Never, until this night, have I dared to stand four feet away from the street, with rows of shouting, screaming high school kids [mostly boys] standing to either side, madly waving and calling to the endless line of honking, screeching, swerving cars,

motorcycles, and dune buggies which contained equally madly shouting kids who formed the moving circles of cars which drove on and around and pass, on and around and pass, etc., ad infinitum. It seemed to me that they should have steel guard rails for North Main: put them up at 7 p.m. and roll them up at curfew.

Many other small towns have a regular circuit of streets teenagers drive around to investigate what is going on. These circuits usually serve as marshaling areas for the dispersal of various smaller groups or cliques of teenagers to more private locations and more intimate social gatherings. But, in Ribley, the circuit is as important for its ability to make persons merely visible to one another as it is for any meeting. People did stop and get out of one car into another. But even if a meeting did not happen, seeing was reason enough to drag Main. One could survey the whole peer group world from the window of a moving car.

Dragging Main is one of those instances where one can see clearly how the social and cultural orders interpenetrate. As we have seen, social life in Ribley is organized in terms of a few simple principles. People recognize the realities of class and do not minimize its potential for conflict and divisiveness. However, the social order rests upon principles derived from face-to-face relationships, not from the social categories that regulate the institutions of the larger society. People in Ribley say, in effect, that one of the advantages of living in the cultural and economic backwash of the society is that one can disregard, to a certain extent, some of the assumptions of the larger society. Therefore, the local social order is predicated on the belief that familiarity breeds trust, although people recognize that sometimes it creates antagonism. Yet for Ribley trust is not the same thing as friendship, love, or intimacy. It is more akin to recognition of the other in a biographical sense, of knowing the private vices as well as the public virtues of the other. One can trust the other because one knows what the other is capable of, and one knows that because one knows what the other has done in the past.

Ribley values tolerance because it believes that people really know each other. And people are known in this way because the culture of the town encourages people to pay attention to the personal characteristics and family backgrounds of others. Thus, the cultural order does not appeal to the innate goodness of mankind, Christian brotherhood and charity or other universal values. Instead, the cultural order depends upon commitment to belief in a commonality that overrides difference and on an institutional order that tries not to exclude or reject anyone who tries to get along with others. And this spirit of tolerance will work for as long as people believe they have good reason to see its results in the experienced qualities of everyday interpersonal relationships. Dragging Main, then, is the most concrete and compelling cultural exemplification of the principles on which Ribley's social order rests.

Social Identities

In Ribley, most people distinguished three levels of the local status system. The system applies to adults and adolescents. Depending on who we talked to, the labels varied. For Tom, they were the country club set, the blue collars, and the lower-class welfares. For J. B., they were "your upper crusts," the middle class, and the lower class. For Mr. Rigdon, they were "your better families, your middle-group students, and your lower group."

Among adolescents, this three-part division of the town was overlaid by other significant groupings. These other groupings are kids who are going to college, jocks, freaks, and hoods. In addition to these identities, there are specific cliques. There were the Beach Boys, and the Barter Boys. The existence of others was purely informal. Cindy and her friends spent much time together, the newspaper clique was often together at the Grill, and there was a regular lunch group at Wilk's, another at Mic's.

The way in which people are categorized reflects something about Ribley: it is just as revealing to speak of a young person in terms of his or her family's social location as it is to identify that person in terms of peer group involvements. In more urban places, there is a greater discontinuity between family background and a young person's social identity in the peer world. That is to say, one cannot automatically determine where a young person fits in peer group affairs on the basis of class or family status in the community. In fact, some scholars infer from this fact that these adolescent social categories have a life of their own (see Schwendinger and Schwendinger 1985). There is a grain of truth in this inasmuch as these categories are collective symbols for experienced divisions in the social world. It is a mistake to infer, however, that one can predict all sorts of positive behaviors (e.g., what sort of delinquency a young person is likely to commit) from knowledge about a young person's categorical identity. What is more probable is that the label young people adopts tells us something about what they are not. Since these identities are often defined dialectically, knowing how young people label themselves reveals the kinds of values they typically reject and the activities they avoid.

The Athletes

In the high school, athletes are subjected to an annual initiation rite. The fieldworker relates a vignette about the costs of being cast as specially favored representatives of the town:

> Mrs. Jones is not aware of all local traditions. For example, several basketball players are in her fourth-hour English class, and one of them mentioned that since homecoming is this week, pretty soon all the basketball players will be going down to the barber shop to get their crew cuts. Mrs. Jones said something to the effect, "Mark you're not going to sacrifice your nice long wavy hair just because the coach makes you?" This stimulated an outburst of comments from some of the jocks such as: "We do it because we want to . . . and that just happens to be what the coach wants [laughter]"; "We are the weirdos now, the individualists, because hardly anybody has short hair nowdays."

One of the changes in youth culture that occurred in the wake of the 1960s has touched Ribley. At one time, being a member of a high school team in a small town meant that one was a "star" in every sense of the word. There was no more enviable position imaginable for young people who dreamed of standing out from the rest of their peers. While being an athlete is still a positive asset in the peer world, it no longer has the luster it once had. Moreover, it is seen, even by athletes, as having some disabilities as well.

"Crew cuts," even in Ribley, are the symbol of ultrastraightness. It is quite embarrassing for a young person to have to appear in public looking like someone who just stepped out of the 1940s. Not only must they cut a slightly ridiculous figure, but, as the comment about weirdos reveals, the athletes are aware that they do not command universal respect among their peers. Freaks, in particular, tend to see them as overgrown Boy Scouts who are still trying to please their parents and act like adults expect them to. Of course, the athletes make a special point of sowing their wild oats in order to discredit this unflattering image.

The Grill Group

The Grill group includes the Baptist Youth Fellowship and the newspaper clique. They are both smaller circles within its larger

orbit. It is difficult to characterize this group in terms of their attitudes since it includes both conservative and iconoclastic youth, by
Ribley's standards. What unifies this group is their sense of being
socially central to the town, though more sophisticated about the
world than many of their peers. And they are confident that they
will be in a position to direct their own lives toward goals that are
personally meaningful to them. While they are somewhat privileged
socially and, to a certain extent, economically, these youth do not
look down at their less sophisticated peers. Nevertheless, there is a
subdued sense of difference that separates many of these youth in
the town even though a number of them have the same conservative, religiously oriented personal ethics as their less articulate
counterparts.

In the following quote, Holden, a member of the Grill group, expresses his detachment from the more parochial orientation of many
of his peers. Yet there is no real alienation or opposition here. In
Ribley, someone like Holden can feel comfortable expressing his
marginality vis-à-vis the preoccupations of the town because he
knows that everyone recognizes him as a person in his own right:

> See, J. B. and I don't get along with anybody else in town. Now
> the girls like Jeannie we can get along with, but the boys we
> don't. J. B. and I hate sports . . . I like sports, I don't like high
> school sports.

Jeannie said, "It's the idea." Holden continues,

> It all has to do with the school. I don't like the way it runs
> the school. Sports rule over academics, especially basketball.
> Not football, because they don't win.

I asked how many kids in town share his feelings. Jeannie and
Holden answered together, "Me and J. B. and Jeannie." [They
laughed.] They went on to admit that really there were a lot of kids
in town who felt that basketball was overemphasized.

It is ironic that these young people who are vocalizing their dislike of basketball hang out at the Grill, which is run by Libby and
her husband who are among the most dedicated supporters of basketball and other sports in Ribley. But they are not out of place in
the Grill. They have some money to spend, they can chat with Libby
about things other than basketball, and their dress and personal
appearance mark them as sociable and respectful young people.
They have been coming to the Grill for years. Their disagreement
with Libby over the emphasis on basketball at school is not as
important as their agreement with her on other issues. One of the

most important of these is the deference due to adult authority. Libby does not allow any "cussin" in the Grill and reports that she has had to kick out only a few kids in her years there. When the fieldworker asked her if anyone had ever talked back to her or refused to obey, she said no, and then added that if someone did do that she didn't know what she would do. The possibility has not even been contemplated.

What distinguishes the Grill group from other groups of teenagers in Ribley is their commitment to striving for conventional success. Their academic orientation, their deference to adults, their suspicion of marijuana, their interest in drama, journalism, and other forms of personal creativity all contribute to the attainment of this underlying goal.

J. B. Buckley is in many ways a unique personality, but his perception of his social position is similar to those of the rest of the Grill group. His reputation in the town is for being hypercritical, bright, energetic. Because of these qualities, he stands out among his peers. When the fieldworker first went to school with J. B., he noticed how frequently other kids called hello to him in the corridor. He was elected president of the Student Council and prided himself on his friendships among many different groups or cliques. He and his friends who meet at the Grill all view themselves as "capable of being one of the student leaders . . . or even a good follower."

There are two characteristics of the Grill group that reflect the normative structure of Ribley. Most young people are aware of the fact that these young people are likely to leave the town when they go away to college and to find a place for themselves in more exciting, prosperous, or exotic communities. Yet, despite the slightly privileged aura that surrounds this group, there are very little signs of bitterness and anger toward them from lower-class youth. This is not to say they are liked, but there is a certain amount of tolerance for their pecularities. Unlike their counterparts in the city, lower-class "greaser" youth do not look for opportunities to physically confront and humiliate "struck up" upper-middle-class youth who go to their school.

Correlatively, there is little in the way of genuine contempt or disdain on the part of the Grill group for the "wildness" or "crudity" of lower-class youth who are noted for their sexual prowess, willingness to get into an occasional fight, and disinterest in anything that has to do with school. From the Grill group's perspective, these young people blend too well into the fabric of comfortable familiarity of the town. One need not distance or insulate oneself from youth whose values, interests, and sensibility differs markedly from one's own. These youth can pass each other by in public places without tension or fear of an encounter that would compromise their sense of self. A slight nod of mutual recognition is all that is needed to sustain the belief that in Ribley it does not take much to get along with others.

"Straight and Middle"

Cal and Bruce are parts of the middle group. Bruce goes to First Baptist and belongs to the Youth Fellowship there. Cal goes to Immanuel Baptist and says of his church going:

> My folks used to go to East Ribley Baptist, and Immanual came from there. They split up. When my dad became a Christian and started going to Immanuel, I kind of went along. I kind of agree with most of the stuff they say.

Bruce is on the football team and sometimes hangs around with the football players. But he also has his friends in the Youth Fellowship. Although he was not a regular at the Grill, his presence there was not considered unusual. On one occasion the fieldworker went camping with Bruce and some of his friends. In the course of the night they talked about who drinks beer, what it means to be rich, sex, and the difference between Ribley and California (where Bruce used to live).

Cal is alert and inquisitive. The fieldworker describes him as

> about six feet one inch, blondish hair long on top but usually not long in back. He always wears old ragged blue jeans and a lumpy army jacket in cold weather. He's very friendly, smiles a lot, speaks with a slightly Southern drawl. His one great interest or hobby is music, and he is forever talking about music with his friends. He plays piano and organ and is learning guitar. Cal is basically straight. He's not high society, not a freak, seldom causes or talks about drugs, girls, etc. Very relaxed, un-uptight kid.

Cal is saving money to go to Lance Junior College and therefore can't hang around with kids who buy beer and drugs, or with those whose parents always give them money to go up to the Grill and buy cokes. He used to play pool up on North Main but didn't like to spend the money on it. He plays Ping-Pong at his church. He can't understand why kids like to spend summer evenings "just sitting up at the Pay-less parking lot." Yet he drives an old Chevy with mag wheels and participates in the central ritual that celebrates youthful autonomy—dragging Main. When the fieldworker asked him why he bought the mag wheels, he said, "It didn't cost me but ten bucks. It's sort of social pressure. Everybody else has 'em. It attracts attention . . . for your ego (laughs). It ran about ninety-five on the way down to Westwood one night. Pretty good for a six-cylinder."

For someone not acquainted with the insularity of adolescent peer groups in urban settings, the reader might assume that this is what "normal" youth are like. And perhaps they are. What is peculiar, however, about being part of the middle in Ribley is that youth do not cling to symbols that accentuate their differences nor are friendships bound tightly to particular types of peer groups. Depending upon individual inclinations and interests, just about anyone can be friendly with anyone else in Ribley, excluding, of course, those groups that have developed something of a distinctive identity and style, that is, the Grill group, lower-class youth, and the freaks and athletes. But even here the principle of exclusivity through cultural homogenity operates in a very weak fashion. There are few breaks in the personal networks that run through the peer group world, and, except for those youth on the top or bottom of the class hierarchy, doing things together is hardly socially inconceivable.

Second, there is a great deal of room in Ribley for young people to develop whatever combination of stylistic elements appeals to them on a personal basis. Cal, for example, can wear the same costume as the Ribley freaks without the slightest feeling that others would cast him in that light. It is this feeling of being unobtrusive because one isn't subjected to the close scrutiny of others that allows teenagers to live an adolescence that is personally satisfying.

"Your Lower Economic Bracket"

Besides not having much money, Jill was new to the town and lived with foster parents. She went home for lunch but usually stopped by Wilk's store on her way to school.

> When we arrived, there were a dozen or so kids standing around. The first thing that was obvious was that they were almost all girls. I asked Jill why this was, and she said, "Man, I don't know. I guess most of the guys that hang around here drop out of school and don't show up." Most of the girls were dressed in shabby clothes, some wearing jeans, some wearing short skirts. They were very expressive, using vigorous gestures and loud speech. Some girls were arguing about something, and they went into a playful fight routine, pretend-

ing to punch and slap each other. It was time to get back to
school, so Jill, Sheila, Kathy, and I walked across the street. All
three of them were smoking. They said it was a real bummer
that they can't smoke in school, that sometimes, after a couple
of hours in the classroom, "you really need a cigarette."

Late one afternoon in February, the fieldworker was driving
around the square. He spotted Jill and Sheila standing in the door-
way of the county building and offered them a ride. Jill was beginning to feel she knew the fieldworker pretty well, but it was the
first time Sheila had met him. As they drove around the town and
out into the country, the conversation covered a lot of topics. At one
point the fieldworker said he was interested in where kids park,
neck, and so forth. The conversation continued as follows:

> SHEILA: The bad thing about parking here, you find a
> parking space, then if kids have had beer
> parties and dope parties there, the pigs are
> watching it.
>
> JILL: If I was going to put a definition on fucking and
> making love, fucking would be someone you
> never saw before and making love would be
> someone you really dig. Like I lived with this
> guy in University City and, like to me, that was
> making love because I really dug him a whole
> lot. Like I don't feel that you have to promise
> your soul forever. It's something good and it
> makes you feel good.
>
> FIELDWORKER: Do you take the pill?
>
> JILL: Yea.
>
> SHEILA: I know all about it, but then I just don't worry
> about it. If I get pregnant, I get pregnant. I
> wouldn't regret it if I really dug the guy that
> made me pregnant.

One of the compensations, so to speak, about being at the bottom
of the social hierarchy is greater freedom about behavior that is
considered taboo in more "refined" social circles. The lower-strata
girls are certainly much more expressive when it comes to sexual
activity and the softer side of youthful deviance than their counterparts in other sectors of the local youth culture. While these girls
are aware that there is a considerable gap between their life chances
and those of more centrally located youth, they spend little energy
commenting on this fact. Whether it is fatalism or realism, they

accept the lack of opportunities to materially change the course of their lives. In terms of a calculus of pleasure, then, girls of the lower economic strata are most deprived and least mobile. They must find adventure and excitement on the local scene while their boyfriends at least can look around for greener pastures in nearby towns.

Sheila was fifteen and a freshman in high school. She said, "I'll be sixteen this month. That's another hassle between me and my old lady. She won't let me quit school." Jill responded, "I don't want to quit school. I quit once, man, and just got myself into a lot of fucking trouble." Sheila answered, "Well, I'm going to be in trouble whether I'm in school or not. I know that much." The fieldworker asked Sheila what she would do if she didn't have a high school education. Sheila responded, "I don't know. I'm just going to think about it when the time comes. I'm not going to think about it now."

When Sheila talks almost nonchalantly about expecting trouble, she is not referring primarily to problems with the law. Rather, for girls of the lower economic strata, trouble is an all-purpose metaphor for the generally problematic character of their lives. Not only do they expect to have fewer of the material comforts than other young people, but their lives are much more constricted than other youth. They have to work whenever they can get a job, and they can expect little satisfaction from working other than a paycheck.

These girls are sensitive to their place in the social hierarchy of the town. They are aware of the fact that there are almost no points of contact between them and what Sheila calls "the so-called high society people." Although they are not happy about being ignored by the socially more respectable sector of the youth culture, they are not very bitter about it either. They live their lives largely outside of the institutions that communicate the town's values, but they do not, for the most part, experience authority as excessively restrictive or onerous. They drag Main with the same élan and enthusiasm as everyone else. Although they rarely attend basketball games or belong to a church youth group, no one makes them feel inferior on that account.

There is, then, a wistful quality to the way young people at the bottom of the status system regard their situation. In keeping with the normative tone of Ribley, they experience the separateness of their way of life, with its pleasures and freedom, as more immediate than feelings of exclusion. Nonetheless, they do not regard youth from the upper social strata with much affection. Tom, one of the boys from the lower economic strata, observed that the fact of knowing a peer for a long time is no sign that any significant social relationship exists. Of J. B., Tom says:

I don't know about if he drinks or not, but I think if he had a halfway decent chance he'd rap to the police. I'm not saying he will, I'm just saying my opinion. I went to school with him ever since seventh grade, and I really don't know him that good. I wouldn't trust him, I'd put it that way.

The normative order of Ribley, therefore, does not negate the reality of class differences between youth. Nor does it obscure the real differences in opportunities available to youth from different class backgrounds. Yet, what makes Ribley different in this respect from many other places is that experiences of feeling rejected by "the country club set" are not powerful or consistent enough to generate deeply felt anger toward authority. Yet, it is easy to overromanticize the sentiment of "rural contentment." As is apparent from the comments of Brad, a young man from the lower economic strata, regarding his chances of dating higher-class girls, not everybody is "content":

. . . there's a few girls around here, a guy may be an intelligent guy, he may be good-looking and everything, but if his family background isn't just right, you know, if his father isn't a doctor or a lawyer or chief of police or whatever it happens to be, the upper class, they don't associate with them. They're the other ones. They kind of look down their noses, well, that's from the other side of the tracks, don't touch that dirt.

Ribley Freaks

The freak culture in Ribley, such as it is, tells us more about the normative order of the town than it does about the meaning of drugs in youth culture. Matters of dress, a tendency to congregate at a local store, an interest in dope, almost exclusively marijuana, gave the freaks of Ribley modest distinctiveness as a social category. Yet the real diversity in the academic bent, friendships, interests, and backgrounds of these young people make it difficult to say that adoption of a style gave specific content to this social identity. Perhaps the core meaning of the freak style in Ribley is that those youth who adopted it felt somewhat freer than others to appear "individualistic" in the eyes of their peers.

Our fieldworker did not encounter female freaks. Whether a group of girl freaks exists or not, it is noteworthy that this style is only marked publicly by boys. In keeping with the cultural parochialism of the town, it is not surprising that males experiment openly with somewhat deviant modes of behavior while females keep their commitments to this identity to themselves. Yet, even in this respect, Ribley freaks do not go out of their way to attract attention to their deviant style. This is in keeping, as we have pointed out before, with the normative order of the town where authorities allow youth enough room to pursue their own interests as long as they do not seriously disrupt the public order or violate the town's commitment to keeping conflict between the generations to a minimum.

Holden really belongs to Ribley's elite group. He was once the best friend of J. B. Buckley and is comfortable hanging around the Grill. But he also has access to Mic's; the store where freaks congregate.

Holden is five feet nine inches tall, good-looking, usually dresses in jeans with patches, old sweaters with the sleeves rolled up. He drives an old V.W. bug, which he is thinking about selling for a convertible.

In most respects, Holden is what most adults would call a straight or conventional youth. He has the classic small-town fantasies made famous in the movie *American Graffitti* about the beautiful girl he has never seen before who picks him up in her elegant sports car:

There's very few girls in this town who go out and lay. I'll put that down right now. They like to make you think they do. Maybe it's part of the new look, social fashion. Hi, I lay. The big thing when we were in high school when I was a sophomore was, Hey, are you getting any? Sure, I get some every Friday night, and really you sit home and watch a moth die on your light bulb.

Holden may complain about the sometimes dull, repetitive quality of life in Ribley. Admittedly, watching a moth die on a light bulb is not exciting. There is a slight note of resentment in Holden's comments. He knows that the more open and direct expression of erotic and sensual possibilities of relations between the sexes is not just rhetoric in the pop culture of the 1970s. However, he is also keenly aware that changes in the attitudes of the girls he is likely to date in Ribley toward intimate physical contact have not been affected by the ideologies of the 1960s.

Ribley's slowness to catch up with the more liberating and, to a somewhat frustrated adolescent boy, exhilarating prospect of doing something more than necking on a date is compensated for by the reassuring stability of the world around him. For an imaginative and slightly restless person like Holden, Ribley is a place where he can experiment with his self-image and test out his new vision of himself on his peers without encountering hostility or rejection. Taking things at his own pace, Holden does not feel pressure to assume a definite persona vis-à-vis his peers in order to claim a niche in the local youth culture.

While he smokes grass, plays tennis, and is the photographer for the school newspaper, what attracts him to the freak circle is that these youth have their doubts about the pieties of American life:

> I really envied Thoreau, the way he could sit down and write something and really not be upset about it. He had that simple life. That's where I'm really caught up because I'd like to go into the society thing where you make a lot of money and all that, and I'd like to go back to a little pond like that and decide if you really want both. But you can't. Not unless you reincarnate or something, which I'm not too seriously counting on.

Yet the note of skepticism about the world is subdued and gentle. The freak style is deeply tempered by the ethos of Ribley. As Holden notes, he lived and went to school in Texas for a year, and he was lonely because no one knew him and he was faced with working his way up "the social scale" of the school. In Ribley, the fact that everyone knows him is powerfully reassuring, and the respect he gets from being "on the top" more than compensates for any doubts he has about the conventional wisdom of adult authority.

Of all the freaks who gather for lunch at Mic's, Abbie Brown is the one who most fits the stereotype. Tall and thin, with hair down to his waist, Abbie maintains a certain kind of aloofness from all his peers. Although his notoriety as a freak was established in Ribley, Abbie never got into trouble. The fieldworker first noticed Abbie at a school dance:

> Abbie started dancing on the outer edge of the dance floor. Generally this is not at all unusual because most of the time with this hard rock music you can't tell who is dancing with whom. Except when Abbie dances. His hands and arms flap around like the wings of a bird, his head rocks back and forth as if his neck were on a spring, and he jumps up and down as if he were running across a bed of white hot coals. I thought it was kind of neat, because I had seen people dance this way when I was in college. But I soon realized that most of the other Ribley kids were slowing down in their dancing and moving away from Abbie as if he carried some infectious disease. They watched him in amazement or shock or awe. Abbie just kept dancing.

Even among those who hang out at Mic's, Abbie is regarded as singular. He is known to be one of the smartest students at Ribley High School, goes to school regularly, and rarely skips class as do some of the Grill group. He complains how boring the classes are but without rancor. He talks about his family and about life in general with objectivity and understanding:

> My father has never really encouraged me to do much. He doesn't even want me to go to college. And he won't take any criticism. That makes it kind of hard on me and the other kids. Like you try to tell him something he's doing wrong, he'll just say, "Shut up while you're ahead or I'll beat your head in." I think it was because he and mom both had unhappy childhoods. He had to run away and she did too.

Abbie talks about how his growing awareness of the artificiality of social distinctions drew him toward the freak style. From Abbie's perspective, the use of marijuana was less important than his feelings about basic human values:

> I think that it's because I started realizing some of the social injustices, like racial prejudices. The way people were biased against poor people. And then I noticed that what was supposed to be the higher social class . . . the way they thought about the lower social class, and I didn't think they were any worse or better people than the higher-class people. It's all caused by ignorance of what other people are really like. And I just decided that what I was doing wasn't what I really wanted to do . . . Once you were accepted into the high social class, you're supposed to start shunning the lower social class. The combination of that and what I read, like about all the protests against social injustice, made an impact on me. Well, you know that isn't just off in some big city. It's happening right here in Ribley. It's happening to me. And I just didn't want to be that way.

When Abbie says, "I just didn't want to be that way," he is talking about all of those feelings that drew him away from joining the elite group in the school and toward the freak identity. Despite his obvious intellectual talent and impressive personality, Abbie preferred to adopt an alternative style rather than become integrated into a social world rooted in what he sees as mindless prejudices. Abbie's stance, however, is hardly one of intense opposition to authority. Being a freak, for Abbie, is a way of leading a nonconfrontational life, one that is consistent with his personal values but does not cause conflict with others. This choice, again, reflects the normative bent of Ribley where the value of tolerance means that one allows others to follow paths that one personally regards as a dead end. Characteristically, then, Abbie does not confront his peers, teachers, parents, or authorities with what he feels is their commitment to superficial values. As long as they respect his right to follow his own lights, he respects their right to theirs:

> Yea, well when I use the word "brotherhood" I mean, you know, the whole counterculture, I mean, that's what I'm talking about. I don't mean just guys, I mean people all over the world. I don't really know if the counterculture is worldwide or not. I suppose there's some in Europe, especially in England. That's what I really mean by brotherhood.

It is difficult to say precisely what this image of the brotherhood of the counterculture means to Abbie. But it is a tangible sign that his feelings about what really matters in life are shared by others. And it is a symbol of the sort of solidarity with those who share one's values that transcends the comforting but limited horizons of Ribley. For Abbie, then, being a freak is a way of reaching out to a world he senses is more to his liking, even though exactly what he will find when he gets there eludes him. Whatever happens in the future, Abbie will never take for granted that it is right and good to move into the niche that others designate as one's proper place in the world. And, in that respect, Abbie is probably the only genuine "freak" in Ribley.

At one time, the notion that a bright young man from a poor family in a small town would get a scholarship and go off to the state university seemed to epitomize the American dream. Even if this young man did not accomplish great things in the world, the thought that he would most likely find modest success was comforting. The feeling that anyone would be permanently stuck in an unenviable spot in the social structure merely because of an accident of birth was disquieting to most Americans. Even if the young man tried to break with his past and failed, most people would feel there was something heroic about risking everything to avoid a cramped and unfulfilled existence.

Abbie hardly fits this traditional imagery. As the fieldworker remarked, it was far from certain that Abbie would go off to college. But, whatever material success Abbie does or does not have in the future, it is already clear that he has a capacity for self-consciousness and reflection that enables him to subject social arrangements and cultural values to critical scrutiny. Even in Ribley, freak culture has added something to the traditional American conception of individualism. It has given support to those who have the ability to succeed on the terms chosen by the larger society but who prefer to reject the invitation to demonstrate their worth by competing against others for fairly conventional prizes. It is impossible to say where someone like Abbie will end up, but it is certain that he will follow a path he marks out for himself:

> I'm just going because I have the chance, I guess. There's nothing else to do right now. I got a grant called an Illinois State Scholarship and they pay all the tuition. I don't really have any goals or anything. I don't really want to do anything but live. If you have goals, I guess they're important to you. But, I mean, what do we need goals for?
>
> You're just saying, well, maybe if I keep trying harder and harder, maybe I'll be happy someday. That's a bunch of bullshit. That's not accepting reality. I don't know. I guess I'm on more of a spirit trip than a physical trip. I mean I'm looking just to purify my spirit and be myself and live. That's all I'm looking for. You remember when I told you I was unhappy with what I already found, the way people try and map out your life for you. I've been looking, and it just seems to make a lot more sense just to accept life for what it is and just try to live.

Conclusion

For middle-class Americans whose occupational careers make most nonfamilial relationships contingent and secondary considerations in their lives, Ribley will probably be veiewed with a certain amount of nostalgia. It will remind them of the idyllic, pastoral versions of a rural America that one sees in the popular media. Here everyone has time for everyone else and proximity breeds a closeness that is neither emotionally suffocating nor spiritually deadening. Neighborliness and genuine charity create bonds that endure for a lifetime, and competition and internal strife never lead to serious destructiveness. This has not been Ribley's history, and its future is unlikely to conform to these comforting but unrealistic images of Rural America.

Needless to say, Ribley is hardly paradisaical. It is not a place where people are free from the pressures created by a declining economy or where people spontaneously help each other out with the daily problems of making a living. Yet there is something about

Ribley that ought not escape the notice of those who value the relatively diminished sense of social envy that marks the lives of its citizens.

As we shall see when we examine the upper-middle-class suburban community of Glenbar, there are communities where most adults are simply oblivious to the fact that relations between the generations involve a genuine concern for young people who are *not* one's children. It is the ability of adults to see young people as persons in their own right and to feel and express concern for their well-being that gives Ribley an especially humane face. To put this somewhat differently, adults in Ribley share a sense of common responsibility for the younger generation. They experience real pleasure in the fact that they are capable of taking care of whatever problems may confront the younger members of their community.

From a young person's point of view, Ribley is an attractive place because the personal, expressive, and communal aspects of one's social existence are woven unobtrusively into the institutional life of the community. There is almost none of the nervous, looking over one's shoulder that plagues adolescents in much more competitive status systems. Here some young people fear that their peers will find them without social merit, and they will be shunted aside and ignored. This feeling of having to keep on one's toes socially and in touch with the currents of the peer world is foreign to Ribley. Regardless of whether one's friends change or remain the same, a young person in Ribley does not worry about social recognition because the very fact of having grown up in the town guarantees that others know one in more than a superficial way. Moreover, knowledge about the social identities of young people is shared by the generations in Ribley. Thus, young people do not feel that only their peers understand who they really are as distinct persons.

In Ribley, youth are not subject to the pressure of intensely competitive standards of individual excellence—save in basketball. Consequently, there is very little sense among youth that a demanding, impersonal, and, in many respects, unsupportive academic apparatus is making them run faster and faster to keep up with the rest of their peers. In sum, the reasonableness of authority is manifest both in what the youth of Ribley do not have to deal with and in the protective and nurturant response of adults to their difficulties and deviance. While the community cannot obliterate the harsh realities of class, it tries to make life as comfortable and unrestrictive for youth as it can. It is not surprising that youth accept authority in Ribley.

3

Patusa

Community Setting

Patusa is a peaceful and conventional American town. It has low unemployment, very few members of minority groups, and no aristocracy of wealth. When the fieldworker first inspected the town, all the houses looked alike to him. There is one "better" residential neighborhood, two new subdivisions, and one mini-slum near the fairgrounds, which he only discovered by diligent looking. It is the only neighborhood in town with a name: Greyson. There is a small two-year college on the outskirts of town with a few hundred students living on campus, the Patusa Christian College, a new institution dominated by the town rather than vice-versa.

There is a striking correspondence between the landscape and the culture of a town like Patusa. Ribley is set in a region of rolling hills, twisting roads, and valleys. The traveler can see from the physiognomy of the land how each town in the area might develop an inward-looking orientation. And, when they are not marred by mining machinery, one can still feel the presence of untamed nature in the wooded fields. Though it is a bit larger, it would be easy to think that Patusa is smaller than Ribley because it is located on a flat agricultural plain that is open to the world on four sides and traversed, as are all towns in the area, by highways.

In this region, there is a certain studied ordinariness to towns like Patusa, as if no place wanted to appear any different than its neighbors. Moreover, the openness of the town, the ease with which one can move through it, almost proclaims that there are no hidden secrets here, no history that is not on the surface and available for public inspection. At the same time, the very sameness of towns like Patusa also has special meaning for those who live there.

The clean, well-kept appearance of their town testifies to its safety, quiet, and prosperity. Patusa is situated in the heartland of American agricultural productivity. At the time of our fieldwork in the 1970s, the land value of the farmland which abutted the outskirts of the town would have impressed an urban real estate developer. The perception that the town was an integral part of what was considered the most successful agricultural enterprise in the history of mankind gave a subdued confidence and pride to towns like Patusa. And, in places like Patusa, there is a deep-seated feeling that local civic traditions set the moral tone for the society as a whole.

Patusa is more prosperous than Ribley and more centrally located vis-à-vis large cities and urban culture. It is in driving distance of large college towns and a fairly large city. Yet, proximity to more urban places is something Patusa prefers to play down. Instead, the culture of Patusa emphasizes small-town stability, consensus, and homogeneity. Equally important, Patusans believe that their peace and security must be protected from disruptive influences in the surrounding culture.

The values of tolerance and accommodation that characterize the culture of Ribley are not experienced by townspeople as opposing the culture of the larger society. In Patusa, however, many people are aware of the tension between the local emphasis on order and security and the larger society's fascination with change and innovation. New life-styles, ideologies, and values are something Patusa identifies with the disorder of urban life. The local middle class, which sets the cultural tone of Patusa, is not oblivious to the images of cultural sophistication that portray the new, the adventurous, and the different as exciting and pleasurable. But, as far as this town is concerned, this sort of imagery is fine as long as it is confined to television commercials. The normative structure of Patusa is deeply invested in keeping cultural change and experimentation to a minimum, and, correlatively, in making certain that young people show proper deference for authority. Whatever may be going on in the larger society, Patusans have decided that there is considerable merit to the old adage that young people ought to be seen but not heard.

There is a defensive posture to the culture of Patusa. It is much easier for those in authority to say what sorts of behavior and activities they will not permit than to speak about those sorts of qualities they would like to see young people develop. Though the basic norm is made explicit in practice rather than stated as public policy, youth in Patusa are expected to keep out of trouble. This means not drawing negative attention to themselves in public situations.

If we think of the culture of Ribley as arising out of its sense of what makes living in this community worthwhile, then we can think of the culture of Patusa as a reaction to what it fears. This is perhaps too stern a contrast between the communities because Ribley is not without a sense of threatening urban influences (e.g., drugs) and Patusa does value what can be called the middle-of-the-road way of life. But the responses of these communities to youthful deviance are so strikingly different that the normative structures of the towns are almost mirror opposites.

Social Outlooks: Locals

John Cox, who has lived in Patusa for most of his life and taught at the high school for twenty years, describes the town:

> It's a small town, even though it is a town of nearly 18,000 people. The thought is still, "Let's stay small, let's not get too big too fast." Patusa is unusual in that there are a large number of people who have grown up here, got their education, and come back. There's a surprising high percentage of teachers who graduated from Patusa High School and went through Patusa elementary. It is a somewhat closed town. Which makes it difficult for the average outsider to move in. Yet it doesn't totally set up all kinds of barriers. In other words, a person has to want to get into community life. The community doesn't go out and seek him. But on the other hand, if he sees a way in, he can get in.

Cox's comments are ostensibly about what it takes for someone to be socially accepted by long-term residents of the town. The metaphor of a "closed" town implies that an outsider has to make oneself known to other people for an extended period of time before they will feel comfortable including that person in local affairs and groups. However, it also implies that Patusans distrust the new and unfamiliar on principle. It is not only that newcomers have to go out of their way to let people know that they would like to get to know townspeople on an informal basis. They have to convince local people that they are not anxious to change the way things have been done in the past or question the way in which local institutions operate.

One person who came to Patusa and found a way in was Ronald Shafer. He has lived in Patusa for twelve years and is a member of the school board. He describes the process of getting in:

We had to show up in different organizations. We belonged to
the Newcomer's Club, Jaycees, and Edna belonged to a couple
of card clubs, and Marathon bridge. We had to join these different organizations to feel kind of accepted in the community.

Listening to Cox and Shafer talk about Patusa, the culture of the
town seems rather paradoxical. On the one hand, there is a clear
line drawn between those people who "belong" to the town, who are
on the "inside," and people who live in the town but do not belong
and are on the outside. On the other hand, it seems like there are no
special criteria for membership; no one is included or excluded for
specific reasons or purposes. All it takes to join the inner circle,
according to these men, is time *and* effort.

But it is precisely these qualities, a willingness to devote considerable time and effort to the civic life of a small town, that clearly
differentiates between people who are committed to Patusan values
and norms and those who are not. Unlike small towns where an
invisible political elite manipulates civic institutions from behind the
scenes (see Vidich and Bensman 1960), the Patusan "elite" are simply people who participate in the church suppers, fraternal orders,
and all of the associational activities that are the institutional life-
blood of small-town America. From the Patusan perspective, it is
natural and right that people who believe in hard work, patriotism,
respectability, neighborliness, law and order, and similar civic virtues should represent what the town values about itself. From this
point of view, the elite of Patusa are simply those people who believe in its normative orientation and are ready to put these values
to work in everyday life.

In a town like Patusa, the fact that there is a social hierarchy
makes people uncomfortable enough not to discuss it openly as they
do in Ribley. In part, this is due to the peculiar criteria for membership in the town's "inner circle." While Patusa is egalitarian in
some respects, it is also aware that it is exclusive in other respects.
Since membership depends on showing goodfellowship and fitting
smoothly into local activities, the town culture cannot easily reject
or accept people on the basis of the relative merit of individual accomplishment. On the other hand, hierarchical arrangements are in
a very real sense the concrete realization of the town's desire for
order and predictability. Hierarchy insures that everyone knows
where they ought to be.

Parkville is one of the cities of about 100,000 persons within an
hour's drive from Patusa which represent the problems of urban
America. Parkville is the state capital, and Hillcrest and Col-

legeville are both university towns. A high school administrator, born in Patusa, comments on the differences between Patusa and these cities:

> Patusa would find more in common with a town like Kostka [pop. 2,500] than with Parkville. They don't see themselves try- ing to compete with those big towns. A certain dislike for the largeness of those towns, and those towns are small when com- pared to some places. This town has not been forced to experience things that large towns have experienced. The stu- dent unrest of the late sixties never did get here. The demand for student rights and all of these other types of things, the large towns were hit—Hillcrest, Parkville, Collegeville—and missed the small towns. Change around here has been gradual and has not been that unsettling. The status quo is pretty much a guideline to follow. Patusa is very heavy in the middle-class bracket, maybe not so much in dollars and cents, but certainly in attitude it's very much middle class, with great respect for education, for law and order. And if you had a sudden tremen- dous push of the lower class, this would be an upset. There would undoubtedly be many repercussions in the schools.

What is striking about this administrator's comments is the ex- tent to which cultural differences are experienced as more powerful in Patusa than class differences. When he speaks of Patusa as being "heavy" into the "middle-class bracket," but quickly qualifies this by saying that it is really not a matter of money, he puts his finger on a basic normative orientation. For Patusans, class is primarily a symbol of cultural commitments. Although poor people are effec- tively disqualified from full participation in civic institutions, that is about as far as money intrudes on a person's ability to feel central to the town's culture. Patusans experience the town as open and friendly to the extent that they share its values and see those values as reflections of core American values. For those who experience those values as parochial and constricting, Patusa is anything but open and friendly.

The primary fear in Patusa is not related to class, even though the administrator speaks of a "push" from the lower class. What Patusa wants, above all else, is order and stability. Anything that promotes that value is acceptable; anything that does not is seen as threatening and alien. For this reason, Patusans feel no affinity to the culture of towns that are receptive to cosmopolitan values. From the Patusan perspective, the future depends upon keeping a firm grip on the behavior of any group that might support conflict and dissent. It is in this respect that this administrator imagines that a "push" from the lower classes, who do not value order and stability, would disrupt the town culture.

There is little sign of class conflict in Patusa because lower-class people are not credited with being anything more than deficient in the values the town endorses. In Patusa, lower-class people are socially invisible. Ribley is an instructive contrast in this regard since people there who are in positions of authority are sensitive to the difficulties of poor people.

The state-run facility in Patusa adds to the town's defensiveness. The hospital employs 15 percent of the town's labor force, and the economic contribution of the hospital to the town is well known. But this institution is run by outsiders. The local people who work there are mostly service workers and paraprofessionals. The managers and professionals who staff the hospital come to the town with urban, cosmopolitan, and university-based values. They often look down on the locals who are under their direction. Friction between locals and outsiders in the hospital is common.

But Patusans are not extreme in their zenophobia. To strangers they are usually genial, polite, and genuinely friendly. Where they draw the line is with respect to personal ties. They keep strangers at a distance until they prove their commitment to Patusa.

Cosmopolitans

Beside those who came to Patusa to stay, there were other outsiders who did not expect to remain for life and did not share the town's values. They remained on the fringe of the town's social life and, for the most part, resented their exclusion and disliked the town.

The Brands were a family who had taken root in Patusa. Mr. Brand was a home owner and engineer for a power company, Mrs. Brand taught primary school, and one son was a popular high school student known for his talent in several extracurricular activities. They had lived in the town for ten years, but Mrs. Brand still had not adjusted to the gossip network. Our fieldworker reports a conversation with her:

> Mrs. Brand said that she had been getting phone calls all day about what happened at the Recreation Center last night. She said this is an example of how things get around in a small town. She wished she could find some place to live in peace without everyone in town knowing what's going on in your life.

She is from a big city and she misses the anonymity . . . She said that she and her husband were just talking about how it's almost impossible to get accepted here unless you were born here or have a lot of patience. She said it's always the women who suffer. Her husband has an interesting job, and she is the one who has to put up with life in a small town.

Mrs. Brand's comments highlight the difference in the culture of Ribley and Patusa. In both places, people are familiar with many of the details of other peoples' lives that would go unnoticed in the city. Beside the lack of anonymity, there is a good deal of talk about those events that add a little spice to the even flow of social life— what city dwellers call small-town gossip. Yet the crucial difference between these places is not what is discussed but how it is discussed.

In Patusa, gossip serves to reinforce the norm of restraint on adolescent expressive behavior and control over the admission of cosmopolitan values to public forums. Mrs. Brand's son was involved in a trivial matter. The response of the town, however, was to caution her about allowing her son to be seen as someone who gets out of line. It was not the seriousness of what he did but the simple fact that Kevin's behavior drew attention to him that was communicated as potentially threatening. Thus, familiarity to Patusa implies surveillance. For Mrs. Brand it was like living in a fishbowl, wondering whether an expression of difference would be interpreted as a sign of intent to violate the town's injunction against youthful displays of exuberance. Moreover, by listening to the gossip, Mrs. Brand was forced to go along with the town's values rather than asserting her ow, namely, that there was nothing about her son that merited this kind of response to his behavior. In Ribley, on the other hand, this sort of gossip is an assertion of connectedness and familiarity. The tone would be one of amusement over the incident rather than, as in Patusa, tension over its possible (but remote) implications for a young person's reputation.

Frank Carpenter is a professional member of the staff of the hospital. He reveals how uncomfortable the town can be for someone who does not approve of its values:

He thought this place was a closed, conservative society. He told me some problems he had about getting his appliances serviced and trading his Volvo in for a new Ford. Unless you can prove that you're from the town and that you work here, they give you a hard time. Whenever he wants to relax, he leaves town. I asked him why he stays. He said that he is doing very well in his work at the hospital and is accomplishing a lot.

Patusa is a perplexing place for middle-class professionals whose occupational identity is a central aspect of their sense of self. These people find it odd and, perhaps, even a little distressing when local institutions make a point of ignoring their expertise. What is even more unsettling is that local people seem genuinely disinterested in knowing anything about the aspect of their professional lives in which they have invested so much time and energy. It is quite conceivable that a professional could spend a lot of time in local organizations, like the Shafers have, without ever being accepted on his or her own terms. In the following incident, a city-born social worker describes a little vignette that discloses how tightly the town closes itself off from what it regards as foreign influences:

> He came over to the high school to introduce himself to the principal. When he told him he was a social worker from the Tri-County office, located in Collegeville, the principal was very reluctant to see him. He wouldn't even let him in his office saying he didn't need any social workers coming down from Collegeville. Then when Jack told him he had just bought a house in Patusa, he was immediately invited into the office, offered a cup of coffee, and treated very well.

Looking at this incident, one can see the potent symbolism attached to the idea of being a permanent resident of the town. Even though this social worker's professional credentials were enough to arouse the distrust that goes with being categorized as an "outsider," the fact that he lived in Patusa was enough to suggest to the principal that this social worker might share their values. In small but significant ways, one can see how the moral boundaries of this community are delineated and protected. Encounters that have ostensibly little bearing upon a person's commitment to the town's values are interpreted as occasions for finding out where a person stands. If a person in authority suspects or knows that an outsider is antagonistic to the norms of town, avoidance and distance are the preferred ways of dealing with the situation. Adults who do not accept the dominant social consensus are put off and ignored rather than stigmatized and extruded. The case is quite the reverse where young people are concerned.

Since so much of the conflict between the generations has been cast in a mold of political conservatism and radicalism, it is important not to read political meanings into the cultural bias of Patusa.

While the culture is certainly congruent with some conservative political values, its normative order is not grounded in these values. That is to say, being "liberal" has a rather different meaning in Patusa than it would in a city. In Patusa, people with a decidedly liberal bent in national politics can fit into the town, providing that they see that its stability depends upon maintaining a nonpluralistic local culture. That means that a person becomes a member of the group that controls local institutions on the basis of his allegiance to Patusan culture. There is a tacit agreement to keep controversial social issues out of local forums, although those issues can be addressed without any fear of alienating townspeople if they are stated as issues concerning the larger polity.

This explains what seems to be an anomalous case: a local citizen with decidedly liberal political allegiances who fits smoothly into the cultural style of the town. Kenneth Grant was born in Patusa, went to the city where he established a career, got married and started a family and came back to Patusa. In 1972 he was a local organizer for George McGovern's candidacy for president:

> I lived for five years in the big city. Sometimes I thought I
> would like to live there, but I really didn't want to commute. So
> we moved to Patusa, and it solved that problem for us. To me,
> being a native of Patusa, it's a perfect-sized town. The Chamber
> of Commerce is interested in their own thing instead of trying
> to attract more industry. But I like Patusa, I like its location, I
> like its size. It was easier for me because I could come into a
> business that was already established. And some of the advan-
> tages that the big city has, well, we go back a lot. But it's not
> attractive for young children. Patusa hasn't changed that much
> in thirty years. It still has all the good things it had before.

Grant, like many people in small towns, recognizes the existence of class at the same time that he denies its role in the social life of the community. He says that while there is no "class structure per se" in Patusa, the class structure does not go "much higher" than the upper-middle class and "goes all the way down" to the bottom of the social scale. While this sounds like a contradiction, Grant goes on to point out that what really counts in a town like Patusa is the feeling of cultural homogeneity: "I think the people who go to opera are the same people who go to the drive-in." Although that may not be literally true, it points to the belief that the town's culture arises out of a common way of life.

The phrase, "a common way of life," is easily misunderstood. In urban areas, a common way of life is predicated on sharing economic interests, social aspirations, family backgrounds, and similar social factors that create distinct social worlds. In a town like Patusa, people can have differing politics, economic interests, religious affiliations, and so on without ever doubting that they share a common way of life. In places like Patusa, the marks of a common cultural style are pervasive and easily recognized in face-to-face contacts. Social differences that would strike an urban observer as potentially divisive are seen by local people as just differences between individuals.

Thus, it would be wrong to interpret the hegemony of the local middle class as having been imposed upon resistant groups by a politically and economically dominant social stratum. Rather, as Grant notes, "everybody in Patusa kind of mixes it up." He contrasts this free-flowing sociability with the exclusiveness of social circles in college towns divided by their commitment to different values and life-styles. By keeping cultural diversity to a minimum, the normative order of Patusa has gained clarity and sharpness.

The Social Status of Youth

In Patusa, youth serve the symbolic aspirations of the adults. One of the central tasks of the athletic teams and extracurricular activites of the high school is to entertain adults and to make them feel that their town can compete successfully in the wider society. Basketball in Patusa was not just a game but a spectacle.

> The visiting team had been on the floor for about a minute when the twelve-piece Patusa pep band started playing "Sweet Georgia Brown" and the Patusa Eagles came out. They were wearing green warm-up suits with flared legs. Each player had his name on the back of his suit. They were carrying red, white, and blue basketballs. The entire gym erupted in cheers and rose to its feet when they came out. The two team captains stood under the basket, and the rest of the team formed into a semi-circle in front of them. Then in time to the music they went through a series of choreographed warm-up exercises using the basketballs. They had a precise routine, and everybody knew what he was doing. After about three minutes the performance ended with everyone spinning the ball on his index finger.

This ritual occurred at all games. At key football and basketball games in the town, the parents of all the players were introduced and honored. Cheerleaders pinned corsages on each of the mothers. At his first football game, the fieldworker remarked:

The adults I was sitting with were really into the game. I overheard conversations which amazed me because of the knowledge of football history that was displayed. I heard tonight's game compared to last year's game against Collegeville. I heard players compared to their older brother or father. I heard people who seemed to know the name of everyone on the team. The people I overheard were both men and women, middle-aged and older. I moved around in the stands and got the same picture.

Adult involvement in high school sports is not unique to Patusa. But in Patusa all the public activities of adolescents are not only adult managed but also adult oriented. This principle that youthful activites should be subordinate to adult concerns applies even to those special occasions reserved for youth. This becomes evident in the way adults stage, control, and eventually take over the senior prom. In Patusa, the experience of being displaced by adults is not unusual. The fieldworker describes a conversation with a disillusioned student:

> One of the students was telling me the whole thing [the prom] is ruined by the principal who is always telling everyone what to do. There are two couples who lead the activities, and everyone has to do what they do. The prom is held in the school gym, and it is always packed with parents. The kids soon get tired and sit down and then the adults get up and start "jitterbugging."

Patusa High School

Patusa High School embodies the town's central values. The school is, in part, responsible for Patusa's good standing in the outside world—through its athletic programs, the quality of its physical plant, the modernity of its curriculum. Its investment in the decorum of the traditional middle class, and its commitment to unchallengeable authority over youth makes the school an "invulnerable" institution. Not everyone in Patusa agrees with the values expressed by the high school. But those who do disagree are marginal to the town's social structure or unsure of what bothers them about the way the school is run.

The Physical Plant

The new physical plant was built in the early fifties. It stands in a spacious setting on the edge of town, amid the corn and soybean fields which cover most of the county. The classroom building, gym and pool, shop building, power plant, and football stadium serve 1,400 students. Every morning and afternoon on school days, the large parking lot between the classroom building and the state highway is filled with a long line of those distinctive yellow buses seen all over America.

The rectangular outlines of buff brick with louvered windows have been constructed in hundreds of towns across America. Inside, the corridors have the pastel tones of asphalt and ceramic tile, buff-colored metal lockers, and a waxed and shiny cleanliness that are an established part of the institutional decor of many American public schools. The whole complex speaks of order, efficiency, and modest affluence. Nothing is opulent, but everything works.

The high school represents a considerable investment of local, state, and federal funds. Officials are well aware of what the school costs, and its budget is very carefully managed. The citizens of the town take pride in their school. It is as good as any in the state for a town of its size. Its football teams have a respectable record. Its musical and dramatic productions are well-attended and professionally done. Its basketball teams are often contenders for the Class AA state championship.

The high school enforces the value local culture places on youth's unquestioning obedience to official authority. There is also a minority position on this issue. A few teachers and officials dislike it—mostly those who deal with the poor and disadvantaged—and some parents are uneasy about it. Most of the students dislike it, but they are also resigned and fatalistic. Their chief solution is to get out of town: parking on the back roads; driving to Collegeville, Parkville, or Hillcrest for a night of entertainment; or making plans to leave for good after graduation.

Patusa seems to be a model of order and efficiency, a place where traditional authority relationships between youth and adults work with little evidence of conflict. But, as we shall see, this system has its costs. From the viewpoint of many adults, the costs may seem negligible. What is missing in Patusa is the expressive freedom one finds in Ribley. In Patusa we will see that the bonds of authority so constrict the development of adolescent expressiveness that most youth culture styles hardly exist. There is simply a choice between conformity to adult norms or keeping one's reservations about conventional wisdom to oneself. Therefore, in contrast to Ribley, we can see that there is little social space given to adolescents in Patusa to work out their own relationships and develop their own modes of sociability. That accounts for the great emphasis in Patusa on proper conduct in public places. It is here that the meaning of authority is communicated most forcefully and directly to youth: if you get out of line you will lose your place in the sole institution where young people are allowed to congregate—the school.

Tracking

There are three academic tracks in the school: the advanced courses, the normal courses, and the remedial courses. The field-worker describes an encounter with the official who sets the policy for the school:

> One of the secretaries handed me a teacher's schedule while I was waiting for Chapman to return. We went over the list of the teachers, and Chapman had me circle the hours of the ones that agreed to have me observe in their classes. I thanked him for his help and asked how I could contact teachers outside of the class. He pointed to a woman over at the faculty mailboxes and said, "There's Mrs. Moses now." Mrs. Moses asked me if Chapman had explained to me about tracking. He had. When he gave me the teachers' schedule, he told me not to let any of the students see it since it has the tracks that the teachers teach on it. He said that I should keep it on the "q.t."

Chapman, who is the school disciplinarian, is hiding something everyone knows is public knowledge. This is not as irrational as it might seem since the point of not letting the students see the schedule is to reinforce a significant norm. School policy is not a legitimate matter for even casual discussion between students and authorities. The latter decide policy and the former conform to it. It is as simple as that. Moreover, this atmosphere of secrecy has additional benefits as far as the administration is concerned. It lets the teachers as well as the students know that everyone has their proper place in the school and that the lines of formal authority dictate who has a right to say how things are to be done. Teachers can privately disagree with tracking or any other aspect of school policy, but the norm is that one does not confront authority with those doubts about the way things are run in Patusa.

Mrs. Brian was a new teacher who taught junior English. After observing one of her classes, the fieldworker talked with her about it.

> Then she asked me if I knew about the tracking system they use in the school. I said I did. She said that she doesn't believe

in it. She treats all kids the same, and she has found out that she gets very good things out of the kids that she has been told couldn't do anything. She said she's found that the kids usually do what you expect of them.

In Patusa, the academic tracking system reflects the idea that privilege and achievement are interchangeable goods. That is to say, those students who are able to demonstrate excellence as a publically certified accomplishment (e.g., scores on standardized tests) deserve the resources to further develop their talents. This is seen in Patusa as the very incarnation of the principles of equality's individualistic essence. Those persons who have the creativity, strength, motivation, and intelligence will do what they have to do to put themselves in a favorable position to get ahead in the world. Those who lack these qualities will not be left out in the cold but will, as Mrs. Brian implies, get less because adults expect less of them. Though she does not quite say so, Mrs. Brian suspects that these young people will grow up feeling somewhat inferior to the rest of their peers.

Yet, for other teachers, tracking reflects differences in ability. It is a privilege to teach the "higher" classes. Our fieldworker remarks:

> I couldn't help but compare Mr. Wolf's class with Mrs. Brian's. I thought of what Mrs. Brian had told me about her views on tracking. Mr. Wolf had told me about his Advanced Placement class before his average class even got started. I got the feeling that he was afraid I would judge him as a teacher by the performance of his average class. If I wanted to see what was really going on, I should come to his better class. Mrs. Brian's class is more chaotic than Wolf's but the kids in Wolf's class seemed bored in the extreme.

Mr. Wolf, like many teachers at the high school, sees the academic hierarchy as a source of occupational rewards and liabilities. He feels that being personally involved in the lives of youth who seem to be going somewhere indicates that he has the qualities that go along with being successful in the world. Conversely, having to cast his lot with students who are, in his eyes, ordinary and nondescript means that there is nothing that will bring out his native creativity. He lets the fieldworker know that this kind of teaching is a routine activity.

In spite of the care authorities take to conceal tracking from the students at the "bottom" of the ladder, they are aware of the stigma associated with their situation.

I asked York about Title III. He told me it was a program for students with reading disabilities. His job is to teach science without using a text, since his students don't read very well. I asked him if his students are aware of being Title III kids, and he answered, "They are aware of their disabilities. Title III offers them science, reading, math, and English especially designed for people with reading disabilities." He said that in the past these kids were just ignored because no one wanted to work with them. With Title III they have a chance to get something out of school. Toward the end of the class almost everyone had put their packets away. The class started to ask Mr. York about the Diversified Occupations program again. One boy asked him directly, "Will they let Title III kids in?" Mr. York said he was sure they would since that was the whole point of the program.

Mrs. Pulaski, another English teacher, pointed out that other students are also conscious of the tracking system's status implications:

I asked her if the kids know about the tracking system. She answered that everyone with the possible exception of the freshmen knows about it. Once they find out about it, it's very hard for them to change their self-image. Some of them even look around when they go into a class, to find the "lowest" person there. Once he's been spotted, they know where they are and what will be expected of them.

Faculty Divisions

Styles of teaching in Patusa are closely related to the school's "managerial philosophy." Mrs. Brian represents the minority view:

She knows that a lot of kids are doing dope because she hears them talking about it in her class. She added that "because I'm young" they ask her if she smokes. Of course she has to tell them no because she doesn't, and she couldn't tell them even if she did. I got the feeling that Mrs. Brian had been waiting to tell this to someone for a long time. She said that the same things that go on in the town go on in the school too. She was almost fired for trying to run her classes the way that she thought was the most effective and conducive to learning. Mr. Chapman did not like what she was doing. All the first year untenured teachers were videotaped, and the department heads and people in the office had to evaluate them. Chapman said her classes were too noisy, and the kids weren't disciplined enough. He said that she had better tighten up or she would be out of a job. So she had to put more restrictions on the kids. She did not know what to tell them since she had already told them she didn't believe in strict discipline. So she didn't say anything, she just did it. There was some grumbling, but none of the kids asked her about it.

It is not surprising that Mrs. Brian had to put more restraints on the freedom with which students moved about the classroom and expressed their opinions. But what is particularly noteworthy is that the students accepted the change in Mrs. Brian's demeanor without comment. Before, she had encouraged individual initiative. Now, she controlled classroom routine with a much firmer hand. Students do not openly question the right of authority to demand conformity to the rules over issues that elsewhere would be viewed as a matter of individual inclination. But, in Patusa, minor issues about how things are done become major concerns if young people appear to be deciding for themselves how the rules should be interpreted.

However, this seemingly unyielding demand for obedience to authority does not intimidate some teachers who are sure of their position in the school.

Mr. York told the class about the most recent faculty meeting he had been to. There was a speaker talking about "the open classroom" concept. The whole idea got most of the faculty "up-tight." One of the books the speaker had used was *Teaching as a Subversive Activity.* York said he already owned a copy and so he brought it to school the next day. He started reading it in the teachers' lounge, holding it high so everyone could see the title. He said he could hear the gasps of shock and dismay when the older teachers walked into the room. He told his students there was one section he wanted to read to them. Just as he found the place, the bell rang. He grinned and told them he would read it to them on Monday.

Mrs. Brian later left the school, but Mr. York remained. His presence is evidence that the present authority system is not as monolithic as it may seem to the students. As it stands, adult authority rests upon two premises. First, the adult authorities must let young people know that the rules must be taken very seriously, and, in instances where authority decides that they have been willfully violated, there is no effective means of escaping the penalties for misconduct. The second principle is less obvious.

As we saw earlier, Mrs. Brian mentioned that she felt she could not discuss smoking grass with her students in an open and non-judgmental manner. This would be seen by Chapman as a breach of a basic but unstated norm: adults in their official capacity as authorities cannot have fraternal relationships with youth unless that sort of informal contact works to the advantage of the established authority structure. In Patusa, therefore, authority rests upon the social distance between the generations. Anything that would diminish the feeling of distance would undermine the present system of authority. It is for this reason that new forms of teaching which might shift intergenerational relationships toward a collegial or collaborative model is experienced by Chapman as threatening the established authority structure.

Patusa is sensitive to "outside" influences that might first appear as innocuous additions to the curriculum. Courses that focus on personal experiences, such as psychology and behavioral science, make it difficult for teachers to maintain formal barriers between themselves and students. Thus, anything that might reduce the sense of social distance between students and teachers is something the authorities at Patusa High regard with suspicion. The fieldworker notes how carefully the school monitors change:

> I told Cox I was surprised that there are no behavioral science courses being offered. He told me that there will be two next year: General Psychology and Introduction to the Behavioral Sciences. I asked if they were going to hire new teachers for that. He answered that he didn't know about the psychology course, but the behavioral science course will be taught by the band teacher. Cox said that he didn't even know if the band teacher was going to get paid for that extra course.

It would be a mistake to imagine that the student body of Patusa High School is seething with unsatisfied intellectual curiosity or that they are dissatisfied with rigid teaching methods. A young high school teacher remarks that while the adults are concerned that teenagers will be swept away by threatening changes in the larger society, youth are less critical in Patusa than in other places:

I think there are a lot of stereotypes kids learn from their parents or relatives or neighbors or maybe even from their churches. That comes out in English classes. Reading a story, and it deals with somebody who is black or Puerto Rican or Jewish or any minority group. The kids usually have prejudged opinions, and very few of them are open-minded. Of course, it also depends on how much a student is willing to talk freely in a classroom situation with a teacher and the other students. So I don't always get a true picture, except for those very brave people who are willing to put themselves on the line as a truly biased person or a truly open-minded one. Very few of them are willing to be honest.

Not only are students intellectually passive in class, they are also not too enthusiastic about the school's academic programs. The fieldworker's description of classroom activities is full of references to a great deal of dead time and routine. By and large, students simply go through the motions in class without investing any real energy in their studies. Apathy is so widespread that it is difficult to elicit either negative or positive sentiments from the students. A typical response to the fieldworker's question about the favorite part of school was:

I don't know . . . after school. Let's see, probably lunch. In our P.E. class, if you get showered and dressed real quick, you can leave into C lunch. It's never more than five or ten minutes, and I go out and talk to Rick.

Discipline

In Patusa, troublesome youth are handled principally by the high school rather than by the police, and in the school they are handled almost exclusively by the dean of students, Gerald Chapman. Chapman's position in the town is quite extraordinary. Parents of teenagers, ministers, and officials who deal with youth responded immediately when asked about Chapman. Jack Kent was a school social worker whose territory covered three counties:

He told me Chapman has a very dirty job but enjoys it. He has an old-fashioned attitude toward drugs. Until recently, any kid caught with dope was thrown out of school. He is reluctant to accept the changes that are going on with youth. One of the determining factors in how much trouble a kid gets into around here is who the kid's parents are. Chapman is known to bend the rules according to the influence the kid's parents have. He told the story—I had heard it before—about a basketball star stealing a car from the parking lot. He said Chapman "bent over backward" to give Wright a break. He told about a kid in the band who was punished severely for drinking on the bus during a band trip. He told about some football players who only got a warning when they broke into a swimming pool after a game in another town.

Chapman gives some youth a "pass" when they are caught violating the rules without feeling that he is contradicting his posture in the community. He gives those youth a pass who he knows will not see this as a sign of softness and who acknowledge that they are getting "special" treatment from him. The idea that authority has the right to decide when and to whom it will make a special exception strengthens the image of its power and invulnerability. However, this is entirely different in Chapman's mind from the notion that authority ought to negotiate the rationality of the rules with youth. The idea that youth should have the right to even comment on the judgment of authority in particular cases would be an anathema to Chapman.

Mr. Gates, the county probation officer, grew up in Patusa. His view of Chapman is as follows:

> He comes across as a very rough and gruff man who doesn't seem to give a hoot about the kids. Then again, I've seen him behave quite the opposite, and has taken in some kids who have really done screwy things and deserve to be kicked out and has sat down and talked to them and, well, not really let them off the hook, but at least explained to them why he's doing what he's doing, and has given them a chance to level with him. For the most part, I think, he pretty much shuts kids off and is pretty harsh in some punishments. Those kids who have a history of behavioral difficulties he's pretty rough with, doesn't really give them a chance to explain any extenuating circumstances of their behavior.

Chapman's own rhetoric on the nature of youth is far from punitive cynicism. He talks about youth warmly, saying that he tries to give them a break whenever he can. As long as offenders defer to his authority he is willing to forgive. But to anyone who seems to dispute his right to define unilaterally the moral correctness of behavior, he is severe and unrelenting. Chapman's philosophy of social control is illustrated by his relationship with a student we call Glen who was, in Gates's euphemism, one of those kids who have a history of behavioral difficulties. The fieldworker relates a story about Glen:

> Glen got on the wrong bus with three girls he didn't know very well. They had several bottles of coke and were drinking them in the back seat. One of the girls threw her empty bottle out of the window, and it broke on the street. The bus driver didn't notice it. Then Glen decided to try the same thing, but he got caught. The bus driver asked him for his name. Glen told him that it was Leroy Jones, which Glen thought was hilarious. He said that the whole bus was laughing about this. The driver didn't think it was very funny and said that he had better give him his real name or he would be in big trouble. Glen refused to tell him and got off the bus. The driver asked the people on the bus if any of them knew Glen's name, and no one would tell him. A girl who he used to go with was on the bus, and even she didn't tell. He said that it made him feel good that no one would turn him in, maybe Patusa wasn't such a bad place after all.

The next day, however, the fieldworker observed the following:

> In Mrs. Brian's class one of the basketball players came into the room with a slip for someone to go down to the office. Usually Porky goes down, but Mrs. Brian read the slip and told Glen that it was for him. His face got very pale. He took the slip and went out without saying anything. In about five minutes Glen came back. Kevin asked him what was going on. Glen said, "I'm kicked out of school." Glen told me that Chapman said that if he didn't give the names of the three girls on the bus, he'd get thrown out of school. Porky said that he had been in the same situation last year. He had been caught racing with another guy in the school parking lot. Chapman said that if he turned the other guy in, he would let both of them go. So Porky turned his friend in and neither of them got into any trouble. So he advised Glen to turn in the girls.

The following day the fieldworker walked with Glen on the way to his after-school job.

> On the twenty-minute walk Glen told me that he had turned in the names of the three girls who were on the bus with him. All that happened was that Chapman said he couldn't ride the bus for five days. He didn't know what happened to the girls. I asked him if he had talked to the girls first. He said he hadn't. He seemed reluctant to talk about it.

The incident reveals how authority operates in Patusa. Chapman did not tell Glen whether he thought that throwing a bottle was serious enough to get him suspended from school until *after* Glen decided to give the names of the girls. It would have been one thing for Glen to face Chapman solely on the basis of what he did on the bus. It was quite another thing to have Chapman make his judgment of Glen's conduct contingent on Glen's willingness to acknowledge Chapman's authority over his loyalty to his friends. That was an especially pressing issue because these girls had refused to turn him in on the bus. Now he was being asked to betray them.

By forcing Glen to choose between his own survival in the school and his feelings for his friends, we can see how effectively authority in Patusa severs the solidarities that constitute meaningful peer relationships. In Patusa, authority individualizes youth, both in the way it distributes exceptions from the rules as well as by the way it punishes. Young people are forced to stand apart from their friends and deal with authority on the basis of whatever authority believes is efficacious as far as enforcement of the rules are concerned. The only mitigating circumstances for youth are those that work to the advantage of adult authority.

In Chapter 1, we distinguished between the rationality and the reasonableness of authority, and this incident is a good opportunity to explore the differences between these concepts. No one, including Glen, would seriously question that his act of throwing a bottle out of a moving bus violated the standard of rational behavior (i.e., it creates a potential hazard that could injure other persons). But the way Chapman responded to the incident involved a strange inversion of the notion of reasonableness. Chapman told Glen that he was willing to be "reasonable" as far as his behavior on the bus was concerned with one proviso: that Glen sacrifice his integrity by an act of disloyalty to his friends. Note that this is not intended as a public act of contrition, nor was Glen's "punishment" meant to deter others from throwing bottles out of moving vehicles. Chapman exacted a peculiar sacrifice from adolescents that has nothing to do with the rational basis for discipline. He demands that those he designates as official malefactors relinquish their expressive spontaneity.

In other words, Chapman wants a very special sort of deference and compliance from young people he suspects will assert themselves in ways that would upset the equanimity of adult authority. As persons who have publicly cast aspersions on the inviolability of authority, students like Glen must do the very thing that undermines their sense of dignity and personal worth. They must give up the feeling of being a fully acceptable and, perhaps, even admirable person in the eyes of their peers. Needless to say that for a sensitive, if not always prudent, person like Glen this meant shame and humiliation.

About a month after this incident, Glen was suspended from school for possession of marijuana. He had come to school in the morning high, bragging about it. When school was over for the day, Chapman met him on his way out, took him to the office and had him empty his pockets. Glen had ten grams of marijuana on him. He was suspended from school until the next school board meeting. The suggested punishment to be discussed by the school board was a one-year suspension. Glen's response to this was acknowledgement of his own stupidity, and contingency plans for moving away from Patusa if indeed he did get suspended. The fieldworker also talked to a Patusa police officer who said that Chapman had called the station about the case, but they told him to handle it. The officer then told the fieldworker in a disgusted tone of voice that Chapman should know there was no way they could touch it, with an illegal search like that.

We have seen that there are teachers, youth officers, social workers, and other authorities who have doubts about what they see as Chapman's inflexibility and arbitrariness. Yet these people also know that how they feel about dealing with a young person's problems does not make a difference as far as the community is concerned. It is tempting to ascribe this policy to the charisma of one person. But it is more realistic to believe that Chapman did not create the culture of Patusa but is only rather adept at putting its norms into practice.

The Peer Group World

Adults who had contact with young people on a regular basis distinguished those who they believed used dope from the larger mass of "straight" teenagers. Most adults thought that a few youth used drugs and that their appearance and demeanor made them quite visible. Aside from the fact that more teenagers use drugs in Patusa than adults would like to believe, the fact of "using dope" is only a significant social category for the adults. For teenagers, smoking marijuana is an important choice in life, but most of them do not make it on the basis of their identity.

Social identities in the youth world are largely based on class. There is the majority of straight youth and the minority of working-class greasers. This term has negative status connotations in Patusa. The fieldworker recounts the following incident:

> Kevin parked in front of a store called "the Bargain Center," down by the railroad tracks. It's a cheap, run-down–looking store. He apologized for going in, saying that he knows it's "a greaser store" but there is a jacket he saw there that he wants to get. He showed me the jacket. It's a short, black, canvas one. It exudes "greaser." Kevin asked me if I didn't think it was "a cartoon." I said I was surprised he would like anything like that. He told me that if he were new in town, he wouldn't wear it. People would think he really is a greaser. But since every one knows he's "hip," he can just enjoy it without having to worry.

When a particular social identity is salient in a community, one assumes that the style that is associated with the identity has considerable substance—that people who adopt the identity do so because certain activities, relationships, and personal attributes mean a good deal to them. However, what is peculiar about Patusa, and yet so in keeping with the normative orientation of the community, is that almost all youthful social identities are nearly contentless. In other words, being a greaser in Patusa says little more than that one is likely to dress in a certain way, come from a working- or lower-class background, and spend some time in the company of youth in similar circumstances. Besides these rather superficial characteristics, there is nothing that "greasers" do vis-à-vis each other, their peers, or adult authorities that makes them much different than any other youth.

In order to understand how unusual this situation is, we might think of Ribley where the term "greaser" is not nearly as common as in Patusa but where lower-class youth have a distinct content to their identity. Here there is a way of life based on a rural sort of toughness, excitement, and adventure that involves getting into fights, hard drinking, chasing after women, and, generally, raising hell. Unlike their urban counterparts, these youth in Ribley do not confront their middle-class peers with a belligerent attitude. Yet there is real substance to their social identity. In Patusa, the power of authority to extrude youth from the school is so great and the community is so deeply committed to surveillance over youthful behavior in public places that the greaser identity, like other youthful identities, is little more than a pallid gloss on an otherwise colorless adolescent social existence.

Moreover, the central symbol of the greaser identity revolves around challenges to conventional adult authority. The range for this sort of behavior is wide. A greaser can affirm his or her identity simply by defying respectable norms of behavior, as they do in Ribley, without openly defying adult authority. But in Patusa even this quite tame "wild" conduct would be seen as a dangerous form of youthful rebellion.

The youth of Patusa recognize other social identities, but they are even less salient than that of greaser. One category is the "farmers," but it does not have any status connotations for most teenagers. As one youth said, some farmers are high class, some are greasers, some are freaks. Another social identity encompasses a small elite of teenagers, including cheerleaders, athletes (especially basketball players), and other student leaders whose central identifying characteristic is that they get along well with authorities. Another social identity could be called the fashionable freak. These are youths who abstain from certain symbols of solidarity with adults, dress flamboyantly, and the boys wear their hair long. Among friends they are open about their interest in marijuana, sex, rock music, but still stay out of trouble. They view themselves as higher in social status than the grubby freaks. Still another social identity encompasses those youth who are publicly oriented toward religion. They go to a church-sponsored party on prom night and belong to a church youth club.

The majority of teenagers in Patusa go through life without acquiring one of these social identities. They live private lives in the undistinguished middle. But it would be a mistake to call all of them "straight." The fieldworker once found out that one of his young friends who did well in school, worked hard at a part-time and summer job for a local farmer, also sold about a pound of marijuana a month to personal friends.

The Greasers

In Patusa the term "greaser" itself is synonymous with working and lower-class youth. Talking with the seniors of an advanced placement class, the fieldworker heard the following:

Someone mentioned the skating rink that had opened recently. They said it was fun when it first opened but now it's "a greaser hangout" and none of them go there anymore. Amy said there might be more to do around here but the "greasers" have taken over a lot of the places. One of them said that with a college in the town you'd expect more to be going on, but it isn't. On weekends you have to watch out for the greasers. They don't hurt anyone, but as Amy said, they're just "so crude" they spoil everything.

Greasers are distinguishable from the hip denim look by the carelessness of personal grooming. Greaser youth clustered heavily in the remedial and Title III classes in school, although a good number of them made it to the average track, and a few to advanced placement courses. They had a loose network of meeting places to go to, the pool tables at the recreation center, the two commercial pool halls, out behind the welding shop, the bowling alley out alongside the interstate. But these few meeting places had no regular patterns of use. Only six youths regularly hung out together at the pool tables of the recreation center, and the chances of meeting someone you knew at the pool halls or the bowling alley were usually slim.

In almost all small-towns, having a place where one can meet one's friends on a casual basis without having any special plans or reasons for being there is taken for granted. In fact, adolescence would be unimaginable for many young people if they could not drive up to the local drugstore or hot dog stand to see who was around and what they were doing. To suggest that the community would not condone such behavior would be incredible to most adolescents. It would be tantamount to denying what they felt was an inalienable right. Patusa does not actually proscribe such behavior. Yet adult scrutiny of adolescent behavior is so thorough that occupying public space without express permission would only elicit uneasy glances and suspicious stares.

The greasers had very little organized social life. They most often saw each other in class, and the most reliable meeting place to arrange doing things together was right outside school immediately after classes. One night when Glen had just bought an ounce of marijuana, he had to make several stops, drive about fifty miles and spend three hours before he could find someone to smoke it with. When he finally did locate someone, it was at the pool tables in the recreation center. When they went out to smoke the pot in a parked car in the center's parking lot, they discovered another carload of their friends toking up nearby. Glen honked at these friends, and they smiled and waved back. Much of the leisure time of these young people seemed to be consumed by just looking for someone to do something with.

Most of these young people worked part-time, some for a family business, others in gas stations or at local supermarkets. A few of them had access to cars, but most did not. As for drug use, some profess great enthusiasm for soft drugs. Others condemn drugs. Mark was a young man whom the fieldworker got to know fairly well.

> As we were walking out to the car, Mark pointed to a girl walking home from school. He said, "That girl over there is a real drug addict." I asked him how he knew that. He said, "Oh, she's always high on something. She comes to school and wanders around with these big dopey eyes." I asked if he knew what kind of drugs she uses. He said, "She probably just smokes grass like everyone else, but she's still a drug addict."

About a week after this, the fieldworker again talked to Mark:

> I asked him if he had gotten high anymore since the last time I talked to him. He laughed and said yes. He told me that he gets his dope free. A friend of his—Mark wouldn't tell me his name—always has a lot of it and so he gives it away. He said that he really likes doing it. I told him I was surprised at this after what he had been telling me before. He said he had never tried it before, and so he didn't know what he was talking about.

On the surface, this minor incident merely appears as if another item is added to this youth's technology of intoxication. But how Mark acquires marijuana and how he identifies a peer as a "drug addict" is symptomatic of the low level of the development of youth culture in Patusa. Mark is neither dull or so removed from contact with his peers that he could not, for example, tell the difference between the star of the basketball team and someone who could not pass gym class. In other communities, a socially competent person like Mark would know how to identify a peer who was deeply involved with drugs even if Mark had no personal contact with drugs. In Patusa, it is remarkable how little peers actually know about each other's lives when they are not in their company.

In most communities, young people know how to identify peers whose lives revolve around drugs because "freaks" and "burn-outs" are common actors on the scene. Their demeanor, appearance, and group activities set them apart from occasional drug users. In Patusa, the notion of a "freak" identity was so devoid of content that it was practically useless as a way of identifying those who were committed to drugs. Moreover, there was no common knowledge about the effect of sustained drug use that Mark could draw upon when he looked for external signs of this sort of deviant behavior.

Even if one does not personally use drugs, one usually knows whether one's friends are doing so. And that knowledge usually tempers one's attitudes toward drug use. That is, it makes one more tolerant unless the use of drugs gets out of hand. In Mark's case, he did not know much about his friend's deviant activity until he was let in on the secret. In most places, he would have known about the "secret" long before he was ready to try something new.

Deciding to use drugs in Patusa has few, if any, substantial ramifications upon one's position vis-à-vis peers. It is without much value as a marker of change in one's identity because, in Patusa, all of these activities remain part of a private sphere, shared only with a few friends. In communities where there is normative space for genuine youth culture, a young person's "deviant" activities such as drug use become negotiable socially. They serve as a basis for affiliation and for public recognition—other youth know who one is (in the sense of what sort of person one presents oneself as being) even though they may not know one personally. In Patusa, almost none of this "personal" information is communicated by public behavior because youth do not draw this kind of attention to themselves.

Drug use is not restricted to greasers. Steve was the son of a well-to-do businessman, a lifelong resident of Patusa. Steve wore his hair down to his shoulders, but also dressed very neatly. On one occasion the fieldworker had a telephone conversation with Steve about marijuana and some wine for a party. Steve's father overheard part of this conversation on an extension, but only the part dealing with the wine. Steve later reported to the fieldworker on the aftermath:

> Steve said his father was extremely upset. He calmed down when Steve asked him if he could tell him one time when he came home drunk or got into trouble because of drinking. His father couldn't think of anything. Steve admitted that he drank, but told his father that, if he stays out of trouble, he doesn't see why he should be upset. His father seemed to buy that.

Steve's father responded to what is almost a code word in Patusa: getting in trouble. This does not mean doing something that is forbidden by one's parents. Getting into trouble means allowing the violation of the rules to become *visible* to the authorities. There is a distinction, therefore, between doing things that one's parents disapprove of and allowing those activities to become public knowledge. Steve could reassure his father about his drinking because he reminded him that he did not get into trouble. And it was an encounter with authority, not the deviant behavior per se, that Steve's father was worried about. The former could be seen as sowing one's wild oats while the latter could effect Steve's future in the community. In Patusa, then, many parents are quite sensitive to having their children acquire a "reputation" for being brought to the attention of authorities, and they will look the other way, so to speak, as long as they are sure that their children's behavior will not get them into trouble.

When Glen got caught with marijuana at school, Steve observed that

> Glen was "stupid" to take dope to school like that. He still has a pound left that he has to find a good place to hide. Steve didn't think Glen would tell where he got it, but he doesn't want to take any chances. Steve said I do everything Glen does, he just doesn't know how to be cool about it.

The key message that youth in Patusa get from their encounters with authority is that it is not what you do but how you do it that makes all the difference. Drugs are not a moral issue as far as Steve and his friends are concerned. Instead, they are a political issue inasmuch as buying, selling, and using drugs safely depends upon where and how these activities take place. No "smart" person, according to Steve, should forget the nearly omnipresent surveillance of authority in places like the school where body and locker searches are not uncommon. Outsmarting authority is merely part of the game. But what the players, both youth and adults alike, do not see is that this diminishes the respect that might otherwise be accorded to authority. This is a case where the sacrifice of the reasonableness of authority is masked by the smooth efficiency with which it operates in Patusa.

The Fashionable Freaks

The principal of Patusa High School kept a list of students' names in his office he suspected of using drugs. Kevin Brand was sure that his name was on it, but he had not been confronted by authority. In school Kevin did not do well academically, but he was a star in the musical production of the school. Kevin and Glen attended the same English class, and through our fieldworker the two of them found occasion to spend time together outside of school. On one occasion Kevin got into trouble when he rejected the attentions of a girl who was interested in going out with him, and she angrily walked out of a party and disappeared for two days. When Mrs. Brand saw her son in the company of Glen in the fieldworker's car, she became very upset and threatened to forbid her son any further contact with him. After the fieldworker told her that Chapman had accepted his research role in the school, she relented. She explained that she and her husband had been afraid that the fieldworker was "an undercover agent." They didn't want their son getting into trouble because he was seen hanging around with "undesirable people."

The irony of this situation was that neither Glen nor the fieldworker had any real influence on Kevin and his friends. Kevin rather looked down on Glen for his lack of cool and had numerous sources of companionship quite apart from his association with the fieldworker. In fact, only a week after Mrs. Brand's description of this "crisis" in her son's life, the senior Brands went away for a vacation. While they were gone, the fieldworker was invited to a party at the Brand residence. The fieldworker found six young men quite drunk and smoking a considerable amount of marijuana. During the evening they talked at great length about politics, and their rhetoric was of the New Left variety. They also spoke for a long time about the rigidity of Patusa High school and the conservatism of the town and made one obscene phone call. During the course of the evening, the fourteen-year-old daughter of the elected official showed up, and she showed no surprise at the tenor of the gathering.

The social sources of this form of peer sociability are rooted in cosmopolitan culture. Kevin and his friends showed no consciousness of having taken part in any deviant behavior at this gathering. Kevin, in fact, indirectly compared the party to the "stag films" shown "every second Friday night" at the Moose Lodge of Patusa. The alternation between the drudgery of work and school and the fun of drugs and sexual activity was an established part of mainstream American culture, as far as Kevin and his friends were concerned. Although they adhered carefully to the separation of these two worlds, and maintained the required demeanor of respectability at school, they looked upon both as normal parts of life.

Though the atmosphere of Patusa may seem restrictive and cold, it is not experienced that way by the more sophisticated youth like Kevin and his friends. They are just marking time, doing the things that interest them and keeping a low profile when it comes to deviant activities. Nor do they experience much anger over the controlling nature of authority. Since they know how to get the sort of things they want from the school and how to enjoy officially forbidden pleasures, the authority structure of the town is irrelevant unless it impinges directly on their private lives. And, for the most part, these youth are clever enough to evade the strictures of authority without even being noticed by those who enforce the rules.

Religious Youth

The Christian Church, with 2,000 members, has the largest youth club. The youth minister of this church described the Youth Club's meeting place:

> The Youth Club has the use of the Youth House, a house that the church bought for them located right behind the main church building. He told me that it's unfinished and that's the way the kids want it. The adults want it fixed up and pressured the kids to put up some drapes. However, the kids know that if they fix it up it will soon be taken over for adult activities. The kids also had a wall that they covered with graffiti, but the adults were greatly upset by it and made them paint over it. He told me that Youth House is open as often as they can get supervision.

The youth minister had some difficulty setting up an active program for the youth group. Although Bible study was an accepted feature of the youth gatherings, it was not the central attraction. The teenagers of the youth group were more interested in the group's social possibilities. Yet, even in this controlled environment, some adults fear that deviance lurks in the shadows and that vigilance is necessary:

> Bob, the youth minister, said that the adult church members have a certain narrow-mindedness about the young people. He showed me a letter he got today with a clipping from the newspaper enclosed. The clipping was a picture of one of the girls who belongs to the youth group. She is on the swimming team, and in the picture she is wearing a two-piece swimming suit. The anonymous letter said this was indecent and called on Bob to do something about it. He said he would ignore it since it was obviously some kind of crackpot.

While the bathing suit incident may seem extreme, one can see how sensitive this community is to the remotest possibility that youthful deviance could take place under the auspices of respectable institution. This church is the largest in the community and is not worried about being viewed as slightly off-center by other congregations in town. Rather, the attitude of many of the parents toward youthful deviance expresses the basic normative orientation of the community: authorities cannot be too careful, and, in these matters, an ounce of prevention is worth a pound of cure. The field-worker describes adult resistance to a church-sponsored, youth retreat:

> Linda said she thought there was no parental support for the retreat. One mother didn't want to send her daughter because the retreat was for the whole community and not just church members. After it was over, she heard that it had been "just like a rock festival." Bob said he could not understand how the woman had gotten that impression. The kids had stayed up late and there were records played, but it was certainly nothing like a rock festival.

In Patusa, many adults feel that youthful deviance is much like a disease that is just below the surface, ready to break out when conditions allow it to spread throughout the body. There is a certain cultural logic to this supposition. Patusa tends to equate spontaneous adolescent forms of expression and sociability with deviance.

One of the most striking features of the church youth group is the passivity of its members. While the youth minister tried to get young people to take an active role planning future activities, there were heavy silences when the minister asked for suggestions. Though the young people had things they wanted to do, such as hearing from people with unusual points of view (e.g., an atheist), they knew these off-beat ideas would be vetoed by adult authority. Moreover, they knew that there was a limited range of activities that adults considered suitable and that it was not really possible to stray beyond these boundaries. Yet there was little overt evidence of resentment at authority. They had come to accept, for the time being at least, the pervasive control that adults exercise over their activities.

Youth Elites

There are three distinct segments of the youth elites of Patusa. The student politicos, the athletes, and the brains of the high school each have different bases for high status in the peer group world. Seen from below, they are all beneficiaries of official privilege. Seen from within their own ranks, they are three separate groups who do not associate with and do not even particularly like one another.

Mike Hale and Vicki Kilgore were the best-known student politi-

cos in Patusa High School. One day while the fieldworker was hanging around the school auditorium talking to the students getting
ready for the school play, he noticed Mike Hale—president of the
student council—sitting by himself. The fieldworker comments:

> While we were talking, Mr. Smoot—the band teacher—came
> over. He asked Mike who he could expect trouble from on the
> senior class trip. Mike mentioned four names, none of which I
> knew. Mr. Smoot said those were the ones he had in mind too.
> He told Mike that the most trouble would probably come on the
> bus ride down there. Mike said he would see what he could do
> about getting them on separate buses.

When the fieldworker interviewed Mike and Vicki, they both
complained about being misunderstood by their peers. They said
that other students thought they had an "easy life," but this was not
true. Dealing with adults was not at all easy, and they had to take a
"lot of shit." But easy or hard, Mike and Vicki did act as brokers
between the bureaucracy and various clusters of students.

This sort of arrangement with authority is possible only when
youth subcultures are as underdeveloped as they are in Patusa. In
communities where youth have their own strong basis of peer affiliation, it would be embarrassing, to say the least, to be publicly
identified as an adjunct of adult authority. This is not to say that
young people must keep their distance from authority in order not
to be seen by peers as its lackey. Certainly in Ribley many young
people felt free to approach adult authorities on a friendly and open
basis and were not afraid to air their complaints or grievances. But
that is an entirely different matter than acting as an authority surrogate, or intervening in "private" student affairs with the interests
of authority foremost in mind.

In most communities, students who openly acted as agents of
social control would be met with considerable hostility and vitupera-
tion. While these youth might not win a popularity contest in Patusa, there is no evidence that they are the object of widespread
animosity. This, again, demonstrates how powerful the grip of adult
authority is on the youth world and why distinctive youthful styles
and identities have so little substance.

The situation of the athletes was not too different. The senior
and junior basketball players regularly functioned as hall monitors
and messengers for the office. In the eyes of most of the youth of
the school this gave them a special status. But they were not particularly envied. There was resentment against the special treatment they often got in disciplinary matters, but the fieldworker

saw the basketball players playing pool at the recreation center with greasers and freaks. Everyone appeared to see basketball as a talent or trade which put a person in a peculiar relationship with adults and officials. But it was a relationship about which they had few illusions. Many of the athletes came from socioeconomically deprived backgrounds. They were essentially employees, and if they did not perform well they would lose their privileges. This was the way the system worked, and no one could be blamed for taking those few advantages that were given out so cautiously by authority.

The third segment of Patusa youth elite were the "smart" students. Most of them came from upper-middle-class families, and their families were solidly established in the status structure of the town. By taking advanced placement courses, they prepared to go to college and to get out of the town. Meanwhile they complained about the emphasis on basketball and spent their free time with small cliques of close friends. Yet taking many of the same courses together and having similar opinions about Patusa did not bind them into a connected friendship network. The fieldworker describes an accidental encounter between some of these students:

> Tim said that most of the time they spend just riding around. He told me about "the route." They go along Greenwood Road either to Frontage, that runs along the Interstate, or sometimes all the way out to Memorial Park. Then they get on Fifth Street and come back to the square. Then they take South Street back to Greenwood and around again. Rosemary said, "Is that the route you take? We do that too." One kid said there are more hamburger places on Greenwood Road than in any other town in the area.

This seemingly trivial fact is perhaps the clearest indication of how deeply the normative orientation of the community cuts into the youth world. The emphasis on tight control over youthful behavior has been translated into a highly fragmented pattern of youthful association. Without the space to congregate freely, such as dragging main in Ribley, young people in Patusa do not know how youth, other than their close friends, spend their free time. For those who believe that youth culture develops largely outside of adult institutions, Patusa shows how effectively adult authority penetrates into the way young people organize their own lives. In Patusa, it is not only the adult world that is on the defensive. Youth retreat into their safe but socially restricted private friendship circles and thereby increase their freedom from adult surveillance. But at the same time, youth sacrifice the pleasures of moving in a social world comprised of peers.

More sophisticated students like these upper-middle-class youth complain about the power that local merchants have over school policy such as persuading the administration to drop open lunch hours. Leaving school grounds was punished by three days of detention. Students pointed out that local merchants were still upset about the abolition of the dress code at school. Yet this sort of awareness of how the authority structure of the community translates its values into policy does little to change youth's basic response to their situation. In Patusa, young people learn a vital lesson: that you cannot fight city hall when the powers that be represent ones' parents values and aspirations.

Conclusion

One of the questions that may arise in the minds of people for whom the culture of Patusa seems claustrophobic is why adults allow authority to be concentrated in one person's hands (i.e., the disciplinarian at the high school) and why those who are uneasy about the situation never raise their voices. In Patusa, there is a fear that if authority is legitimated by dissimiliar interests and values it will disintegrate. One way to grasp this is to think of the difference between consensus that requires absolute unanimity (everyone must think the same way about the issues and express their agreement in the same terms) and consensus that allows for difference of opinion and judgment. In the latter case, all that is required for consensus is that all parties recognize the issue and that the final resolution of the problem take account of minority positions.

In Patusa, the latter image of consensus goes against the grain of the local culture. An open discussion of whether authority is reasonable would, in the minds of many Patusans, pit group against group: administrators against teachers, parents against the school, traditionalists against cosmopolitans, and so on. Consequently, even those who privately dissent from the Patusan consensus probably agree on one point: it would be too costly to the order and security that the town has achieved in the face of threatening outside forces to risk opening themselves up to change.

One of the unintended consequences of the Patusan commitment to order and stability is that the town does not confront the dynamism inherent in the school's dedication to certain goals. In other words, Patusa does not face the paradox that while it officially endorses the values of individual initiative, competition, and success, it does not cultivate the personal qualities upon which these values are based: individual autonomy and independent judgment. There should be little wonder about the fact that many students seem enervated and listless. The inversion of the reasonableness of authority subverts the younger generation's faith in the efficacy of the means to commonly valued ends. That is to say, many young people in Patusa hold back from investing themselves in the educational process because, as far as they can see, it does not yield substantial rewards that are personally meaningful. Doing well in school, at best, helps one's future opportunities, but it does not widen the scope of one's freedom during adolescence.

In general, Patusa is a place where dissent and diversity do not mar the polished image of authority. However, those who object to the harshness of authority would miss the point. For Patusan culture, the message to youth is that we are all alike. Sameness is the guarantor of our being able to recognize each other as being worthy of respect. If we did not feel this way, the logic of the culture suggests, we would be an agglomeration of individuals driven by private interests.

Part II
Working-Class Communities

CAMBRIDGE AND Parsons Park are blue-collar, working-class communities. Cambridge is situated in the nearly all-white suburban belt that runs along the western edge of a large city. Parsons Park is an urban community located in the path of the movement of the black population out of the inner city. Viewed from the usual sociological perspective, we might expect Parsons Park to have more serious youth problems than its suburban counterpart. Parsons Park is threatened by a "racial invasion," and there is considerable anxiety about the viability of established patterns of social life under external pressure for change. In this light, a community like Cambridge must look like a refuge from the turmoil of racial strife.

Where youth are concerned, the situation is quite different. There are racially motivated incidents between the youth of Parsons Park and black youth at football games and other places where these groups come into contact. Yet, for youth, much of this occurs at the periphery of their social world. It is not a central preoccupation in their lives nor does it have the same ideological significance as it does for the older generation. In Parsons Park, the authority of parents and the parochial school is experienced as rigid and unyielding. Youth resist the idea that deviance is equivalent to moral corruption and resent the older generation's refusal to discuss their harsh response to minor deviations from the rules. Nevertheless, there is an underlying bond between the generations. This solidarity is rooted in a powerful common identity. They see themselves as working-class Catholics who share a common religious heritage and value their ethnic backgrounds. They are proud of their status in the larger society and secure in the knowledge that membership in the community affords them privileges that are not easy to obtain.

In Cambridge, there is a chasm between the home and school. The school embodies the values of success through academic achievement. The faculty is comprised of middle-class professionals whose status is dependent on their formal education. This is an alien environment for parents who have skilled manual or service jobs. While they see the school as the route to upward mobility for their children, they are aware of the gulf that separates them from sophisticated social circles. For the youth of Cambridge, the school stands for ambitions that run against their sense of themselves as autonomous persons. Adult authority is experienced as infantilization at the hands of people who have no sympathy for their desire for independence from adult controls.

The character of youthful deviance and the nature of adolescent social identities in these two communities reflect the differences in their cultures. In Parsons Park, youthful identities are quite similar, and there is a good deal of contact between youth whose aspirations and personal values differ. While fights, drugs, and open disrespect for authority are not uncommon in Parsons Park, very few youth base their social identity upon the rejection of adult values. There is a spirit of fraternal solidarity in the youth world which stresses experiences that bring different youth groups together.

The situation is markedly different in Cambridge. Not only does the reaction of youth to adult authority have a much more aggressive character, but the youth world is also split into groups that despise one another. In Cambridge, drugs and fights often have serious repercussions. Youth who are seen as compliant to adult authority are targets of real hostility, and a code of personal honor that is hypersensitive to insult sets youth groups against one another.

In Parsons Park, authority is perceived as rational and as only partially unreasonable. It is rational because it is predicated upon values that unite all the institutions of the community and bind the generations together over time. It is unreasonable because it allows for almost no negotiation or compromise but nonetheless embodies qualities these young people admire.

In Cambridge, authority strikes most youth as patently irrational and unreasonable. It is irrational because it has no instrumental value. Going to college and moving into the professional middle class is a pipe dream as far as most youth are concerned, and, for some, it is an unappealing prospect as well. It is unreasonable because it humiliates and embarrasses them. Being treated as errant schoolchildren is more than they can bear. For these young people, nothing matters more than respect for themselves as persons who can manage their own lives.

4

Cambridge

Community Setting

Cambridge is one of many suburbs that run along the western boundary of a large industrial city. Its population is about 15,000, but it has a work force of over 100,000. The town's southern boundary is defined by a large railroad yard and the northwestern boundary by an interstate expressway. The streets along its southern and eastern boundaries accommodate continuous heavy truck traffic which moves in and out of factories and warehouses.

Despite the industrial character of the area, the residents of the town think of it as a desirable place to live. The streets are clean, and the lawns and exteriors of the homes are in good condition. About 90 percent of the people who live in Cambridge own their modest frame or brick homes.

Cambridge is a reasonably prosperous working-class community. According to the 1970 census, it has a mean family income of $13,000. About 3½ percent of the families are below the poverty line. Thirty-six percent of the people over twenty-five in Cambridge completed high school, and about 3 percent are college graduates.

North Lansing High School

North Lansing High School serves Cambridge as well as other nearby suburbs in a large, modern two-story building which has a light, open atmosphere. Classrooms are clustered around a central plaza. The school has a full range of facilities including a gym that many colleges would envy. Administratively, a single superintendent is responsible for both North and South Lansing, its sister school.

The Dean

The dean of students is a disciplinarian and negotiator. He is responsible for spotting potential trouble and determining what ought to be done to resolve problems between students and teachers. The dean makes the crucial decisions about a student's fate in cases of academic failure, violations of school rules, or challenges to a teacher's authority. Although the dean is charged with upholding the established order of the school, he also tries to make school bearable for young people who find it absurdly restrictive. Speaking of a "survival" group he ran for students who were expelled or "counseled out" of school (a term for convincing a student that it is in the student's best interests to voluntarily withdraw from school), the dean says:

> One of the kids in my summer group said he had to smoke a joint before he came to school. Then he named the teachers he had and said, "How the hell do you think I can get through school with those bastards." I sat there and thought to myself, that's not the best way to do it but you couldn't logically argue his point of view. To me the kid who has to smoke a joint during the day is a kid who can't face reality and has to run away from his problems.
>
> A student who is expelled has to develop a record of all kinds of educational disturbances that's usually capped off by some sort of specific event such as hitting a teacher or selling drugs. Then we have to prove, with the exception of selling drugs, that we have tried everything possible to help the kid such as referring him to an outside agency like Family Services, doing a psychological [test] on him with the counselor, with the parents, and the social worker involved. We pull out all the stops before we're ready to expel a kid.

The dean's comments illuminate one side of the tension that makes the school the cultural battleground of this community. On the one hand, community culture demands that adult authority make its presence felt. This community cannot tolerate the idea that young people who break the rules will feel that authority is weak or vacillating. On the other hand, this school represents what these hard-working, blue-collar parents want for their children: a passport to a prestigious and well-paying middle-class job, or, at the very least, a skilled manual occupation. Thus, the school pushes troublemakers out but, at the same time, is committed to pull the majority of these youth up the class ladder.

Values and Aspirations

North Lansing sits on a tax base ordinarily associated with affluent suburban communities. The school has approximately 2,000
students. The assessed valuation of taxable property for each student enrolled in the school is $140,000 and for the school district is
approximately $500,500,000 in 1971.

North Lansing High School does not get clear directives from the
community about its educational policies. This is evident in the
dean's remarks on the lack of parent involvement in the school:

> We don't have a high percentage of parents that turn out at
> parent-teacher night. We've always had the feeling since I've
> been here that the community is not that concerned about the
> kids' education. But, on the other hand, I've always had the
> feeling that the parents that did come have respected the school
> and the teachers for being teachers. They never really ques-
> tioned what we did. But I also had the feeling [of a lack of active
> support at North Lansing] compared to the suburban school I
> taught in before where we had national merit scholarship win-
> ners and where 70–80 percent of the kids were college bound. If
> you're talking about the percentage of kids here that go to a
> four-year college and eventually come up with a Bachelor's de-
> gree its still around 20–25 percent.

When the dean says that the community is not concerned with
education, he is comparing Cambridge to an affluent suburb.
There parents were attentive to the indicators of their children's
academic progress, and felt they had the right to intervene when
they thought the educational process was not working to their
child's advantage. From the dean's perspective, the parents' ambitions were easily transformed into student motivation for good
grades. Yet the dean appreciated the latitude professionals had at
North Lansing where parents left teachers alone, except in the
crucial matter of discipline in the school. However, the dean's remarks about the small percentage of students going to a four-year
college pinpoints the place where the school falls notably short of
parental expectations.

For the last eight years, the drop-out rate was 18.5 percent. The
drop-out problem is just one symptom of a wider discrepancy between the school's performance and the expectations of the community. Although we do not know how North Lansing compares to
other suburban schools on nationally standardized tests, by its own
reports its academic success is disappointing. Teachers, counselors,

and administrators hinted about what they saw as their collective Achilles' heel. The dean would remark that the community's preoccupation with security made it difficult to encourage the sort of creativity that produced National Merit scholarships.

In addition to the school's lack of progress toward high levels of educational performance, it has concrete reminders of its difficulties. In 1970–1971, the percentage of students failing one or more courses was 28 percent for the first semester and 28 percent for the second semester; 21 percent and 23 percent, respectively, were failing one or more courses during 1971–1972.

While half of the seniors have part-time jobs, a study group appointed by the school board felt that "disciplinary difficulties" were the primary cause of the excessive drop-out rate. They recommended abandoning the modular scheduling program that allowed students maximum freedom to schedule their own time and returning to a "closed door" policy with respect to leaving the campus. This recommendation fits into a pattern in school/community relationships: the community demands and the school acquiesces in imposing stricter controls, closer surveillance, and tighter security over the students.

What is left undiscussed is whether the goal of a college education is realistic for the majority of students. Raising this question would burst the balloon on which the school rides. It would focus the community's attention on their own expectations. Lower expectations for their children might be translated into lower investment in education as a vehicle for upward mobility. The dean says:

> I was talking to two of the older teachers who feel that there are many kids out here who shouldn't be in school. They're just being carried [by the schoo]] and they think they'd be far better off working because they're getting absolutely nothing out of school. These kids get thrown out of school everyday, but the problem seems to be that their parents want them in school, and the administration can't admit that some kids just aren't making it in school. The older teachers said that if they brought something like that up at a meeting—that possibly some of these kids would be better off working even though they are only fifteen or sixteen—they would call that negative thinking: everybody has to finish high school.

A less overt element in this situation is the teacher's and administrators' attitudes toward working-class people. There is a discernible undertone of contempt for the uneducated and, in their opinion, boorish manners of working-class persons. The fieldworker reports:

I was talking to the older of the dean's two secretaries about the socials the teachers have every Friday, and I said, "Why don't I ever see you there?" She said, jokingly, "That's for high-class people—that's for administrators and not for the clerical people." I said, "I didn't know that, I'm not an administrator," and she said, "But they consider you to be on their level." I said, "You're kidding," and she said, "Oh, no, most of the teachers out here are very, very sensitive about that. They'll let you know in no uncertain terms that they're teachers and you're a clerical person. A lot of them are always making comments about the people in this area, about the factory workers drinking beer and using rough language. They kind of consider them to be low-class people; it's like they're doing them a favor by teaching out there." Then she laughed and said, "Of course they don't act that way on payday." I said, "What do you mean?" She said, "Because of all these working people out here and the factories, the taxes are very high, so teaching salaries out here are higher than in the city or anyplace else."

High school teachers in this community exemplify the social and intellectual skills that distinguish the educated, middle-class from the skilled working class. What is at issue here is the symbolic aura, so to speak, of middle-class professional expertise, competence, and self-confidence. Teachers are at home in the literate, paper culture and can manipulate the verbal symbols that are its stock in trade. But these qualities do not make them perfect role models as far as the parents are concerned. As much as many parents would like their children to emulate the career patterns of middle-class professionals, they are, at the same time, aware of their low opinion of working-class people. Moreover, in the eyes of many parents, teachers and administrators have a slippery way of avoiding tough issues.

The dominant undertone in Cambridge is one of not measuring up to a not clearly articulated standard of comparison. At first glance, one might suppose that these families would celebrate their good fortune and evident success. Unlike working-class urban communities such as Parsons Park, Cambridge is not surrounded by groups that it fears may eventually push them out of their homes. Moreover, in Cambridge most families have two tangible aspects of the American dream: comfortable homes and a good school system. Why are these people so defensive?

In order to answer this question, we must look at the situation of the working class as a whole. As Sennett and Cobb (1973) point out, people who have skilled manual and lower white-collar jobs are in an anomolous position: they are not economically marginal, but they are beset by doubts about their own worth. Since American ideology stipulates that success or failure is a sign of personal talent, these people feel that they are missing some undefined qualities that would enable them to rise about the mass of people in their situation. As Sennett and Cobb remark, the issue is not having as much money, power, or status as the educated middle-class but rather what these things signify about the self.

What these people admire and, at the same time, resent about professionals is their self-control and self-determination. Middle-class professionals seem to know what to do in complex situations but are also experienced as manipulative and duplicitous. What people in Cambridge want for their children is the autonomy and self-respect they associate with occupations that require formal education.

Despite their cultural superiority, administrators defer to the economic power of the community. The fieldworker describes a typical scene:

> These two guys with Ph.D.'s in education, the principal and the superintendent, were really catering to two guys on the school board and to the parents. You got the feeling that these guys really felt that they were dependent on these people for their jobs.
>
> Everybody becomes very attentive when one of the board members comes around and they're very friendly. The dean changes his character. Usually he is the kind of guy who's out to say something with some kind of sexual overtone, kind of a little joke. But he becomes very serious, and he introduced me to the school board member and I found myself becoming the same way.

In contrast to the rest of the faculty, the athletic coaches at North Lansing are proud of the fact that they have risen from the ranks of the working class. They see themselves as persons who subjugated their youthful disrespect for authority to the discipline of competitive sports. Moreover, the coaches realize that winning an athletic scholarship is the only way that most working-class youth can afford to attend a four-year college. For this reason, the athletic program is the crucible that tests the determination the coaches believe is essential to get ahead in the world.

Most student athletes have few illusions about how difficult it is to attract the attention of talent scouts for college programs. Yet they are aware of the fact that the school, their parents, and the community at large views them as exemplars of what is best in youth. Nevertheless, this injunction to better oneself can be experienced by a young person as a statement about the value of his family background. Identifying with those who have made it "out" of the blue-collar world can lead a young person to assume that there is something humiliating about manual labor. A coach talks about a "model" student who is embarrassed by his mother's "lowly" job in the school cafeteria:

> I was talking to the football coach about this kid and I've heard several other teachers talking about him. They say now there's a kid you should talk to. He's out for football and basketball and is one of the starters on the basketball team. He's a good kid, he's polite, he respects everybody, he's likable, and he gets along well. In other words, the teacher wants this kind of kid to represent the school.
>
> The football coach went on to say, "It's too bad Joe can't quite accept his mother." I said, "What do you mean?" and he said that his mother is one of the matrons who works in the cafeteria. He knows that the other kids know that his mother works there, and he's ashamed of it. The coach said that he couldn't really like the kid, he thought something was wrong with a kid who didn't respect his mother no matter what.

The coach is sensitive to this young man's embarrassment at seeing his mother in a low-status job. This impulse to deny one's origins is something the coaches have had to come to terms with. For the coaches, the desire to better onself has to be tempered with the kind of loyalty to friends and family that will enable one to stand up to people who will try to take advantage of one. In this way, a person may bend to those in power but not relinquish that ultimate right to confront those who were demeaning. From their perspective, the young athlete has lost the most precious part of his background: the ability to tell anyone that he is proud of who he is.

This young man is unusual in another respect. Many youth in Cambridge do not think it is unrealistic to try to assert their will against authority. They fail to see, however, that their demeanor does not endear them to those who guard the doors to success in the larger society. That is, how one knocks on the door makes all the difference. This young man has learned that a polite knock is all that is necessary to catch the eye of many teachers and administrators. Many of this young man's peers, who occasionally walk through the door and demand to be recognized, are quite surprised that the rules of the game are not as egalitarian as they were supposed to be.

Students and authority

Many students do not accept the authority of the school. The fieldworker describes a scene in the dean's office:

> This kid came into the dean's office on a referral. He had been sent home but was seen in school that day. He was talking to some kids in class, and the teacher told him to be quiet. He maintains that it was between him and the teacher, and it was no one else's business. The dean called his father and told him that the kid would have to stay home until one of the kid's parent's came to school. The father took the kid's side immediately and said that legally he couldn't send the kid home.
>
> The kid told the dean what he doesn't like about it is "that you guys [teachers and administrators] are always right no matter what happens. You're just like the cops, like the government: we're always wrong. We are just working people but we never win." The dean said, "There are certain rules here and when you break them you take the consequences."

For working-class males, having one's parents called to school is equivalent to being told that they are not mature enough to handle their own affairs. In this youth's eyes, it is the same as saying that he is still a dependent child who cannot stand up for himself or take responsibility for his conduct. He was not denying that he violated the rules or that he gave the teacher a hard time. What he was asserting was that neither the teacher nor the dean was man enough to work the problem out with him.

This young man's comments about the bias teachers and other "government" officials—that is, authority figures—have against the working class carries considerable symbolic weight. It is one way of saying that he is aware of the fact that middle-class professionals like the dean looked down at people like him. That was good reason as far as he was concerned not to respect the rules they imposed on his conduct. To do so would be tantamount to experiencing himself as weak and impotent vis-à-vis authority.

Insistence on a strict adherence to the rules is more ideology than operating policy. The school is flexible if it feels that the violation of the rules is not a real challenge to its authority:

> Sammy was in the dean's office for coming into class twenty-five minutes late. He wanted a permit to get into class, and the secretary checked his records and found that he had been late five times. She said that he had to see the dean, so he was

kidding around with her. He said, "That's the way it is, a kid tries to go straight and you won't give him a chance." You get the distinct impression that if a kid is not a real troublemaker he gets a break, and Sammy is one of those kids. So she started to write his name down, and he gave his brother's name just jokingly, and she wrote down his real name so he knew he was in no trouble. He got in to see the dean, and the dean suspended the whole thing.

However, this flexibility disappears when teachers sense that students are deliberately flouting their authority:

I was in the outer office when an English teacher came running in out of breath. She said, "You won't believe what just happened. I caught this little . . . I won't even say it, lighting up right in the hall. When I asked him his name he said he didn't know, and I asked to see his I.D. card and he said that he wasn't from the school, and then I said come with me and he walked away." She started describing him to some students and the secretary. She was really beside herself. She was going to find out who he was and make sure he got written up. When nobody could think who he was, they started going through yearbooks, and a half-hour later when I left she still had two students sitting down, going over the yearbooks.

In this incident, the usual relationship between students and teachers is reversed. Without being aware of it, this teacher experiences how it feels to be treated as a person who is not worthy of respect. Her anger at being denigrated by someone who considers her inferior does not allow her to see that approaching students in the school as if they were recalcitrant children does not elicit compliance. In the teacher's eyes, contempt for her authority was illegitimate because she, like many professionals, has been taught that justice is a matter of formal rationality. That is, what is fair is dictated by following rules that facilitate the instrumental aims of the organization, and the student who was smoking was flagrantly violating them.

It would be unimaginable for teachers to think that they might reasonably negotiate with students about the grounds for their association. It would be tantamount to throwing everything away that gives them pride in their professional status. Teachers know that most of the sanctions at their disposal to deal with students who refuse to listen to them are ineffective. Detentions, failure notices, and so on do not intimidate these students. However, they know that the power of the school to express disapproval of the student will triumph over resistance to their authority because that student's family will ultimately be powerless to contest this verdict of personal failure.

Many teachers interpret a student's refusal to recognize the rules of proper behavior as a rejection of themselves as credible adults. The fieldworker describes an incident with a student who got into a lot of trouble in and out of school:

> I met Tommy Joe coming down the hall. He was red in the face, talking to himself. He came into the dean's office; he had an argument with a teacher. The dean said, "Well, look, let's go down to talk to the teacher and try to see what the problem is and work things out." Tommy Joe said no. He was going to punch the teacher out. The dean said, "What good is that going to do? I might have to throw you out of school this time [for the entire year]." Tommy Joe said, "That's fine with me. I want to get out of this damn place anyway."
>
> What happened was that Tommy Joe started to put his coat on and the teacher told him to hang it up until the bell rang. Tommy Joe said that the teacher came over and told him to get his fucking coat off and nearly ripped it off. He was obviously exaggerating, but it seems that the teachers here are very much into showing kids who's boss—if a kid says something a little out of the way they can't take it lightly. The teacher was peeved, and if he had an apology everything would be all right.

As much as teachers take a certain amount of deference on the student's part for granted, they have a difficult time understanding why students are so sensitive to the way they ask for the student's compliance with their orders. Students, in other words, do not seem to object as much to the substance of the command as they do to how it was said.

It is almost impossible for a person who is immersed in rational images of authority to grasp the significance of its expressive meanings for the self. Middle-class professionals have been taught to objectify themselves in ways that treat the expressive significance of face-to-face contacts as inconsequential. What makes a difference are calculations of what one has to put into a relationship in order to get certain things out of it. Consequently, teachers are adept at experiencing themselves in terms of the functional properties and expected utilities of the roles they play in formal organizations.

Thus, teachers cannot penetrate these students' state of mind. Why, teachers want to know, don't students ask themselves a question that would make life easier for everyone? What would I have to do to convince this person (i.e., an authority figure) that I am the sort of person he wants me to be or at least someone who does not feel it is a matter of personal honor to transform every situation into a struggle of wills? What this question presupposes is something these students do not accept. The norms of polite social conduct often strike many of these students as a contrived evasion of the real issue. It offers a way out for persons who lack the courage to face those who refuse to acknowledge them as moral equals. Of course, most teachers see students like Tommy Joe as irrationally belligerent.

Apologies from students do not come easily. They resent being treated like children. The rationality of the rules escapes them because they see few benefits that come from compliance to them.

> A kid came into the dean's office this morning. A teacher had written him up for wearing a Levi jacket with a lining in class. The dean said, "You're a senior and you're going to graduate in June. Can you go along with the program until you get out? Does it mean that much to you?" The kid said he was thinking about not graduating rather than go along with something that stupid but he finally decided it would be O.K.

The discussion that dean had with this young man illustrates how passionately these youth resent authority dictating what they feel is their personal business. In a very real sense, their dignity is on the line. If they accept the right of authority to tell them how to conduct themselves, many of these youth feel that others will see them as people who can be pushed around. That is something no self-respecting young person in this community wants others to think about him.

The dean's role in this little affair deserves some comment. In the dean's view, the teacher's action was regrettable, but the matter was not one of abstract justice or equity. What he sought to do here, as he does in many similar cases, is to intervene in a way that does not allow the power differential between authority and the student to become a matter of public contention. The respect given to the faculty is so fragile and the support of the community for the school is so equivocal that the dean instinctively realizes the entire system cannot stand great stress. Consequently, he invokes the student's legitimate interest in graduating in order to get the student to drop the issue.

When these incidents reach crisis proportions, the dean tries to "counsel" students out of school rather than expel them. This strategy often works, but leaving school is often a grave blow to parents' hopes for their children. Even though staying in school may be intolerable, these young people know that their parents are disappointed and embarrassed by their failure.

> A kid came into the dean's office and the dean said, "I understand you're not going to class." The kid replied, "That's right, I am not going to class." So the dean said, "Why don't you quit?" And the kid said, "O.K. I want to quit." I found out later that the kid works part-time at night and needs a credit and a half to graduate, but he said he's so fed up with it that he can't stand it anymore.
>
> I was there later when the kid's father came in. The father was about sixty-five—the kid is nineteen—and the poor guy was just bewildered. He said, "I don't know what I'm going to do with the boy. He's crazy to quit now. He ought to finish high school." When the kid found out that his father was coming to school, he jumped up and ran out of the dean's office. I've seen other kids do this. They're not scared of their parents coming to school, but I get the feeling that a lot of kids are ashamed of their parents. Particularly if the father is older and wearing work clothes.

The farther down one goes, so to speak, in the hierarchy of the school, the more sensitive students are about their personal dignity. Perhaps the most poignant incident occurred when a student at the bottom of the educational ladder—he was in a special classroom for Educable Mentally Handicapped—confronted the teacher:

> A kid came into the office besides himself with rage. He was so mad and upset that he couldn't talk. Finally, he said, "Where does it say that a teacher can hit me?" And then he took his hand and knocked all the stuff off the dean's desk, breaking a little statue, knocking the papers off, and he stood there screaming in front of the desk.
>
> Apparently this teacher hit him, and his mouth was kind of red. The dean settled him down by walking all over the building with him. The kid wouldn't talk to anybody and wouldn't respond to the dean. All he could say was that he was going to kill the teacher. He went down to the teacher's room, and the teacher was out in the hall. I guess the teacher was slightly scared. I thought the kid was going to hit the teacher, his fist was doubled up, but we got him away from there. The dean said, "Haven't you ever been hit before, your parents have

certainly slapped you or something, haven't they?" He said, "Yah, but that's different." To have a stranger hit you, boy that just hit home, to have someone not in his family hit him really hurt him [emotionally] badly.

This incident illuminates the dean's dilemma. He is in a unique position in the school because he knows which students are likely to provoke their teachers or resist an otherwise innocuous order. This student did not fall into that category. Moreover, as the dean realized, he was vulnerable in a way that most students are not. By having to attend a classroom designated for "slow" learners, this student must deal with a label that reduces his sense of worth among his peers. The dean had no doubt that what the teacher did was morally indefensible. Yet the dean, as in previous situations, acted to defuse the possibility of open conflict before exploring the student's right to seek restitution from the teacher.

At first glance, the dean's behavior in the incident appears to be in the service of a self-aggrandizing rationality, namely, whatever will protect the school is good for the student. However, in a community where young people do not value negotiation and compromise when they have been insulted, the dean cannot reasonably suggest that filing an official complaint would satisfy this young man's sense of wrong. In other words, he has to personalize the issue for the young man. But he must do so in a way that reduces the possibility of a physical confrontation. So the dean analogizes the situation to one of physical discipline at home. But, on this occasion, the dean makes a symbolic misstep. This young man replies that not only does the teacher not have the right to hit him (i.e., he is not his father), but the teacher looks down upon him as well.

School Authority and the Community

The issue of control penetrates to the core of the culture of Cambridge. During the time we were in Cambridge, the community pressured local authorities for greater surveillance over the "bad" kids who were attacking the "good" kids. The fieldworker described a PTA meeting where the question of why their children were being "harassed" in school came up. After the meeting:

I was standing there talking to the dean and the principal came over and said, "Boy, I had to put an end to that. It just got down to where the topic was what's wrong with North."

The question, "What's wrong with North?" was specific. Two recurrent issues faced the administration: drugs and violence. These two issues were not unrelated inasmuch as the school perceived the same sort of student as the source of both problems. The school felt it acted forcefully against students who were distributing soft drugs. But the school was often confronted by a bewildering response from parents. The public consensus on the evils of drug use was unwavering. However, where the school's right to enforce community norms was pitted against a family's loyalty to its children, parents sided with their children.

> This athlete overdosed a few days ago on downers [barbituates] and almost died. He told who he got the stuff from. The dean called the father of the kid who sold the dope and told him that they were going to try to expel him. Well, the kid's father was irate. He didn't think his son should be thrown out of school. And the dean really got irritated. He said, "Maybe you don't understand. I'm telling you that your kid almost killed another kid; he sold him some dope and he almost died from it." And the father's reply was, "Yah, but that's no reason to throw him out of school." The father wasn't upset with his son; he was upset with the school because they wanted to throw him out.

Parents demand a harsh policy toward this sort of deviance, but when authority turns to them for support, it evaporates. What administrators do not see is that one of the reasons why parents are so unwilling to back them up is that the parents distrust of official authority is as great as their children's. From the parents' point of view, authority will deal with their children in a way that causes the school the least trouble, and authority will not go out of its way to look at extenuating circumstances. Although that is, in fact, what authority tries to do in Cambridge, this message falls on deaf ears.

Conflict between Jocks and Badasses

These incidents become matters of community concern when trouble is perceived as being part of a widespread conflict between the "jocks" and the "badasses" or "rednecks." The community, of course, does not define the conflict in terms of the opposition between peer group identities. What the community sees is a group of "bad" young people whose sole joy in life is in tearing down everything the community has worked so hard to build. The fieldworker attended the school meeting for concerned parents:

The room was full. The dean, the superintendents of both schools, the principal of North and the assistant principal were there, and the police chief of Cambridge and the youth officer also was there. They went around the room and each person said what they thought the trouble was. Mrs. Bronsky told about her younger son being harassed and beaten up by two kids and about her older son having all the windows and lights on his car smashed. Some other people told about their kids being beaten up. One kid had been hospitalized which resulted in another kid being sentenced to the House of Correction. One woman told about phone calls to their house about how they were going to get their son. And they talked about the dope in the school. Several parents said that their kids knew you could get anything in the world you wanted there, that there was dealing in the halls, and one woman said that she was sure some of the teachers were on drugs themselves. It got to where people were making really outlandish accusations.

In order to understand this scene one must understand something about the nature of physical violence in this community. This is not a case where easily intimidated youth go running for adult protection from schoolyard bullies. Much more is at stake here. In the first place, physical confrontations often result in serious injury. For parents, these incidents are not the usual animosities between rival groups but represent a real threat to the peace and order of the school. Parents who insist that their sons abide by the rules refuse to see the depredations of "criminal" youth as exaggerated reactions to a common situation in the community (i.e., sensitivity to personal insult).

The collective response to the problem was not only to identify the malfactors and to punish them but also to use the problem as evidence that the agents of control and order—the school and the police—were not doing their job. It angers these parents to think that the youth who represent what they believe is decent and good become a target for what they feel is perverse and evil. They were caught up in the morality play of a Western movie when the spineless sheriff and his deputy were hiding under the bed while the "bad guys" were riding roughshod over the hardworking and Godfearing townspeople:

One woman said that she talked to a lot of kids and none of them respected the dean, that he wasn't doing his job, that he was real easy on the redneck kids and let them go, and that he was really hard on the athletes. She said the reason was that he was scared of the rednecks and that all of the teachers were scared of them. They painted a picture of terrorism in the school which isn't there at all.

They jumped on the chief of police for not protecting people and for not sending these kids up [to jail]. Two or three of the men said that if they ever caught these guys they were going to take care of them themselves, and they wanted to know if they would get into trouble with the law. These people were really heated up, they were angry and they were out to get somebody. They wanted to know whose fault it was, and they thought it was the dean's and the police, and they wanted something done about it.

Even though the dean and the chief of police were under heavy pressure for "failing" to employ the full extent of their power against these youth, the dean could not admit that the problem was not black or white but had shades of grey. In other words, he could not point out that there was a continuum of extralegal behavior among the student body and that the group of youth under discussion were the most visible representatives of much broader patterns of behavior. It was essential, in the dean's opinion, not to contradict the illusion that "bad" behavior was located among a very special group and had not "infected" the school as a whole.

The community's image of deviance draws heavily upon moralistic notions of right and wrong. Deviance has strong connotations of malicious disregard for the rights of others. There are two classes of people in the world, and it is a sign of fuzzy thinking to blur the distinction between good and bad behavior. Authority has no choice but to punish malefactors to the full extent of its power. Otherwise, Cambridge fears, the temptation to violate the rules will spread. The assumption is that people will respect authority only if they see that the penalties for predatory behavior far outweigh its advantages. The stress is on the restraints the community must exercise over deviance and not on the rewards that come from conformity with the rules.

Underlying all of this, there is a view of human nature as essentially aggressive and self-aggrandizing. People need to be held in check for everyone's good. This explains the apparent contradiction between the public insistence on strict enforcement of the rules and each family's willingness to protect their children against authority. If deviance was treated with tolerance and understanding, social life would be difficult indeed because everyone would use this official latitude to press their own self-advantage against the rights of others. On the other hand, parents in Cambridge assume that the personal motives of those in authority are no different than anyone else's. Authority will ride roughshod over their childrens' rights if it is in its interest to do so, and there is little faith that justice will be administered in an even-handed manner. Those persons who have the "right" connections will get a break, and those who do not will have to bear the punishment for those who go free.

One of the paradoxes of the culture of Cambridge might be stated in the following way. Most of the adults were raised in working-class communities and got into their share of trouble as youth. They probably were not more law-abiding than the present generation. Why, then, are so many of these parents insistent that there are no redeeming qualities to adolescents who get into fights and use drugs?

It is important to remember that Cambridge is socially homogeneous. Unlike urban areas, these adults are not struggling with other groups for control of civic institutions. They actually represent authority in its complete political sense. Cast in the role of making policy for local institutions, it is not surprising that people in Cambridge feel they must endorse the official order vigorously. At the same time, there is private cynicism about how democratic institutions really operate. Through their activities in unions, these people know how vital connections are for getting good jobs. They also know that someone who obeys all the rules all the time is probably incapable of looking out for his own interests. In the final analysis, people in Cambridge feel that every family has to protect itself in the best way that it can.

The dean's strategy was not to confront the community's image of deviance with one based upon notions about the strains and stresses of adolescence. Instead, he did not dispute the notion that a small band of evil-doers was responsible for youth problems in the school. Rather, he stressed the limits of the school's authority, and, more specifically, the restrictions that the courts have put on the school's right to discipline and expel students. That is, he tried to direct parental anger toward the legalistic separation of the powers of the school and the home. He implied that the school and the police were caught in the middle between parents who demand that authority employ strict measures and the courts that have taken due process and individual rights as their standard of justice.

However, for these parents, the solution was straightforward:

The people actually wanted the chief of police to go out and beat up these troublemakers and throw them in jail. They want a policeman with a gun in the school, and they want the door locked. They want the teachers to have the authority to slap a kid if he uses bad language. They wanted tough action from the police, and when the police said the law wouldn't allow them to do that, the people were frustrated. They said goddamit, if they ever caught them they'd deal with them their own way.

Although the vigilante response to the problem never materialized, the dean's role was based on a contradiction that neither he or the school could transcend. On one hand, it was perceived as an institution whose primary responsibility was enforcing respect for authority. Within these limitations, the most the dean or the school could do was to thread a thin line between presenting a harsh face toward the parents and a flexible one toward the students. Near the end of school year in June, the dean was talking to one of the students who had been repeatedly caught stealing and whose family had a history of serious problems:

> The dean gave the kid a lift home with his bike. Before they left, this kid, George, wanted to smoke, so he asked the dean if he could smoke and the dean said, "Go ahead, but don't mention it." So the kid sat there and smoked a cigarette and he told me that this must be a first. The kid told the dean that he told the police that the dean was a nice guy. The dean said, "Don't ever tell anybody I'm a nice guy. As long as I can go around and see written in the washroom, 'The dean fucks pigs,' and 'The dean sucks,' I know I'm doing my job. If I ever see that somebody has written that the dean is a nice guy, I know I'm failing."

The dean's compassion for youth who have a hard time in school must, in this community, be hidden behind his official stance as someone whose loyalty is to law and order. His role, in fact, is built around trying to ease a difficult situation where parents and children cannot talk to each other about what matters most to each of them. Adolescents cannot tell their parents that their academic expectations are onerous and unrealistic. They cannot say that they see no reason to do any better than their parents who, by all appearances, have done rather well for themselves. Parents cannot communicate how it feels to give their children a chance to get ahead in the world that they would never have dreamed of when they were young. It is hard for them to say that they do not want their children to make the same compromises, to experience the same frustrations, and, most important, to feel less worthy than people who wear white shirts and ties to work.

Youth World

Adults in Cambridge are largely unaware of the meaning of local adolescent social identities. They perceive an undifferentiated mass of "average" youth and pick out either young people who excel in sports or who are known as troublemakers. Those youth the school holds up for others to emulate are not perceived by the rest as the embodiment of all that is virtuous and good. While the school believes that the "rah-rahs" and the "jocks" merit special privileges, there is no consensus in the rest of the youth world that their style is better than anyone else's.

Rah-Rahs

The rah-rahs are not an "exclusive" social circle. In general, rah-rahs are distinguished by their affirmation of conventional values. The rah-rahs know that the badasses think of them as "goody goodies" who go out of their way to curry favor with teachers. They sense that the intent behind the charge is to cast them in the role of dependent children who are afraid to assert their own independence. Many rah-rahs are aware of the risk involved in trying to tread the narrow path to success. They know that there are many contingencies that may subvert their determination to make something out of their lives. It is precisely this attempt to follow a torturous route to success that badasses see as compliance to authority.

This theme is apparent in the case of a stunningly beautiful senior who was captain of the Pom Pom girls—a group that assists the cheerleaders at athletic contests. Besides being on the Pom Pom squad and being editor of the school newspaper in her junior year, she works continuously at a number of jobs after school and on weekends. Until her senior year, she made the school honor roll. Her commitment to conventional values grows out of her distaste for the selfish attitudes of her parents rather than a desire to rise above her social origins. For the Pom Pom girl, the image of a decent life that transcends her parents' base motives goes to the core of her personal values:

> My father and my stepmother think I should go on the pill as soon as I'm eighteen. It shouldn't be a cheap thing: it has to

bring you closer to a person. The thing that keeps you going is the goals you have, and I have a lot. I want my kids to love me. I don't want to be rich but just to have a nice house. I know you have to work for things. I don't mind working for it as long as you get it eventually. Its kind of bad when you keep on getting cut down.

The note of doubt that crept into the Pom Pom girl's description of what she wanted out of life reflects her perception that even superhuman effort on her part will not guarantee that she will find the kind of life she wants to live. Her commitment to what she considers to be a decent way of life may, she suspects, be crushed by forces that she cannot control. It is a far cry from this girl's view of her prospects to the Walt Disney image of the beautiful cheerleader who has the world at her feet and unbounded faith in the goodness of the world around her. Hers is a very guarded optimism. She worries that school may be the only place where she will experience a sense of accomplishment and self-worth:

I've always reached out because I didn't have a home. Even if I did reach out at home, there's nobody who has time for me. That's probably what made me the person I am, reaching out in school. Being in pom-poms makes me feel part of the school, part of somebody. It is not that I belong to a certain crowd. Its more that it makes me feel good. It's a feeling for somebody else, to help somebody or to let somebody else know that you care and you're there.

This young woman's aspirations for the future are vulnerable in a way that is new. She recognizes that the "promises" that are implicit in the rewards the school gives rah-rahs may not be negotiable currency in the larger world:

I realize that once you're out of high school you're on your own. But when you are in high school it's like a whole little world in itself, and there's a chance for you to be something. So take advantage of it because once you get out of high school it's going to be so hard. So many people, so many brains, so now is the time. I mean you could be something in high school and that might be your only time. It's so hard in the world.

Like the Pom Pom girl, athletes have a very realistic view of the pitfalls on the road to success. For athletes, the school's rationality is tied to the benefits that come from achievement in sports. One athlete says:

Most of the guys who quit [the team] or don't go out are guys
that get discouraged. [They feel that] they don't get a chance to
show themselves, and they think they have it. You can't blame
the coaches because they go for the best guys.

This individualistic ethic, however, is tempered by the solidarity
of the peer group. It is possible, in other words, for ambitious working-class youth to use sports as a means of social mobility because,
unlike the purely individualistic significance of academic performance, the experience of being part of a team reaffirms the experience of remaining close to one's friends:

I think this year's team is the way all the teams should have
been. Everybody was out for each other; nobody was cutting
each other down; they were just patting each other on the rear
end; helping each other along. Nobody was down on each other;
no individuals, they were all teamwork.

For almost all athletes excellence in sports is the only realistic
way to plan for the future:

My family asked me a long time ago what I wanted to do. I said
I wanted to be in as many sports as I can. I'm working over the
summer to make money for college and play baseball, that's
why I'm going to college. I've got to write a few colleges and let
the season go by and see how good I do. Maybe I could get a
scholarship. I'm hoping for it. I'd like to go all the way if I
could. But that's pretty hard.

Athletes know that the connections and goodwill of the coaches
is vital for their future. Since many are called but few are chosen
for scholarships to four-year colleges with major sports programs,
there is a "reserve clause" in the tacit contracts athletes make
with the school. If an athlete cannot get a scholarship, he can go to
the local junior college. However, the junior college route is most
likely a dead-end. Bronsky, one of the better basketball players on
North's team, describes what happened to him in his senior year:

After the game the coach came up to my mother and said he had
a "ride" [i.e., a full scholarship—room, board, tuition, and
books] at school. So in the next couple of days we got a letter
from the university of some college out west somewhere. They
said to fill out this information and I filled it out and turned it
back. The coach came up to me and asked if I received anything
from the college since I sent in the application. I said, "No," and
he said, "When you do let me know." That's the last thing I've

heard about it. I didn't ask for anything else, so I just left it at that. When I graduated I enrolled at Wilson Jr. college.

Beneath the disappointment and, perhaps, sense of betrayal, there is a stubborn refusal to sacrifice his personal dignity by begging for help. Even for the rah-rahs and the jocks, not being compliant in order to get the most out of the situation is a value that runs through the whole of working-class youth culture. Bronsky knew that he might be on a treadmill to oblivion:

> If I do good next year in football, then I'll stick it out for the second year. You have to wait for your second year [for scholarship offers] before you know where you are going to go. If I don't get no scholarship or nothing then I'll just forget about school.

Unlike most teachers and administrators, the coaches are more closely attuned to the undercurrents of the youth world. They know that they are in competition with youth styles that reject their values. They are determined to stand fast rather than overlook what they see as the self-indulgence of the "badass" and "freak" styles:

> I was talking to the football coach about Sam, this redneck— but they have to want to play badly enough to make it in school too. He mentioned another kid who was the best sophomore football player South ever had, and he was also a very good wrestler. Then something happened. He grew his hair down his back, got into drugs, and changed completely.

These disaffections do not weaken the coaches' resolve to stress making a choice between competing values because the coaches have themselves experienced this decision personally:

> This one coach told us that sports financed his college education. If it hadn't been for sports, he said he wouldn't have amounted to anything. The only reason he studied or made any kind of grades at all was so he could stay eligible for sports. He did well enough to get into college on a basketball scholarship. He felt that sports made the difference between his being a bum and a high school coach and teacher.

One might argue that the coaches overdramatize the choices that face ambitious working-class athletes. Part of the reason is obviously financial. Most of these families do not have the money to send their children away to a four-year college. Yet, one could argue that going away to college is not the only way for a working-class youth to get ahead, and that is certainly true.

There is a symbolic element in the way coaches experience this choice. In their youth they felt the powerful pull of their peer groups toward activities that interfered with making something out of their lives. Getting into trouble and taking school lightly seems to come naturally to boys who grow up in these communities as far as coaches are concerned. Interest in academics is not something the coaches feel will motivate working-class boys. In their opinion, competitive team sports combined with individual discipline teaches these youth how to get ahead in the world.

Coaches stress the sharp line between success and failure. Discipline, self-control, and personal sacrifice are necessary at every step along the way. Coaches insist that a young person cannot afford to lose his grip, even temporarily, on his goal. In effect, the coaches work to channel the antagonism toward authority of working-class boys into the controlled aggressiveness of competition. Winning is intended to replace personal autonomy as the sign of manhood, and, in light of the difficulty coaches have recruiting to the athletic teams, this is only a qualified success.

The tension between commitment to success through discipline and an ethic of personal autonomy is illustrated in the career of the "badass" athlete Sam. Sam straddles the line between these two competing values. He went out for the football team but was constantly in trouble for disregarding their rules about training and for missing team practices. This negative attitude toward authority is hardly confined to students like Sam who adopt the badass style. The fieldworker noticed a student who was particularly athletic in gym class and wondered why he was not out for a team sport:

> He's well coordinated and you can tell the guy could be a good athlete. He went out for tennis as a freshman. He said he kind of wished he had hung in there. I said, "It's strange because you'd really be good." He replied that he likes to play but that he didn't like the discipline—being told what to do. Peter is no redneck by a long shot.

There is a limit, as we have seen, to what working-class youth in Cambridge will allow someone in authority to tell them to do. Consequently, the image of rah-rahs and athletes as youth who give up their personal autonomy in return for conventional rewards must be carefully qualified. These youth can only be perceived as compliant within the framework of a working-class community. In middle-class communities, these young people would be experienced by authority as self-assertive and, at times, hostile to adult direction. Rah-rahs and athletes made it clear that their respect for teachers is dependent on being treated with respect by the teachers, and they are not afraid to voice that sentiment publicly:

> This kid had been referred to the dean's office when I was in the outer office talking with a couple of rah-rah girls. He was really mad and called her a bitch and said she was always picking on him when he wasn't doing anything. The referral slip said that he had his feet on a chair which is against the rules, and he was sitting there when she told him to sit somewhere else. The dean said it was more or less her privilege since she is the teacher, and it was up to the kid to get along with her. Well, the kid was arguing with the dean, and one of the cheerleaders spoke up and said that she didn't see it that way at all. She thought the kid ought to respect the teacher but that the teacher should respect the kid. Somehow the issue of teachers hitting kids came up, and this girl said that if a teacher hit her she would hit her back. She said respect was a two-way thing, and all the kids in the office agreed with her.

Rah-rahs have no pretentions about being any better than they are. On one occasion, some of the rah-rahs were joking openly with the dean and the secretaries in the office about their sexual involvement with their boyfriends. When they left, everyone in the office agreed that these girls were truly "wholesome." These adults sensed that the rah-rahs know how to violate community norms selectively, and they do so without challenging authority. That was appreciated in a community where open resistance to the rules is common. Yet open violation of the rules occurs among rah-rahs, and in the following incident one can see that they are not so different from their badass brethren:

> On the last regular game of the season the senior cheerleaders decided to celebrate and got drunk before the game. One girl fell in a mud puddle and got her uniform dirty and wet. Another girl passed out in the washroom. Their sponsor—this fiftyish-looking teacher—was saying that she was ashamed of them and called the mother of the girl who passed out. She told this other girl she couldn't cheer anymore—not tonight and not at the tournaments next week. And this girl was going around saying, "I don't care what she says, I'm going to do it. She can't stop me." When the game started the sponsor wouldn't let her cheer,

and then two of the other girls wouldn't cheer because their friend couldn't.

Ordinary Students

Most students at North are not deeply committed to either the rah-rah or badass style. Rather than looking at these students as colorless young people who work, go out with their boyfriends and girlfriends, and plod along in school, most of these "ordinary" students are suspended between committing themselves to a more or less washed-out badass identity and conventional working-class adult concerns and interests. The element of continuity among the identities of "average" students and the badasses rests on a denial rather than a commitment to common values. In one way or another, most of the "average" students reject involvement in school as something that means more than just "getting by." These youth have a limited commitment to school because of their conception of what it takes to become a working-class adult. They do not see going in college as essential to getting a reasonably well-paying job. Almost all the students except the rah-rahs feel that much, if not all, of the academic part of school is irrelevant to their lives. A seventeen-year-old boy who works hard after school and hopes to go to college comments:

> You just don't learn anything. It's that simple. Classes where they have you reading SRA themes and you take tests on them. That doesn't do you any good. Is somebody going to ask you about an SRA tape. They give you nine weeks and they say you have to have fifteen SRA themes done. So you wait until the end of the eighth week and you copy the fifteen off your girlfriend.

As another boy who was not a badass put it:

> If a teacher says, "Well, read your book and just sink your head into it," you don't like it. You hate her, well, you don't exactly hate her, but I don't think nobody likes to sit and bury their head in a book for an hour.

Badasses

Young people who adopt the badass style are very sensitive to affronts to their personal honor and resort to physical force if they feel degraded or demeaned. Yet it is possible for a young person to hang around with badasses without forcing other people to respect one's physical power. One youth told the fieldworker:

I hang around with guys that fight a lot, and if they fight I'll walk away or try to avoid it. They know I don't like to fight, and so they go, "pimp," and I'll say, "O.K. so I'm a pimp." The first couple of seconds you think [of going along], but then you think, "I got a life ahead of me." Why should you hit anybody? Half of the time they don't know who it is; they don't even know the reason—they just fight.

Even though this young man thought that the badass interest in fighting for the sake of fighting was irrational, he would not question the appropriateness of using force to defend one's honor. Nor do these youth question letting other people know that you are tougher than they are if you are willing to back up what you say with your fists. A young man who was not known as a badass but who identified with the style was beat up by some of the local rednecks. Our fieldworker comments on the aftermath:

They put him in the hospital for a couple of days and strangely enough he didn't seem bitter about it. He said, "Well, I had it coming. I learned that you don't go around wiseing off and shooting your mouth off—that's kid stuff." He said he learned not to wise off to anybody unless you're pretty sure you can beat them up or unless you have your friends with you. It was all right then.

There is a group of badasses known as "hard guys" who have no contacts outside of their extremely tight-knit circle. Most of the older tough guys in the area would talk in a friendly way to the fieldworker. But the "hard guys" maintain a belligerent attitude toward anyone who has the faintest aura of authority. Even within the group there are continual demonstrations of power:

These guys are never really friendly. Their idea of being friendly is to walk up and hit a guy hard on the shoulder, and say, hi, jagoff, and pour beer on him. One of these guys who was sent up [to jail] for assault got a beer out of his car and opened it. It started spewing over two or three people standing nearby, and he just let it happen. If they didn't like it—tough.

Among these youth there is a strong connection between their insularity, distrust of adults, and their commitment to power as the sole means of making their mark in the world. There are many youth in the community who get into trouble but are receptive to helpful adults. However, for the "hard guys" all adults are the same: weak or hypocritical. This strange insistence on denying any validity to intergenerational ties creates a very constricted vocabulary of motives within their group. These youth seem to be able to talk to each other only about those things that confirm this inflated image of their toughness. They try to convince each other that they have the ability to survive on their own and need no support or guidance from anyone besides their "buddies." Moreover, they look with contempt at their peers who are afraid to make their presence felt by the sheer force of their will.

These badasses put loyalty to their friends above all other considerations. The fieldworker was out in Willard Woods one night when hundreds of local youth were drinking beer, taking downers, and milling around:

> These guys [i.e., the hard guys] never smile and they never joke except about kicking someone's ass. Well, this guy, Tommy, came up to me to see if anyone had a car. He said his friend was too fucked up that they couldn't hitch (back to town) with him and that they were going to have to carry him so that nobody will give them a ride. We got the guy in my car. He was really ripped. He couldn't walk and he couldn't talk. He had done some THC, some acid, and was drinking beer. He lived in the jungle, but we took him to his older brother's house. On the way over this guy really got bad, he kept trying to go to sleep. They knew it was dangerous and were saying, "We can't let him go to sleep, he may never wake up."
>
> The thing that struck me is that these kids may not care about anyone else, but they are loyal to each other. One of the guys said, "Look you take care of him, I really have to get home." Another guy replied, "O.K. jagoff, go ahead run out, fuck you," and then the first guy said, "All right man, you're right, I'll stick." There is no way these guys would have left him.

One of the advantages of looking at "extreme" cases is that they often disclose principles that are harder to see in more conventional situations. Most of badass youth thought that the "hard guys" carried their investment in physical prowess beyond the bounds of reason. They confused fear with respect. The ordinary badass demands respect. That means any sign of condescension on the part of others will be met forcefully. But the hard guys were seeking absolute dominance. As any experienced badass will say, "There is always somebody who is tougher than you think you are." Nonetheless, the hard guys were not seen as bizzare or deranged by the rest of the badass world because they exemplified one virtue upon which the entire style rests. Loyalty to one's friends comes before all else. The importance of peer group solidarity—the feeling of comfort and security of being with people who know one as a person—is something these youth cannot articulate easily. But this experience is so fundamental to a sense of self-worth and recognition, and it is so absent from their contact with adult authority, that peer group relations assume the quality of an ultimate value.

The badass style is obviously masculine. But girls too are often ready to fight each other, especially when one girl feels that another girl is "stealing" her boyfriend. Girls who are drawn to this style have a problem with boys: they are attracted to the tough and independent boys and, then, discover that having sexual intercourse with a boy has little effect on his continuing interest in them. Moreover, the tougher badass boys approach girls in the same way as they do boys.

> They are really rough on the girls. They say, "Fuck you bitch" when a girl comes up and says "How is it going?" And they'll say, "Suck my dick," and the girl will laugh or say something back. The girls who hang around with the rednecks in the park have a much more traditional role, they're much more in the background [than freak girls]. The guys are standing there drinking beer or passing a joint around and the girls sit there and don't join in. They stay together and do it later by themselves.

The response of badasses to school is direct. When the fieldworker asked one girl what she thought of school, she replied, "It sucks." When he asked a badass boy whether he gets anything out of it, he replied:

> You get an education and stuff out of it; you get a job but it doesn't do anything else for you. Like they have history and they have like Christopher Columbus discovered America. When we go to work people aren't going to ask us who discovered America.

A recurrent theme in the life of badass girls is getting thrown out of school, feeling elated about it but later feeling that they are somehow excluded from something which, in some indefinable way, will affect their lives:

Sally [who does a lot of drugs] tells me that she finally got expelled from school. This makes her very happy. She won't have to put up with school anymore. She said she couldn't stand it; it was ridiculous. She's seventeen. A kid named Dennis quit and he was very happy about that, and they were kind of congradulating each other.

For many of these youth, dropping out of school is not permanent. Though they find being in school intolerable, they also feel a vague sense of loss when they leave school. While they may not admit it to their friends, most of these young people are well aware of the fact that dropping out of high school is seen as a sign of personal failure by most adults. Consequently, many youth try school a number of times before making an irrevocable decision to leave, and there are alternative means of getting a high school certificate for those who want the degree.

Another young girl rejects school because it makes her appear dumb. Nothing is worth the embarrassment that comes from failing repeatedly and having others look down upon her as an incompetent human being:

I didn't want to go back to school. I'd rather work, but everybody says they want me to go back. All the people that go to school make me feel really dumb because they talk so smart and I don't know what they're talking about. Like I took some classes my counselor said were supposed to help me, learn me more and talk to people a lot easier. If I don't like a teacher I won't talk to them. With school you don't think you're getting anything out of it, but when you're working it seems that you've got something to show for it—money in your pocket. If they [teachers] talk to everybody else and leave a couple of people out including me, hell with them. I'm not going to do nothing in their class. They don't care about me so why should I do anything.

Many adults in Cambridge believe that badass youth are oblivious of the implications of their disinterest in school. While these youth do not focus on the long-term economic consequences of dropping out of school, this girl's comments about feeling dumb in school exposes a soft spot in the badass identity. These youth are aware of the fact that a modicum of education is necessary to maintain one's self-respect in the larger society. And they know that their basic skills in such subjects as reading or mathematics may be very shaky. But, as this girl remarks, it is very painful to go to school to face the reality that she does not measure up to the other students. Furthermore, she experiences academic rejection as part of the impersonal treatment that is her lot in this institution.

As this young girl remarks, the deepest insult is that her teachers and counselors do not recognize her as a person. They see her as a deficient and ill-motivated student. Both parties are at an impasse. The faculty cannot reach her because they do not understand that she, like other youth in Cambridge, puts being treated in a reasonable fashion by authority above the rational basis for staying in school. On the other hand, the badass style and the culture of Cambridge has a very poorly developed sense of how young people can legitimately ask for support from nonfamilial adults. The culture of Cambridge emphasizes the adult role outside the home as preventing youthful deviance from getting out of hand. It provides no coherent image of nonfamilial adults as persons who can guide and assist young people in times of personal difficulty and uncertainty.

The Outpost[1]

The outpost was part of an experimental youth outreach program which was funded by a federal agency. It was staffed by a metropolitan youth-serving agency. This program was designed to reach young people through contacts with the school, street work, and its "drop-in" center in an unused, decrepit garage. It was partially funded with local moneys that came through the block grant program of the federal government. The outpost was supposed to counsel youth with problems and provide crisis intervention services to youth in trouble. The fieldworker's description of the outpost captures the "refuge"-like quality of this program:

> It's an old city garage made out of old concrete blocks which look as if they were put up in a couple of days. It is kind of greasy, and the floor has never been cleaned up since they got the trucks out of there. It has all this old junk furniture that came from all over town. There is a stereo that is going as loud as they can play it. Kids can come there and do just about whatever they feel like doing. There's absolutely no structure except that on certain nights they have these groups where the kids and staff get together and talk about their problems. I've seen ten-year-old and twenty-five-year-old kids there. They can talk and lie down on the couch and sleep. They are not supposed

1. See Schwartz (1981) for a fuller description and analysis of this situation.

to do dope there—there is group pressure to keep this from happening. Some of the rednecks have past histories of being violent, and there are some long-haired freaky kids who do a lot of dope. But for some reason the outpost is like neutral territory—kids come in really high and no one bothers them—they pass out on the couch. Sometimes I've seen waterfights going on for hours and I'm thinking that any minute somebody is going to get mad and a big fight will start. But somehow it never happens. There may be anywhere from five to ten kids at night, and you never know when they are going to be there.

One of the most interesting features of the program was the role of "volunteer," some of whom were paid small sums for their services. They are an adjunct to the regular social worker. The volunteer reflects the changing character of the working-class freak. Initially, the working-class freak was nothing more than a badass who used soft drugs and listened to rock music.

For the older youth who gravitated toward this new style, however, there were major changes in their social identities. In the first place, they could retain their resistance to conventional adult authority as a freak and not abandon the image of manliness rooted in physical power and courage in fighting. But this new style allowed older males to find an honorable way out of the pattern of aimless violence that marks this sector of the youth world.

Equally important, the freak style was infused with the ethos of the social workers at the outpost. It was no longer seen as effeminate by males to talk about their personal feelings in group contexts. "Rap groups" which explored relationships with others had given some of these young men an alternative vocabulary for dealing with problematic situations with peers. Recourse to force was not the only viable alternative in their interpersonal repetoire. Moreover, the pleasures of a more relaxed, less confrontational mode of life appealed to some of these young men. It was more enjoyable sitting around listening to music stoned than riding around looking for trouble.

The transition to the freak style had two implications for the older girls. It introduced a new note of personal sophistication into their cultural horizons. They adopted an urban sort of "hip" orientation without the emphasis on economic success of middle-class culture. It also introduced a new way of looking at their involvements with men. While few of these girls broke free from a subordinate position vis-à-vis males, they could talk about their romantic dilemmas with social support. They had a developed image of an intimate relationship that was different from the traditional role of wife and mother and more akin to the companionate model of the middle class.

Youth came to the outpost because they were not regimented or watched. Almost anything that did not openly jeopardize the center, such as drug dealing on the premises, was tolerated. The field-worker comments:

> They were tripping over each other and throwing pillows and wrestling. It is something to see kids pushing and shoving each other, running about, giggling, and never getting mad. The outpost is open till 11:00 and looking around the whole place is messed up. Furniture overturned, pillows all over the floor, coffee cups and pop bottles, cigarette butts and papers. Rod [the program director] said, "This place reminds me of a scene out of the movie, *The Hunchback of Notre Dame*, where the beggars, the lame, the poor people and thieves have a Carnival of Fools where everybody is crazy." Some of the kids are high, some are drunk, there are lonely kids, a lot of them have no place to go, and they have problems at school and at home.

Despite the apparent chaos, the workers exercised considerable influence over their clients on the basis of nonauthoritarian relationships with them. When conflict between youth activities and the rules that protected the outpost from external interference occurred, violations of the rules were interpreted as violations of trust. In the following incident, Sonny, a local badass who was in perpetual trouble with the police and school, was caught dealing drugs in the outpost:

> Three staff members chewed him out for about an hour. At first he was defiant, and then he resisted by saying how do you know it was dope or how do you know where he took it. But he kept getting less offensive and finally, near the end, he was going to give the kid his money back, never going to sell or do dope again. He just about agreed to any of their conditions as long as he could come back to the outpost.

Sonny did not want to be cut off from the outpost, but, more significantly, he did not want to give up his relationship with its staff. For someone like Sonny who spent a good deal of time in police stations and being thrown out of school, it was an unusual and gratifying experience to have a personal relationship with the workers at the outpost. Although no one had any illusions about his activities, he was not stigmatized by his deviant identity in the community. For Sonny, as well as for many other badass youth, this was a powerfully confirming experience. They were knowledgable older people [though most workers were in their twenties or thirties] who would accept him as he was and still try to find common ground for a friendly relationship.

The kind of control the outpost had over youth rested on a shared feeling that they were allied against a hostile community, and that meant that they all had to be careful about how outsiders perceived what was going on there. These young people intuitively appreciated the fact that the workers were not only people whose sophistication and social skills they could emulate but were, in fact, people who cared about what happened to them as persons. Tommy Joe, one of the notorious troublemakers in school, was at first quite suspicious of the workers, but he began to change:

> I didn't like to be around this kid before we went out with the workers to eat tonight. He was just too damn obnoxious. I mean, he was really loud. No one could talk around him because he was always interrupting and putting down whatever you had to say. Well, he was just a model of good behavior. He sat there and listened to us. If we talked about something he felt he knew something about he would make a comment and listen.

The Outpost and the Community

The outpost's success in attracting badasses and freaks, however, did not go unnoticed by the adult community: it was becoming a staging ground for "bad" kids. Local authorities recognized the potential of the program for dealing with troublesome youth. But the latitude they had in supporting the outpost was narrow indeed. They kept from becoming publicly identified as allies of this program and made it clear to Rod, the program director, that they could not bail him out if he got into trouble.

The atmosphere of the outpost began to change as its reputation for allowing young people to congregate spread among the youth. The staff was caught on the horns of a dilemma. If they failed to enforce the rules about drugs and violence the adult community would rise up in arms against them. If they put young people under close surveillance this would destroy the basis for their alliance with them.

> Its reputation has spread word of mouth that there is a place where people don't hassle you as long as you don't do dope on the premises, drink, or fight. Rod told the kids that if the staff

members had to police the place it would become just like the high school. So they decided that it would be up to the kids to protect their interests by telling a kid if you do dope that's your business but don't do it or deal here.

The notion of youth enforcing these norms was unrealistic as long as different badass and freak groups came to the outpost. It is one thing to exercise some restraint on one's friends. It is quite another thing to tell a peer to stop doing something when this is tantamount to a personal confrontation. In the spring, the youth scene blossoms as young people begin to move about the cars looking for excitement and diversion. It was not long before badasses from nearby towns came over to check out what was happening and to see whether they could impose their presence on the place.

Two guys came up from Winter Park who had been coming around regularly. They were on downers and one of them was particularly wild, and both were acting crazy. Rod was off, but Nicky and Wildman, two volunteers, were there. You can feel the tension in the air. Freddy S., a well-known local redneck, was there with his girlfriend, and these guys from Winter Park were looking for women. They were getting forward, pushing themselves on the girls, touching them and trying to get them to go with them. Finally, this guy grabbed Freddy's girl by the breast and Freddy hit him a couple of times and it was all over.

As an aura of drugs and violence began to envelope the outpost, the police began to see it as a real problem. The chief of police and Rod met over recent troubles at the outpost. The chief reminded Rod that the community was "paying" for the outpost and did not want outsiders coming in and stirring up trouble. At this point, there was no way Rod or anyone else could erect a protective screen around the outpost, although some of the local badasses tried to protect it. But they did so in a way that reinforced its negative reputation among adults.

Dave is an easy-going country kid who works for a company out there. He's really a straight kid that likes to hang around the outpost because he was lonely before now. He's made friends even though he doesn't do dope and has short hair. He likes to help people. Anyway, this girl was on downers and she fell down and Dave was trying to hold her up. Her boyfriend is a super redneck. He punched Dave out because he said he was mauling his girlfriend. It was a stupid thing to do because everybody knew Dave wouldn't do that. So Dino and his brother, they are older rednecks, beat this kid up because he started trouble in the outpost and you are not supposed to do that. You can do anything you want on the street but don't break the rules because you can get it closed.

The Final Act

During this period a serious fight occurred in front of the outpost and one boy was beaten unconscious and kicked into a nearby creek. Only the intervention of Rod and the fieldworker prevented things from getting totally out of hand, but this incident triggered threats of even more dire conflicts between local and outside badasses. In order to circumvent the inevitable, Rod decided to close the outpost temporarily before the city council did so permanently. Support from the youth commission had eroded.

They said at the meeting that the outpost could have been an issue in this election, and it would have hurt them. They said why bother with those kids anyway. They're no good. When they find out that you're going to help them that just makes them bad. So they see the outpost as making the kids worse.

After officially closing the outpost the youth commission informed Rod that there were just too many complaints about it. The final act in the history of the outpost occurred at a city council meeting that spring.

There was seating for fifty to fifty-five people, and there were people standing in the back. Some people complained about drinking, one woman said there was fights every night, and other people complained about reckless driving. The manager of the Fair View apartments said he had many complaints about the orgies at the outpost and that they have a big investment they stand to lose if people don't want to live there.

Two or three of the mothers who have kids at the outpost gave a good account of themselves. People really tried to get personal with them saying, "We know your kids are in trouble anyway." One mother replied that she knew a few things about their kids that they may not know and that they better find out what's happening with their kids. The general feeling was our kids don't do that and if the kids out here need help let their parents or the police help them.

An alderman said this program came out here on a trial basis and they've been out here a year. I've heard the kids speak and

I've heard the taxpayers speak, and I go with the taxpayers. I think they should be closed. Everyone applauded. One of the women who was so vocal against the outpost has a daughter who is in college now but was doing a lot of drugs in high school. Of course, none of these people would admit that their kids had any problems except those created by the outpost. The mayor said that he personally wouldn't want the outpost in his neighborhood.

There is a strong denial on the part of many adults that public problems are also private troubles. The culture of this community puts a premium on appearing strong, self-reliant, and invulnerable in public situations. To do otherwise would mean that you could not handle one's own family affairs adequately and that one's private life was not as respectable as the next fellow's. This accounts for the fact that, while many people knew that their own or their neighbor's children participated in deviant activities, they would argue that only a small minority of youth did these things. In a community where self-respect is a precious commodity, appeals to liberal values of tolerance for youthful deviance is experienced as a slap in the face. Being told that there is something "wrong" with your children is interpreted by many of these parents as the same thing as being told that there is something "wrong" with them. Consequently, the culture of Cambridge is committed to the fiction that youth problems are not communal problems but rather are better left to agencies of social control.

Youth Scene—Drugs and Fighting

Adults believed that drugs and fighting in the youth world only affected the "bad" kids. But "nice" as well as "bad" kids participated in the drug scene. Similarly, fighting was hardly restricted to confrontations between badasses and athletes. A minor violation of the personal space of another person, such as eye contact, is easily transformed into an insult. This emphasis on one's ability to dominate others creates the feeling that fighting is the moral equivalent of sports. A badass who got beaten rather badly talked about it as if he had lost a football game. One young girl was beaten to death, and, although the police did not find out who killed her, a local youth was a prime suspect. After the outpost closed, the youth scene moved to nearby Willard Woods where drugs and violence became a potent combination. The fieldworker describes a night in Willard Woods:

These guys from Newton had been selling everybody dope, and last night they waited a few hours for everybody to get "greased" and came back and started trouble. Supposedly they beat up four guys and two girls and put them in the hospital. So everybody is going to be ready for them this time.

We went down this road that leads into the forest preserve. It's about a mile long and there is no outlet. You have to turn around to get out. It was getting dark and you could see that people were waiting for somebody to make the first move. I talked to an older guy who is about twenty-five. He said, "We're going to be ready for those mother fuckers this time," and pulled a big pistol he had stuck in his belt. He told me they heard the guys from Newton had guns. Nobody was kidding, and it was tense. A car from Newton drove by or at least they thought it was a car from Newton and this guy from the outpost ran over with a bat and broke the back window in. There were two cars, and they broke the windows in both cars but of course the cars didn't stop. I looked up and saw the metropolitan police [from the nearby city] surrounding the area quietly. It took about twenty minutes to get the place cleared out.

As the summer progressed the crowds in Willard Woods grew, and this Saturnalia became a standard feature of the youth scene:

We saw a girl lying in the road and this guy was trying to get her up and they were stumbling around falling over each other, so we decided to give them a ride. It's really strange to see teenagers so wrecked on downers that they talk and act like drunks. This nice-looking girl came up and said, "I'm sick, I've got to throw up," and this guy helped her wash up, and she said now I want to fuck and he said OK. They started to screw right there on the grass within sight of other people.

If you can imagine a concrete road maybe 200 yards long with about a hundred cars lined up on each side. Quite a few of them have radios, tape players, or stereo speakers on top of the car. And about 400 or 500 kids, mainly 15-, 16-, 17-year-old girls, a few younger kids, and guys about 17, 18, 19, with a few older guys. Everybody is drinking beer, and every now and then a little fight breaks out. Kids are always coming up to you asking for some kind of dope—if you want to buy or sell it.

The fieldworker's observations on this scene contrast vividly with the notion that this sort of behavior is confined to only the most dedicated troublemakers in the community. He points out that the expressive significance of these events lies in being together with one's friends in a way that does not enable adults to place restrictions on one's freedom:

> It would never dawn on any of the kids that they are doing anything wrong or illegal. It's just like everything is right there for that moment and that's it—I guess abandonment is the word. It's like it's never going to end. They don't seem to worry if they have a ride or if they pass out, although most of them stick with friends and they look out for each other that way. They are always asking did you see so and so. I saw Dora who has done some pretty wild things and I was telling her about what happened to this girl and she thanked me. But these girls have to be in that scene. I think that if two or three girls got killed every night a lot of them would come. It's almost as if they feel it's their duty to be there barefooted and getting high.

Conclusion

In the spring of the year there was a major confrontation between local badasses and athletes when the former invaded a house at which the latter were having a party. There was some property damage and fighting. Legal charges were filed in the case. But almost as soon as the tension between these two groups came to a head it began to dissipate. Near the end of the school term some badasses and athletes were saying that the other group was not so bad. While one of the most threatening sources of conflict in the community diminished, there is no evidence that the underlying tensions in working-class youth culture were resolved by this moment of catharsis. Oppositions within the youth world may sharpen or lessen over time. But as long as the school represents the moral superiority of a social world to which the vast majority of youth are excluded and as long as the community demands rigid adherence to the rules of proper behavior, this drama of rebellion against authority will continue.

One should not get the impression that Cambridge is a weak community caught in the grip of a youthful deviance it cannot control. Usually, quite the reverse is the case. The essential point has nothing to do with the aggregate amount of youthful deviance which seems to fluctuate according to historical circumstances that are impossible to predict. What is important in the culture of Cambridge is the tenuousness of the bridge between the generations. Adults in Cambridge present a strong and unified front to youth when it comes to disruptive behavior. Ultimately, adults have the confidence, resources, and power to enforce their will and dampen the level of youthful drugs and violence. But they are much less adept at presenting a coherent image of how two aspects of the local culture fit together.

Youth are given a directive to get ahead in life and to accept the rational authority of the school. This means developing a future-oriented sense of the self that values self-restraint, self-discipline, and individual initiative. Moreover, this kind of rationality treats the expressive qualities of the self as strategic elements in a game of impression management. Like their parents, these young people are receptive to a much less calculating and more honor-bound conception of self. They cannot defer acting on their sense of personal integrity when they feel it has been impugned. Nor do they see the value to pretending that they still feel like dependent children in the presence of adult authority when they, like their parents, intend to protect their sense of personal autonomy in a world that is reluctant to recognize it. For these youth, going along with the official program would entail an extended period of social amnesia, forgetting that they experience themselves as having largely grown up.

5

Parsons Park

Community Setting

Parsons Park is situated in a large city. Its modest prosperity is evident in clean, tree-lined streets of solidly constructed bungalows built in the 1920s and 1930s. The atmosphere is quiet and orderly and testifies to the value its residents put on hard work and financial security. More than three-quarters of the people are Roman Catholics. Parishes are important bases of identification and affiliation. Ethnic ancestry looms large; one is identified as Italian, Irish, Polish, or Lithuanian. The majority of the working adults are either skilled blue-collar workers or clerical and service workers.

Not many of the parents have been to college, but they want their children to go, boys first, then girls. About 40 percent of the youth of Parsons Park families go to Catholic high schools. The public schools are attended by children of families of other religious backgrounds, the poorer or disaffiliated Catholics, and children from other neighborhoods. All the public high school districts serving the area overlap with contiguous areas of very different social composition. The neighborhood is named after the mile by half-mile city park which lies roughly at its center. The residential tracts which extend out from the park on all sides for a distance of a mile or so contain a population of roughly 60,000 persons.

Parsons Park developed as a residential area at the turn of the nineteenth century when surface transportation lines provided easy access to the central city. The area's population tripled in the period between 1920 and 1940. At that time, the large Lithuanian colony was established in the community. There are few factories in Parsons Park proper, but industrial plants run along the railroad lines that mark the western, southern, and eastern boundaries of the area.

148

Pressure from the Outside

A massive railroad viaduct forms the eastern boundary of Parsons Park. To the west of this boundary, the neighborhood was all white. To the east, it was all black. In the early 1970s, black families were just beginning to move west of the tracks. The neighborhood just north of Parsons Park is called Donahue Park. It was also primarily white. The district for Donahue Park High School includes much of the area east of Parsons Park and Donahue Park as well as the two white neighborhoods. One reason for this is that so many teenagers from these areas go to Catholic high schools. The result was that Donahue High's student population was about 60 percent black in 1972.

In the fall of 1972, groups opposed to racial integration organized a boycott of Donahue Park High School. Parents joined their high school–aged children on the picket lines. The school officials sat out the boycott, and eventually school resumed again. The embattled posture of this community comes across clearly during a Christmas Eve mass at one of the largest churches. The fieldworker comments:

> St. Boniface seats about 2,500. It was full, and about 500 people were standing. There was not a single black in the audience although the church is only about a mile from the racial line. The sermon began running down the places at war in the world. The priest said, "And here in this city there are people who want to kill you for no reason," making it quite clear that blacks were reasonless killers after their lives.

This implacable response to the movement of blacks close to their community was not confined to ideological pronouncements from the pulpit. An excerpt from one of the many block club newsletters conveys the intensity of the feelings among many residents about the prospect of living in a racially mixed community:

> Everything of importance to us in this community is being taken from us by individuals who are well-organized. Our homes, our friends, our businesses, our churches, our schools, our peace of our own personal safety—everything is being denied us by the combined efforts of the real estate speculators, panic peddlers, rumor spreaders, the Board of Education, the Federal Housing Authority, the criminal element, and our own weaklings. Stand together or we all lose.

The culture of Parsons Park stresses the institutional representation of familial values. There is little separation between family concerns and community preoccupations. The private and the public are two sides of the same coin. In Parsons Park, school and church are much more than institutions that serve particular needs and are responsive to particular constituencies. The church and the (parochial) school are microcosms of the social macrocosm.

The school and church embrace those values that this community endorses as moral virtues. That is, young people are taught to develop the kind of social character that the community recognizes as both good and respectable. It is not easy to distinguish, under these cultural conditions, who one is from who one knows: one's identity in the wider society draws heavily on local ties and personal relationships. Ethnic traditions, religious faith, family patterns, political involvements, and economic prospects are woven into the fabric of local institutions. Social life is not compartmentalized or fragmented. The urban parish gives a solidity to neighborhood ties that they lack in more heterogeneous areas.

While this culture has some historic depth, it can be undermined by demographic change. This marriage, so to speak, between the normative commitments of family life and the values of local institutions rests upon uninterrupted continuity in the recruitment of like-minded people to these institutions. In the city, where demographic change is almost as constant as seasonal variation (Hunter 1974), this is a tenuous basis for institutional stability. The intense localist spirit, protecting one's hearth and home from "outside" threats, reflects the vulnerability of institutions that depend upon cultural homogeneity.

Parsons Park is a community trying to build a wall around itself. Part of the problem is the obvious disparity between the sentiments of local residents and the city government's official commitment to racial justice. Parsons Park feels abandoned by those groups they have worked to put into power and duped by people who they thought shared their feelings about the sanctity of their neighborhoods. But it would be a mistake to overemphasize the external threats to the culture of Parsons Park at the expense of the younger generation's doubts about the wisdom of its authority. For some youth, parochialism is no longer synonymous with security and certainty, but it raises disquieting questions about living apart from the pluralism and cosmopolitanism of the less localistic parts of the city.

The Family

In the early seventies, there was a striking parallel between tensions within the community and the family. Taken-for-granted assumptions about the principles that ordered both spheres of social life was experienced as being under attack by "alien" forces. In the family, relationship between children and parents, husbands and wives, brothers and sisters were complicated in new ways and were resistant to old solutions. The rules for courtship and marriage (no sex before marriage), sex role in family life (the working wife and mother, the domestic and virginal daughter, the deferential son), the loyalty to Roman Catholicism (unqualified respect for nuns and priests), and the emphasis on unquestioning deference to the authority of the older generation were in flux.

Most young people did not categorically reject the idea that adult authority has the right to demand obedience and respect nor do the majority openly rebel against the assumption that authority can unilaterally interpret how the rules apply to youthful conduct. Yet it is precisely the nonnegotiable character of authority, rather than the specific content of the values it supports, that creates a good deal of youthful covert resistance and dissent.

The sources of irritation within the family revolved around what young people feel is their parents' excessive concern about the signs of moral depravity in their behavior. The fieldworker describes an incident that shows how quick parents are to interpret their mildest deviance as signs of wayward character:

> Sandy went into the thing about getting her breath clean so that she could go home without her parents smelling alcohol on her breath. She said that she and her parents are getting along a little better lately. They used to yell at her all the time, call her slut and things like that. She said the main reason for the change is that they are directing their fire at her younger sister these days.

There were countless incidents such as this one where the response of authority, parents, and school officials alike to signs of youthful deviance centered on the moral significance of proscribed behavior. In other words, authority did not say that such behavior was inappropriate, dangerous, immature, or stupid. Authority labels it as morally wrong and, equally important, claims that such behavior is a sign of inward spiritual corrosion. If authority does not grab young people on their descent into deviance and force them to recognize the danger to everything that is good and virtuous, then authority is failing in its duties.

Note, for example, a parent calling a daughter a "slut" because she has alcohol on her breath. This is not an isolated instance of excessively figurative language. Other young people reported their parents reacted to infractions of the rules as if this was evidence of a tainted character. Moreover, what might be otherwise handled by both parties as a relatively minor issue escalates into a major confrontation over the moral identities of parents and children. Youth are cast in the role of impulsive and hedonistic people who are without the internal controls that would temper their indulgence in forbidden fruits. Adults become oppressive and unyielding guardians of the established order unable to separate minor derelictions from major violations of the rules.

Conflicts over the interpretation of deviance, then, tends to drive parents and youth apart, as if each lived in opposing camps and could only communicate freely in some sort of no-man's-land. What the culture of Parsons Park lacks is a conception of youth as conscious moral agents capable of making rational decisions about their own behavior. Both sides do not speak about this because young people are so deeply cast in the role of basically passive and reactive persons that this cultural assumption is never openly questioned. Deviance, therefore, elicits such strong emotions from authority in Parsons Park because adults cannot imagine how young people will pull themselves out of it unless they are given a forceful shove in the right direction.

There is a paradox here that is difficult to see unless one compares Parsons Park to an upper-middle-class suburb like Glenbar. In Glenbar, parents are not concerned about the moral significance of youthful deviance. They are much less likely to say that deviance is wrong than that it is irrational or destructive. And they are much less likely to charge youth with being indecent than to threaten them with the consequences of an official response to deviant behavior. It goes without saying that the threatening quality of much youthful deviance is that it can go on "your record" and perhaps reduce one's chances of getting into a good college.

In Parsons Park, parents do not tell their adolescent children who get into trouble that they will not get ahead in life. What concerns both parties is the degree of expressive freedom that is reasonable and proper for young people of this age. Neither side views an instrumental conception of self as having much bearing on the situation. These youth are not pressured to groom themselves to become the kind of persons that the older generation is not. Nor must they split their social selves into two parts: a young person adopts one sort of stance with peers and another with authority. They can be pretty much the same kind of person at home and with their friends. It is what they *do* with their friends that concerns adults in Parsons Park.

The paradox can be stated explicitly. In this case, what seems like conflict grounded in a moral rhetoric that appears to create irreconcilable points of view actually produces solidarity between the generations in the long run. It does so because it does not confound local conceptions of what is reasonable with societal notions of what is rational. Parents and children can argue about how they experience each other's personal conduct, and thereby limit the extent of their disagreement to the expressive significance of violations of specific injunctions and prohibitions. There is little opportunity in this sort of fight for dividing up sides according to basic values and social commitments.

One of the most conflicted relationships in the families of Parsons Park was between fathers and daughters. Perhaps the chief occasion for arguments was the violation of curfew. For a girl to be out of the house "at night" was viewed as dangerous by many fathers. Getting home late was one of the most feared experiences of teenaged girls. The fieldworker describes a remarkable incident:

> Carole who came over to Sally's house was a Croatian whose parents don't allow her out of the house. She sneaked out of the house without permission. This girl said she was going to get drunk and did, but not too heavily. When 11:30 had passed she became very worried because staying out after curfew meant a beating. She was so worried that a group of boys took her home and promised to wait a little down the street. If she was being beaten she was to scream and they would come to her rescue. The guys did not wait around long enough.
>
> When she came home her mother scolded her, and her father, who had been asleep, woke up. Apparently, this was the first time she talked back to her parents and even swore. This enraged her mother who called her a "dirty slut." Carole said, "Yes, I've been a slut for a long time and now I'm going to go out and screw a nigger," and she ran out the door and went back to Sally's house.
>
> Carole told her parents where she had been because the father called Sally's mother and asked if he could come over to talk to her. Sally's mother told Carole to hide in the backroom and not to come out under any circumstances. Sally's mother said, "I have to admit he acted like a perfect gentleman." She tried to reason with him and told him that his daughter was scared to death of him. He responded, "Is she really. You don't know how good that makes me feel. I feel much better already. At least my upbringing accomplished something good."

Authority, in Parsons Park, is seen as commands that are decisive, encompassing, and unambiguous. Problematic issues are not perceived as matters of degree or situational appropriateness. In order to keep this young girl out of trouble, her parents issued a blanket order for her to remain in the house at night. That is seen by authority in Parsons Park as normal and unexceptional. Parents do not worry about how much control they can reasonably exercise over their childrens' lives.

Because of the sharp line her parents drew between obedience and disobedience, this girl invested considerable expressive significance in her violation of their rules. She could not express her sense of the unreasonable nature of authority except by dramatizing the extent of her disagreement with it. She went to the opposite extreme of what her parents considered proper: getting drunk, speaking disrespectfully, and threatening miscegenation. The latter is a potent symbol, to put it mildly, of contempt for parental authority in this community.

The father's response to Sally's mother is instructive. It is difficult to look beyond harsh and punitive enforcement of authority to the cultural grounds on which it rests. What strikes us as cruel seems intuitively wrong. We are tempted to eschew further analysis and insist that this sort of conduct can have no cultural justification. The father's obvious displeasure in knowing that his daughter was scared to death of him is not sadistic delight. In this community, parents feel competent when they know that their children are afraid to violate their injunctions. The idea is not of inculcating fear for fear's sake. Rather, fear of authority is taken as an incontrovertible sign that a young person is afraid of doing what authority stamps as wrong and that person recognizes the power of authority to make that judgment without discussion or qualification.

Physical violence was far from universal among the families we knew in Parsons Park. Yet all youth agreed that their fathers were strict. Everyone had at least a friend or two for whom it was not unusual to be beaten by their father. These young people recognize a continuum of "strictness." Not all fathers use physical violence, but the threat of violence is apparently near the surface in many homes. Thus most of these young people are quite sympathetic to their friends' efforts to cope with excessive physical punishment:

> Marriane comes from a large family of seven kids, and her
> father is fairly heavily into beating kids as is her oldest brother.
> She told us about her sister who had been beaten up pretty
> badly for the crime of ditching mass. Her father beat her up so

badly that some blood vessels in her head were broken and she
was badly bruised all over. Joan said that her father would get
mad but he would never beat up kids as bad as what Marriane
was describing. And Phyllis said she has none of these problems
with her parents.

Helen was a Lithuanian girl who had a mind of her own. She
regularly fought with her parents—mostly her father—over curfew, and he regularly slapped her around. On one occasion the encounter left marks.

Helen came over this afternoon. She was covered all over her
arms and legs with black and blue marks and bruises. She said
there was considerably more over the rest of her body because
her father had been beating her with a belt. She didn't seem as
upset as I was. I said she was quite welcome to move in here if
she wanted to, but Helen said, no, she wanted to wait until her
father kicked her out.

Youth do not regard harsh physical punishment as completely
justifiable parental behavior. On the other hand, the off-hand character of the discussion among youth about "strict" parents and Hel-
en's dispassionate account of what the fieldworker saw as irrational
brutality indicates that youth expect parental discipline to be severe
and unyielding. They do not expect to be consulted about extenuating circumstances nor do they expect a sympathetic attempt to understand what was involved from their perspective. All most of the
parents care to know is whether the rules were, in fact, violated
because their response follows almost mechanically from this information.

One might be tempted to explain the nonnegotiable character of
parental response of deviance as the cultural defensiveness of immigrants who fear that their children will adopt modes of life that are
unintelligible to them. While many parents are second generation,
they are closer to the immigrant experience in Parsons Park than in
other places where the feeling of connection to a European past has
been diluted by secular institutions. However, parents, by and
large, in Parsons Park are as facile in dealing with urban institutions and are as competent in American culture as any nonethnic
working-class community.

There is, however, a general image of authority based on the
hierarchy of the Catholic church that has some bearing upon the
way parents respond to their children. Parents, as we shall see, do
not define what is right and wrong on their own authority, so to

speak. They look to the parish priest and the parochial school principal to establish the norms of proper youthful behavior. In turn, these figures look toward higher authority for moral direction. Looking up from the base of the hierarchy, it is natural for parents to assume that, if it is their role to accept what they are told is the correct way to conduct their lives, it is no less reasonable to ask their children to do the same. The sentiments of awe in the face of the might of the ultimate source of moral authority gives authority an expressive significance it lacks in secular communities.

Children tend to react to their parents in much the same way as the parents treat them. Their response is monolithic and non-negotiable. Helen says she will wait until her father kicks her out of the house because this will be, as she experiences it, a decisive, irreversible break with parental authority. The bond of parental control will be cut forever, and she will be free to do as she pleases. In other words, she imagines decisively turning her back on them in a way that is emotionally similar to the way they have treated her.

It would be wrong to downplay the depth of Helen's bitterness toward her parents. But her remark about leaving home is born of the passion of the moment. The reason these youth do not react with the kind of rage one might expect is that most of these youth experience parental concern with their welfare, even though it is expressed in this most unreasonable manner. Parents work hard in this community *for* their families. This effort does not go unnoticed or unappreciated by their adolescent children. In this community, people are still close enough to the immigrant experience to value the sacrifices parents make for their children. Few families are so affluent that the cost of parochial school is not a major item in the family budget.

There is a symbolic truth to the threat Helen makes on this occasion even though the chance that she will leave home in a way that irrevocably cuts her tie to her parents and family is remote. It invokes an equally powerful moral force against the deviant behavior of her parents. She, in effect, imagines a scene of ultimate retribution for unforgivable crimes against her right to be the kind of person she experiences herself becoming. Her parents' crime, in other words, is against the expressive integrity of the self. She is being forced into an empty mold devoid of any substance other than "don't do this or that."

Underneath the aura of potential violence and bitter recrimination between parents and youth, there is a normative gap. Authority, as it is defined in this community, becomes powerless and ineffective in its own eyes if it engages in negotiation and compromise. And, for this reason, disputes flare up into angry confrontations for which neither side has the means to call a truce, or to look for a solution that does not completely negate either side's interests or point of view. Thus, judgments about the rightness or wrongness of the other party's conduct are stated in absolute terms. If the other party behaves in an arbitrary, irrational, or unreasonable manner, then only force can make them see the error of their ways, even if, in Helen's case, the force is the symbolic break in the tie to her father.

Mothers are much more protective of their children because the culture demands such forceful intervention from fathers. In the following instance a young woman decides after much soul-searching that she must tell her mother that she is pregnant and wants an abortion:

> Janet was calm and said that she wasn't nervous. Her mother, on the other hand, was very upset. She kept on saying that she was old-fashioned and couldn't understand her seventeen-year-old daughter having sex. Yet, despite her great unhappiness, she was pretty supportive and made no effort to tell Janet what she should do.
>
> Her greatest fear was that Janet's friend, Sally, might tell someone in school and what the nuns would say. She was worried that if her husband found out she would get all the blame for being too lenient with Janet. She has been telling her husband that the reason she is crying so much lately is that her mother died in January.

It is not surprising that youthful deviance is defined by adult authorities as something that ruins one's reputation and disgraces one's family. While Janet's mother was genuinely touched by the moral dilemma of her daughter's prospective abortion, she was immediately responsive to how her daughter's pregnancy would affect the family's position in the neighborhood. Janet's mother was worried that the neighbors would see them as defective parents. And she was even more frightened by the disapproval of the church and school which implies a grave sense of moral failure. Yet she stood beside her daughter because the fear of alienating her daughter's affection was greater than the risks she would have to take concealing this embarrassing event from her husband and the community at large.

This protective impulse of the mothers to mitigate their husbands' hard discipline and emotional distance from their adolescent children is a recurrent theme in the lives of the youth of Parsons

Park. It would be a mistake to view the mothers as willing allies of their children, ready to overlook or rationalize whatever deviance is brought to their attention. Rather, mothers tend to be much more sensitive to the implications of heavy-handed sanctions. They feel that excessive disapproval will eventually drive their children from home and create a barrier between them that will be hard to overcome. We can see in the following incident that Lyn's mother tries to downplay her husband's aggressive disdain for Lyn's long-haired boyfriend. She does not approve of this young man's personal style, but this strikes her as too trivial an issue to run the risk of affronting her daughter who is old enough to leave home:

> Lyn has a new boyfriend who has fairly long hair and was over the other night. Her father who was fairly drunk said something about hippies and not liking him. Her mother defended the boyfriend saying that the father didn't know anything about him and not to judge him by his long hair. Lyn's mother said that the father should stop hassling her because, she asked him, was he going to go on telling her how to live her life after she moved out of the house.

Images of Deviance

One of the things teenagers often complained about was that the issues for conflict with parents often seemed so trivial. For boys, one of the important issues was the length of one's hair.

> Moe talked a lot about his long hair and how this was a symbol of independence and breaking away from his parents. But when I drove him home, he put his hair back into a pony tail. He said his parents had seen him with his hair down only once and that was by pure accident. He had just gotten out of the shower, and when they came in the room he immediately went back in the bathroom and tied it back. It upsets them a lot, he said.

Jim talks about his father's irrational response to his hair:

> I feel he's waiting for me. One time when I'm ready to go out he's going to chop it all off, make it look really stupid. I just hate the feeling that just a little thing like letting your hair grow, he's going to kill me for it.

These boys were not incipient hippies or student radicals. They shared many of the same social values and personal prejudices of their fathers, though often in a more moderate and less intransigent form. Yet long hair, in and of itself, was frequently an electric issue. It is difficult to say how much the hair issue is related to their fathers' resentment over the greater sexual freedom of the younger generation. It would be impossible for fathers not to notice the signs in the larger culture of youthful sexual experimentation. Fathers probably look back at their own youth with some bitterness at the straight and narrow line they were forced to follow during adolescence, punctuated by escapades with girls that they might have ignored except for the fact of their sexual accessibility.

The central symbolic meaning of hair length is the emotional spontaneity it implies. Fathers in Parsons Park believe that life is hard. Conformity is not a matter of personal inclination but an unalterable requirement of social survival. The notion that their sons would run off in any direction that their feelings might lead them angers many of the fathers. Growing up to manhood in Parsons Park means doing what one has to do, and that often means doing what one is told by someone in authority. These signs of youthful expressiveness were read as signs of license and self-indulgence and, perhaps, of weakness as well.

Parents are sensitive to signs of moral turpitude in their adolescent children. Kate, college freshman, gets a prescription for birth control pills from her family doctor:

> She told the story of going to the doctor because of heavy bleeding and severe cramps during her menstrual period. He prescribed birth control pills, and Kate thought nothing of it. But when her mother discovered the girl was taking pills, she freaked out and said the only reason was that she wanted to mess around. Kate argued that the reason was medical not sexual, but her mother wouldn't believe her and tried to get her to stop.

Kate's mother's reaction to birth control pills illustrates the fear of dealing with situations that are morally ambiguous. It is not as if Kate's mother could not tolerate any sign of sexuality on her daughter's part. Rather, it was her anxiety about what Kate might do with this freedom, which from her mother's perspective had no clear-cut external controls or normative boundaries and so elicited such a seemingly irrational response. It was as if her daughter were going off into completely uncharted territory without any preparation or guide and would get hopelessly lost in a morass of vice or promiscuity. That she had not done so until now is not seen by most parents as convincing evidence of their adolescent children's growing maturity and good judgment. Rather, it is interpreted as the

result of effective controls and respect for authority. As external
sanctions lose their power over adolescents, parents worry about
what will prevent them from going off the deep end.

There is a good deal of consensus among parents, teachers, police, and other representatives of authority over an acceptable public image for youth. Yet some liberal clergymen and less conventional older youth sponsored an alternative meeting place in what is
generally perceived as an extremely conservative community. One
of the young ministers who worked at the Gemini coffeehouse pointed out that this was the sort of place where the liberal, college-
oriented youth would feel comfortable. The intent here was not to
launch a frontal assault on the moral standards and political sensibilities of the social world of the Catholic parish. Rather, the coffeehouse was a refuge for youth who were moving out of this world:

> The coffee house was full tonight, about forty kids. All of them
> were trying to look hip: long hair, army jackets, tee shirts with
> graphics. There was no entertainment or shows. A bulletin
> board contained nothing controversial except for a small notice
> which read, "You know your rights. Draft counseling. See Al in
> the back."
>
> I talked to one kid who romanticized a bit about the bullet
> hole in the window of the coffeehouse which was apparently
> fired from a passing car. He said everyone was afraid to sit in
> the coffeehouse, but if that is true a lot of kids were doing a
> good job of hiding their fear. He said that the coffeehouse was
> hassled by the cops, and as a result they try to be completely
> noncontroversial. I was told it was the second time a bullet had
> been fired through the window so there is hatred against the
> place even though it isn't clear who the enemy is.

It would be a mistake to interpret cultural dissent simply as a
rebellion against the strictures and constraints of traditional morality. There was a strong grain of straightforward curiosity about the
other ways of life. Even the traditional boys from St. Irene's High
School put aside their racial feelings when they were presented with
the opportunity of meeting sophisticated black friends of the fieldworker. They did not become converts to the cause of civil rights.
They were willing, however, to tolerate a situation in which their
girlfriends expressed some attraction to black men because they
intuitively sensed that this was a rare opportunity to be part of
something that, in their eyes, represented a cosmopolitan urban
style:

There was about twenty kids at the party. Most of the girls were slightly into women's liberation and considered themselves liberal, and they are also open and friendly. It was obvious that none of these girls had any previous contact with blacks. Jenny was especially friendly to Sam, one of the black guys, and at one point Fred, the other black fellow, whispered to me that she spent all her time telling Sam how much she liked Sammy Davis, Jr., Smokey Robinson, and other black entertainers. Later some of the girls were quite tipsy and were sitting on Sam's lap.

Except for Mike and Dan, who are school buddies of Sam and Fred, none of the boys talked to them all evening. Yet all of the guys are quite proud of being racially prejudiced, so I would expect some signs of hostility when the girls were sitting on Sam's lap and openly flirting with him. I could detect none and I looked for them. The guys had a good time and accepted the blacks as part of the free atmosphere of the party. While there was a lot of talk about drugs there was very little indulgence in them.

In all of this, there is fascination with subjects that are thought of as taboo in this community. Rarely do these young people feel confident enough to deal with emotionally charged topics on their own. Thus, the fieldworker was often approached as a sympathetic and knowledgable person who could accept those things that other adults in the community would react to with anxiety or contempt:

> Jane told me that a girlfriend of hers and her boyfriend were looking over the school yearbook and this girl's boyfriend thought that Jane looked exotic. Jane asked me, "Exotic is the same as queer, isn't it?" That night this girl dreamed that Jane was queer and told Jane about it the next day. She really felt better for having talked about homosexuality which has always been a taboo subject. She thought that women became lesbians because they didn't have a father.

The experience of breaking out of the confines of a received and unexamined morality usually occurs when young people recognize that their peers' feelings about "sensitive" issues are similar to theirs. There is a sense of collective release from what each individual has experienced as corrosive doubt about the sanctity of traditional wisdom:

> Jane used to go to Mother of God and is still very close to these girls, but she didn't think an all-girl school was healthy. Her

stepfather supported her decision to change school. She went on to say that her stepfather is a good man who believes in humanity. Other kids immediately picked up on this conversation. Louis cheered when Jane said her father wasn't a Catholic, and at least five kids said that was great or made anti-Catholic remarks. Jane said she was surprised at how many friends her stepfather has. She keeps assuming that people won't like him because he is openly antireligious. Not only was there a generally antireligious sentiment among these kids, most of whom went to Catholic schools, but it was a hidden sentiment which was surprising to the other kids. They seem to assume that their friends have accepted all of the taught views, and in this group most of them haven't discussed the matter before.

These anti-Catholic remarks are not indications of deep religious skepticism or signs of disaffection from the Catholic church. Rather, the ability to distance oneself from conventional gestures of piety and conformity shows that one can make one's own moral decisions. That does not mean that these youth have serious doubts about the moral rightness of Catholic belief and worship. Instead, this ability to question the faith is symptomatic of tolerance for difference. These youth do not find the idea of cultural pluralism threatening. They are willing to grant that people can live according to moral precepts that are quite different than theirs and still be decent human beings. Theirs is likely to be a Catholicism, however, that is different in one basic respect from that of their parents. Because they do not see the "outside" non-Catholic world as unreceptive to their values, these young people are much more likely to practice a liberal form of Catholicism that does not entail obedience to every precept of church dogma.

While many of the young people are irritated by the tight controls imposed by their families and schools, they also experience their background as ethnic, working-class Catholics as a source of solidarity. This becomes apparent on those occasions when the boys at St. Irene play other high school football teams:

> The St. Irene guys consider Sacred Heart a rich kids school, and their attitude was, "Lets teach those rich kids a lesson." Before the game one guy commented, "Did you see the fancy station wagons and big Cadillacs those Sacred Heart guys were coming in." During the game they often yelled things like "Hit that rich bastard." Toward the end of the game when it was obvious that St. Irene had it won, the guys were chanting, "St. Irene Runs It" and "Ghetto Power."

The opposition between these two Catholic schools was based on social class. Thus, symbols of a streetwise, inner-city way of life, epitomized by a black power handshake, were appropriate ways to assert their dominance over "soft" suburban kids. Yet the most powerful symbol of their status as working-class ethnics was the feeling on the part of most boys that they had to stand united against the real or imagined threats of blacks to their way of life. At this football game, the fieldworker observed:

> The guys all seem to use the black power handshake and brag that they are from the "inner city" or the "ghetto." Yet the race issue came up in the usual way. At half-time some of the guys used the word "niggers" and a few girls objected that they were "blacks." They argued a little, and then a guy said, "That's the trouble with you girls; you don't have any prejudice."

The ironic character of the remark about not having any prejudice suggests that these youth are not virulent racists. Rather, they see blacks as competitors for their traditional dominance in a city where the white, ethnic working class have direct access to political and economic power. The fieldworker describes a fight at a football game between St. Irene and a black public high school:

> The cops apparently wanted to cool Tom and Bob off and probably didn't intend to arrest them. Tom didn't realize this and was furious because the cops let the black go and were holding him and Bob. He protested repeatedly to the cops about this, and they finally let him go.
>
> Later Tom admitted that he and Bob had gone off looking for a fight, that he often got that way when he got high. Apparently the blacks had been talking among themselves about what a good game their team had played, and Tom yelled, "But St. Irene won it." This led to words and then a fight. Tom's girlfriend, Sally, objected to this attitude. She repeatedly told him, "You don't have to act tough to be accepted," and that his racism and desire to get into fights all the time was sickening.

Girls feel much freer to express nonconventional sentiments about emotionally charged matters. The boys are more likely to confront authority head-on: to say, in effect, that you cannot make me do this. Yet this kind of overt rebellion against authority is more easily understood and assimilated in the culture of Parsons Park. Here people understand that males occasionally will break free of the restraints of external control. That sort of behavior does not trouble them nearly as much as youth who seem not to recognize authority as a central presence in their lives. After all, it is a gesture of respect to take authority seriously enough to contest its power. In these battles, authority has little doubt about who will emerge victorious. As long as young people have experienced that encounter as a vital and consequential moment, authority feels that its hold on youths' loyalty to cultural tradition is not in jeopardy over the long term. If young people turn their backs on authority, walk away from its presence, and declare its irrelevance to anything that matters in their lives, that is a threat to its legitimacy.

It is difficult to say how much boys differ in their attitudes toward authority. Boys like Tom may get some vicarious pleasure from having their girlfriends like Sally play the liberal counterpart to their traditional stand on the racial issue. To a certain extent, this is a classic instance of the dramatization of sex-role differences: boys are "hard" and girls are "soft." Boys "protect" themselves against the incursions of others, whereas girls are tolerant of differences because they do not have to physically defend their personal integrity against the real or imagined insults of others.

There is more to the differences between these girls and boys. Boys get vicarious pleasure out of watching their girlfriends experiment with traditional culture because it would be socially too risky for them to move into uncharted cultural territory. At the same time, they are not left without some real connection to the cultural pluralism and sophistication of the city. Many of these girls are more aware of different ways of life and alternative values than the boys. Although the boys do not openly admit that in this respect their girlfriends are more adventuresome than they are, they clearly admire this daring on their part. Otherwise, they would offer more than token resistance to their defense of blacks, to interracial parties, and all of their "liberal" attitudes to go directly against the cultural grain of Parsons Park.

At the same time, it would be hazardous to interpret these little forays into more sophisticated ways of life as incontrovertible evidence of cultural dissent that decisively casts off the normative orientation of Parsons Park. Rather, it seems that the more innovative girls are also the most ambitious girls—good students who work hard in school and look forward to going to a good college. They have almost no affinities to the freak or badass culture of Cambridge other than somewhat greater freedom than their more conventional peers where soft drugs and sex are concerned. In other words, most adults would spot them as "good" kids whose dress and demeanor identifies them as much closer to the "straight" than the deviant sector of the youth world.

What is happening to these girls is more complex than adolescent rebelliousness. Much of their protest against the cultural orthodoxy of this working-class community can be seen as anticipatory socialization. In other words, they are rehearsing ways of responding to the world around them that are more appropriate in middle class, cosmopolitan social circles than in Parsons Park. They are trying to be more "worldly" and less "provincial" in their attitudes toward sensitive social issues. Yet it is premature to say whether theirs will be a path that preserves a good deal of continuity with their past or whether they will reject much of their traditional upbringing as so much excess baggage in their movement out into the larger world.

Mother of God High School

While the administration of Mother of God High School was confident of the validity of its social and educational philosophy, the rebellious students in the school saw the moral principles underlying this philosophy as irrelevant to their lives. Restriction for restriction's sake was the way these students perceived authority's attitude toward young people. There was, furthermore, no serious discussion between these two positions over issues of principle.

There was a considerable range of opinion on social issues among the faculty at Mother of God: there were a few liberal priests as well as lay teachers. However, the school's emphasis on keeping "troublesome" topics out of the day-to-day operations of the school was not open to question as far as the administration was concerned. Since the college preparatory orientation of the school was so pronounced, teachers had a reasonable degree of flexibility when it came to curriculum and class discussion. Yet the overall thrust of the educational process revolved heavily around assimilating factual information and building skills that would enable these girls to do well on standardized tests. The total dominance of the philosophy of authoritative control by the nuns penetrated deeply into the minute questions of how teachers would use their "free" time. The fieldworker describes a typical incident where the seemingly "negotiable" issue of a free day for the faculty becomes an occasion for authority to underscore its basic position—that it has the right to make decisions unilaterally:

> There was supposed to be a free day for one of the Catholic holidays. Sister Christina announced that teachers would be expected to organize field trips, and every student would be required to go on one of the field trips. After the faculty meet-

ing, I was talking to four lay teachers, and one of them said, "There is a revolt brewing among the faculty." Another replied, "There's no chance in the world of this group of cowards doing anything about it." They all laughed and agreed that while they objected they weren't likely to do anything. I think that all of them know that a number of lay teachers were not rehired last year because they spoke up about their opinions, and they're not about to do the same thing.

Authority sometimes exercises power simply to strengthen its position of dominance. The message to those who would contest its judgment or disobey its commands is that deviance will be painful and costly. In a democratic culture like ours, there seems to be something eminently unreasonable about authority that acts unilaterally. It would be wrong, however, to see the authority of the school in this light.

In order to understand this, we must understand that from the school's point of view it would be unreasonable to consult those subject to its authority. Consequently, it is the obligation of authority to chart out the course of conduct for those dependent persons in its charge. The metaphor of dependence refers to a person's position in a hierarchical structure, not to some aspect of the personality or will. Those persons, like teachers, are too far down in the hierarchical structure of the school to legislate for the welfare of the whole.

In the following statement, Sister Christina discusses her philosophy of educational administration. Implicit in her view is the fundamental contrast between order and anarchy. Anything that contributes to order is reasonable and just; anything that opens the door to anarchy is unjust and unreasonable. Thus, Sister Christina can say that she allows the girls to voice their opinion just as long as they are receptive to correction when Sister Christina thinks they are wrong. In other words, the image here is that each party has a specific duty, and, if all parties recognize their particular duty, order will result. It is Sister Christina's duty, as a parental figure, to define right and wrong. It is the students' duty to learn from her so that they can live in accordance with good order. Authority, from Sister Christina's perspective, is as deeply bound by traditional conceptions of its responsibilities as are those persons for whom it defines the rules of proper conduct, She says:

> Over the years I've seen the loss of discipline, that permissiveness creeping into the home that I think I have tightened up on. I feel that if they're not going to get discipline

while they're here, they're not going to get any idea of this anyplace else either. One thing I'm going to insist on to these girls that there is a certain respect for authority. Not that you cannot speak up or express your own opinion. I try to watch this very closely with the students; that if you did wrong you come and let me know your side and see if I could show the student where they were wrong.

There are many taken-for-granted assumptions about the nature of authority in Sister Christina's statement. The most important is that the social order depends on an unequivocal chain of command. Parents have authority over children, husbands over wives, principals over lay teachers, priests over families, and, of course, the Church is the ultimate template for the distribution of authority in the world.

Authority, as long as it is truly authority, is categorical. Its judgments about right and wrong conduct are not subject to change because that, in Sister Christina's opinion, would lead to moral chaos. Everyone would presume that their definition of right and wrong took precedence over that of authority. Authority would be left impotent, able to enforce its precepts only on those who were somehow receptive to them. But the test of true authority, in the culture of Parsons Park, is its power to legislate for the whole, to gain compliance from malcontents and deviants as well as from the devoted and obedient. For Sister Christina, then, there is no real difference between the rationality and the reasonableness of authority. Authority is rational when it reflects inherently right moral principles, and it is reasonable when it gets others to recognize the validity of those principles. Anything less on the part of authority is a dereliction of duty.

Moreover, Sister Christina's statement reflects the centrality of the church in the community. It is the center from which moral authority radiates into the community. The role of the church and school is not to usurp parental authority, according to Sister Christina. The school and church sets an example. It provides the leadership that resolves doubt and reinforces parents' commitment to the proper ways of raising children. When Sister speaks of permissiveness, the reference is not to the situation of affluent youth who can afford to indulge every whim. Rather, it is a cryptic reference to the threat of pluralism, of seeing another normative code as having equal validity to one's own, with the consequent inability to defend one's principles as those worthy of respect.

The principle that informs the policies of Mother of God High

School is that parents want to be certain that their daughters are raised in an atmosphere free of moral taint. This means that the school administration feels that they have the right to punish what they perceive as an intent to violate as well as overt infractions of the rules. The idea that proper, ladylike demeanor is the essential virtue of a good education for young women is not imposed solely by the nuns upon the students. There is strong support among parents for the idea that the distinctive mark of moral excellence revolves around proper decorum. This is evident in a letter sent by the Mother of God Alumnae Association to parents of all seniors:

> The seniors are invited to attend the Snow Ball sponsored by the Mother of God Alumnae Association. If you permit your daughter to attend we ask full cooperation on the following. Modest dress, formal or semiformal, which means no strapless or low cut gowns. Neither she nor her escort is to indulge in liquor of any form whatever. Both her reputation and that of the school are at stake at such time. We feel confident that you too are interested in keeping your daughter's name clear of unsavory remarks as to their dress and behavior. Any conduct on the part of the seniors or their escort which would cast a shadow on the good name of Mother of God High School and on the Alumnae Association would compel us to refrain from inviting the seniors in the future. We are confident that both you and your daughter and her escort will keep our standards high and our reputation above reproach.

"The Luggens"—Ethnic Group Formation

The order of nuns who ran Mother of God High School was composed almost entirely of women who apoke Lithuanian as their first language. Admissions were open to all, but understandably the majority of the 600 students were of Lithuanian ancestry. There were several dozen girls from black families and a larger number of Catholic girls from the other ethnic groups of the area. The curriculum was particularly strong in the arts and humanities. The tuition was moderately high, somewhere around $750 a year.

Within the student body groups formed by two sets of standards which often overlapped: ethnicity and the parish grammar school one had attended. Lithuanian girls were referred to as "Luggens," but among them there were two groups: the Luggen Luggens and the modern Luggens. This difference was largely due to the migration process of Lithuanians to America. One phase lasted from the

1890s to the 1920s. A second great influx occurred during and after
World War II. Thus, there were third-generation and second-gen-
eration Lithuanian girls at the school. The third generation made up
the nucleus of the modern Luggens, and the children of the D.P.'s
and emigres from the war and subsequent Russian domination of
Lithuania made up the nucleus of the Luggen Luggens. For many of
these girls, Lithuanian was their first language. The fieldworker
describes a conversation at school with these girls:

> I talked at length to about eleven or twelve of the Lithuanian
> kids who were juniors at Mother of God. These girls are quite
> nationalistic. They ran down a list of their activities, and there
> was something just about every night. One night they learn
> Lithuanian folk dances and another it is the Lithuanian girl
> scouts, which is completely separate from the Girl Scouts of
> America. Simone told me that there are two cliques and hers is
> a little bit less nationalistic. They did talk about the fact that
> most of the Lithuanian girls were friends only with other
> Lithuanian girls and that they were isolated from the St. Irene
> clique because they say that their lives are centered around
> their boyfriends. Deva said, "Can't you see us sitting around all
> day talking about our boyfriends!"

"St. Irene's Clique—Skunks"

The group of girls at Mother of God for whom the values implicit
in the regime at school were invalid were members of the "St.
Irene's clique." This was a group of Italian and Irish girls whose
boyfriends for the most part attended St. Irene High School. Their
interaction with girls from Lithuanian backgrounds was curtailed
by the conservative nature of ethnically based clique formation. But
they did know of some Lithuanian girls who agreed with them and
whose tentative migration from traditional Lithuanian cultural at-
tachments was similar to their incomplete migration from Catholic
working-class values in general.

The educational philosophy of this high school holds that a girl's
moral character and her academic performance should *not* be evaluated separately. However, adhering to the rules of proper decorum
and doing well in academic subjects were not, from the girls' point of
view, something they valued equally. Despite the skepticism these
girls had about the nuns' right to mold their character, they did not
question the idea that theirs was a superior educational experience
to that of the public schools. A strong emphasis on grades and con-

tinual round of testing was accepted as a natural consequence of going to a "good" school.

The principal point of conflict between the nuns and girls came from the former's insistence that a good student was a good girl. The concrete symbol the nuns used to make this point was the student's "record." The fieldworker records a typical incident of "subversive" activity:

> After school Sally and her friends were shouting cheers in the halls. The principal heard them and scolded them for making noise in the halls. Sally and her friends stood up to her and argued that there was nothing wrong since school was over and the halls were empty. The principal made them sign a detention list and kept them in her office for an hour, but none of them would apologize or admit they had done anything wrong.
>
> When the principal could not get them to repent, she threatened them with taking out their records. Sally challenged the principal to bring it out. When the principal brought out Sally's record, Dora said, "Don't forget to bring out mine too." As each nun came into the office and saw the girls in detention, she commented, "Its always the same girls, isn't it."

There is a consistent pattern to the tension between youth and authority in Parsons Park. What seem to youth as relatively trivial issues such as chewing gum in school, fooling around in the halls, or coming home after curfew are treated as serious violations of the rules. In all of this, it is not the unreasonableness of the rule itself, though it is certainly that, that bothers these youth as much as the implication that they are no different than children. It is customary for elementary school teachers to insist on order in the halls or to chastize a child for chewing gum in class. But, in Parsons Park, that regimen continues without significant change into high school. It is experienced by many youth as a denial of an obvious change: that they are older now, much closer in judgment, powers, and rights to adults than children. But this growing sense of their own autonomy and responsibility goes unrecognized by authority. This is the significance of the nuns' threat to put this incident on their "record." From the girls point of view, that idea that a demerit for deportment or citizenship would make a serious difference in their lives was ludicrous. But the principal saw that as a serious sanction, as an official notification of their disobedience. Yet it is precisely the nature of the obedience demanded by authority that is contested by these girls. They think of themselves as young women, and authority treats them as if they were oversized schoolgirls.

There is a slightly different aspect of this situation that seems to go unnoticed by those in authority but which they must appreciate at some level. These girls have a highly developed sense of when and where to pick a fight with those in charge of the school. They have a keen sense of the issues that they can debate with authority over who has the right to define reasonable conduct. In other words, they know how to provoke authority and to make their point without creating deep and irrevocable antagonisms. After all, their behavior in the hall capitalizes on one of the natural assets of adolescent girls: they can critique the illusion that the nuns have the situation under control merely by tapping their normal playfulness and giddiness. These girls, however, are also sensitive to the limits of dissent. When they have made their point by forcing the nuns to think about the appropriateness of maintaining decorum in the halls after school, they stop there. They neither broaden the issue to include more serious matters nor do they intensify the emotional significance of the conflict with authority. Although those in authority cannot say so, it should have occurred to them that these girls demonstrate considerable tact in their attack on the unreasonableness of certain rules.

The overt resistance to unreasonable demands, however, does not encompass the traditional value placed on academic performance. Doing poorly on a test is experienced with considerable anxiety by most of the girls:

> A young lay teacher was giving out history tests, and most of the girls did badly. There were lots of questions about grades, and the girls suggested lots of ways these grades could be eliminated and they could get better grades. The kids wanted to know if they could have a retest or do extra credit work to make up the grade or do work sheets outside class. They complained that other classes had easier tests, but the teacher replied that everything on the test was on the work sheets.

We might compare these grade-conscious rebels with rebellious working-class girls in Cambridge. Ironically, the crucial difference is that the symbols of authority in Mother of God are so stable, palpable, and encompassing that it saps little of their energies to devote considerable time to subverting the nuns' authority. In other words, these girls know precisely what they dislike, why they dislike it, and how to get a rise out of authority without putting themselves in an indefensible position. And they have to do very little to make their point. Teasing a nun is a lot less dangerous than using drugs and alcohol in a forest preserve where groups of young men are looking for a fight.

The comparison goes deeper. In Cambridge, there is a separation between the culture of the home and the school. Parents' expectations for their childrens' success are embodied in an institution that makes them uncomfortable, and their own educational background affords them little in the way of understanding how that goal is to be accomplished. They send their adolescent children into an alien cultural environment in the hope that some of the "magic" that carries people from the working class into the middle class will rub off on their children, although the exact mechanisms that govern this transition remain a mystery.

The parochial school, on the other hand, is an extension of the home, a place where parents have absolute faith that their children are in good hands: its policies and practices have their support and approval. Equally important, these girls compare their situation to that of urban youth as a whole. They are certain that whatever the restrictions, absurdities, and inconveniences of their school, they are a privileged elite. That is, that they are getting a better education by far than youth in public schools and that the environment of their school is without the stresses that make going to school in the city difficult—fear of being raped in the bathroom or of fights in the cafeteria. Thus, it would be wrong to conclude that even the dissident girls at Mother of God are a seething caldron of discontent. The clarity of the target for their attacks on authority combined with the knowledge that they have many advantages other youth lack lends a whimsical, playful quality to their rebellion. In Cambridge, only the physical structure speaks of privilege. Otherwise, school seems unreasonably boring and confining to the majority of students whose situation is no different than youth in a host of nearby towns. Furthermore, attacks on school authority resonate with the diminishment of their parents' dream whereas in Parsons Park these girls can belittle authority without jeopardizing their aspirations for the future.

Perhaps the most explosive point of contention between the dissident girls at Mother of God and the nuns revolved around the latter's assumption that they had the right to pry into the personal lives of their students:

> Sally told me about one of her friends who accidentally left a letter in a book in one of her classes. She was writing to a boy she knows in college and she told about the good time she had the last time she visited his campus, of how she got totally

stoned and she and another girl ended up sleeping in the men's dorm because there was no other place to stay. Sally said there was no sex involved, and it was lucky that the nuns did not understand that there was a difference between being stoned and being drunk.

The letter was circulated to most of the nuns at school, and this girl was called down to the principal's office and given a long scolding, and she received lectures from many other teachers. She emphasized the possible damage this would do to the reputation of the high school and the girl's immorality because she associated with boys who drank. The girl was especially worried because she knew the nun would call her mother so she had to go home and tell her the story first.

Here we can see one of the normative principles of the culture of Parsons Park at work: the interpenetration of the home and the school. It is inconceivable to authority that it does not have the right to intervene in the lives of these girls when circumstances warrant it. The idea that students have "private" lives that are of no concern to authority would strike authority as removing the principal reason for its existence. Authority shapes and molds character. It takes young people and makes them into law-abiding adults who follow the rules of proper behavior in their personal as well as their public lives. Moreover, as the principal emphasizes, students are responsible for the moral standing of the community as a whole. Anyone who falls below the acceptable standard casts aspersions on the moral integrity of the school. The idea that one is responsible for one's own moral destiny is foreign to the culture of Parsons Park.

For the nuns, it is the substance of morality—the literal meaning of what a person does—that goes to the heart of their conception of the self as a moral agent. Following an externally defined model of correct conduct comprises an infallible standard for personal morality as far as the nuns are concerned. For these girls, on the other hand, the way in which one makes moral judgments is as important as their substantive significance. Thus, the principal's insensitivity to moral nuance prevented her from appreciating the relative innocence of this girl's behavior, and thereby foreclosed the central task of authority. It was impossible for those in authority to discuss whether getting stoned or sleeping in a male dorm was the wisest course of action because authority was incapable of understanding that it was possible to do those sorts of things in a more or less reasonable way under certain circumstances. In other words, the inability of authority to perceive the situation in other than black or white terms disqualified it from offering any counsel or guidance that would be heard by this girl.

By their very inflexibility, the nuns risk casting their own moral precepts in an anachronistic light. But, more important, the nuns refuse to recognize that the students are responsive to a value that is endorsed by American culture. One cannot encourage young people to develop the habits of mind that go along with being good students at an elite institution without also promoting autonomy. This, in turn, encourages a sort of moral Protestantism: a belief that one must examine one's own conscience before making decisions that affect one's spiritual welfare. These girls may eventually agree with the Church on most moral issues, but they probably will never relinquish their right to investigate the issue for themselves.

The nuns found it almost impossible to discriminate between willful disobedience and playfulness. Every sign of high spirits among teenage girls was likely to be seen as an indication of lawlessness. The fieldworker describes what happened when some girls were "playing" child-like games:

> Dora, Lydia, Linda, and several other girls went to the drama practice room and found a lot of costumes and decided to play dress up. Sister Constance came in and found Jenny who was lying on the floor in a weird position. When that happened, they all tore off the clothes and ran. She's old and her eyes aren't too good so the sister didn't know who all of them were.
>
> Anyhow, Sister Constance got three other nuns and asked Jenny to tell them who the others were. She refused, and they really browbeat her and threatened her with all kinds of things until she broke down and all of the girls got into quite a lot of trouble. Dora was told, "You've had a lot of straws on the wall, but you've picked the last one. The next time you are out." All of the girls were threatened with not being able to attend graduation ceremonies.

We mentioned earlier that one of the bones of contention between these girls and authority was the inability of the latter to recognize their maturity. The other side of the issue is the tendency of authority to confuse youthful expressiveness with disrespect. This incident began as pure girlish play. In fact, they were playing a children's game of dressing up. To the nuns, any activity that lacked the strict regimentation and prescribed routine sanctioned by the school was an invitation to licentiousness and disorder. Again, rationality is purely a matter of order, of predictability, of time-worn habit. Spontaneity and humor have, in the eyes of authority, an intrinsically subversive meaning. Consequently, the failure of authority to recognize expressiveness as reasonable—as a potentially creative, nondestructive aspect of adolescence—reduces its legitimacy. The language that would enable the generations to communicate their feelings about what really gives pleasure to being in school together is almost completely missing at Mother of God. There is a joyless quality to the way authority insures that its voice is heard and removes whatever warmth it feels for those for whom it is responsible.

The rebellious girls of the St. Irene's clique made their conflicts with the nuns into a symbol of their collective identity. They called themselves the Skunks and had a little cheerleading routine in which they would line up and go through the letters of their names, "Gimme an S . . . Gimme a K . . ." and so on. When the Skunks went on a class trip to California, they referred to the girls who always obeyed the nuns as "the Virgin Marys." They saw obedience as connected to control over sexuality. As for their own sexuality, it was regulated personally and from within rather than traditionally and from without. Thus, when in religion class a set of traditional rules for sexual behavior was given to them, their response was one of incredulity and laughter. It was not only the content of the rules that struck them as funny but the very act of having it given to them on a piece of paper from a teacher.

The disagreement with authority was joined over the question: "Who is in charge here?" "Standing up to the nuns" and "saying what I really think" had a purely expressive significance. It is equivalent to symbolically affirming their integrity as morally autonomous people. Rarely did the girls ever push their point to its limit. They were in fact masters at the short attack: the skirmish that let it be known they were not to be completely controlled but that also did not break the connection with the school:

Sally told about her latest run-in with the nuns. This one was the last straw, and supposedly the next thing she does she is not going to be allowed to graduate. It has to do with "hamburgers," which is what the kids call these kazoo-like instruments you hum into and it amplifies the sound. A lot of kids have them, and the nuns caught them using them. Sally was accused of using one once when she hadn't been and got called into the office. While Sally and some other girls were in the office, Dora and some other girls came parading through the office while the nuns were not around, and serenaded them, but beat it before the nuns could catch them. They did this several times, and the nuns were apparently running around trying to catch them.

Many of these incidents dissolve into laughter rather than tears for these girls. They are likely to remember the inherent absurdity of the situation when they look back at growing up in a parochial school. It is not unlikely that, in time, some of these girls will develop a tolerant regard for the awkward, humorless, ineptitude of the nuns. The nuns scold and threaten, but nothing much happens. In one sense, both parties understand each other too well for conflict to develop a grim sort of mutual hatred. There is a normative space here—a room to grow without taking extreme stance or engaging in destructive behavior—that lends a gentle note to these little dramas of generational discord at Mother of God High School.

The Peer Group World

The teenagers of Parsons Park were a pulsating front of restless, only partially directed energy. One complaint we never heard was that there was nothing to do. During the school year "the kids" were broken up into achievement groups, struggling with school, meeting in small groups for parties and talk, conversationally reprocessing their relationship with their families, and often resting in front of the T.V. set. In summer they worked at part-time jobs but still had the leisure for massing in the park and for consuming prodigious amounts of beer and cheap wine and lesser amounts of marijuana, hallucinogens, and downers.

Among the young people who attended parochial schools, there was little in the way of different youthful social identities. Unlike Patusa, this does not mean either that the youth culture is undeveloped in Parsons Park or that peer networks are weak and fragmented. Despite some differences in the aspirations and personal values of these youth, the young people who attended Mother of God and St. Irene felt very little necessity to segregate themselves into exclusive groups and cliques other than those that were based upon strong ethnic affiliations. Moreover, there is a powerful neighborhood flavor to the character of youthful association in Parsons Park. These young people had grown up together in the same area and continued to get together at parties, in the park, and at homes even though they might not go to the same school. Moreover, younger and older youth associated freely. In general, there was a clear sense of solidarity rooted in the master identity of being from Parsons Park and seeing oneself having the same religious background and family situation.

During the summer, our fieldworker's young friends persuaded him to let them use his house in the neighborhood for a going-away party for Bob, who was about to enter the Marine Corps. They expected fifty or sixty to attend, and about 150 showed up. The party flowed out of the basement, into the back yard, into the back alley, out on the street. The fieldworker describes the scene:

> The noise level was incredible. About twenty or thirty couples were necking and the rest of the place was packed with people standing around drinking and talking.
>
> Simon who was obviously drunk had a near fight with someone. There was at least five or six guys trying to hold Simon down who was yelling and screaming that he was going to get a couple of guys. Apparently Simon insulted this guy's girlfriend, and the guy insulted Simon back, and Simon started the fight.
>
> I was talking to one of the neighbors who told me I should try to hold down the noise because people around here call the cops when the kids are playing basketball in the alley. At this point two cops showed up and went around to the back and walked into the basement, and all of a sudden this huge stream of people started coming upstairs and leaving through the front door. Anyway, one cop was being friendly whereas the other cop said we should bust everyone here, including me. This cop, I found out later, is around the neighborhood, and several kids at the party liked to torment him. But the first cop who was Irish said we should just break up the party and tell everyone to go home and they wouldn't make any arrests and would put down in their report that there was no alcohol on the premises.

In this incident, we can see continuities in working-class youth culture. The similarities between Parsons Park and Cambridge revolve around the traditional themes of male peer groups. There is sensitivity to infringement on one's personal honor, a readiness to answer an insult with a punch, a certain rowdiness in public gatherings, and a willingness to disregard authority when it is possible to do so. But the differences are also striking. These youth feel at home in their neighborhood in contrast to Cambridge where they feel that they must find a sanctuary that is remote from adult surveillance. Getting drunk, making noise, and having the police break up the party are ordinary events in Parsons Park which carry no ominous overtones. Adults intervene, youth protest, and everyone goes home feeling that they have played their usual parts in this drama of excess and restraint. But the essential point is that one rarely sees the genuine anger and bitterness about youthful expressiveness in Parsons Park that one finds in Cambridge. In Cambridge, youth, outside of the home, are looked at as potentially dangerous and destructive people who need to be carefully watched by the authorities—police routinely break up any large gathering of youth in public places. In Parsons Park, there is much less of this feeling, and adults are confident that they can keep youthful activity from getting out of hand.

The Police

In spite of widespread and, in many cases, intense familial conflict and a local tradition of standing up to authority outside of the school and home, Parsons Park is regarded, on the whole, as an orderly and safe neighborhood. There is relatively little serious juvenile crime such as muggings, rapes, murders, robbery, and burglary. As we saw earlier in the remark that the neighbors in Parsons Park "call the cops when the kids are playing basketball in the alley," there is a great deal of informal surveillance over the streets. People have no compunction about intervening if they suspect that some sort of deviant activity is in process. Calling the police under these circumstances is thought of as a normal response to any threat to the public order. Finally, there is a great deal of understanding between the police and youth based upon their similar cultural backgrounds. When the young people get into trouble and become difficult, the police tend to react as older brothers rather than as impersonal officers of the law.

When Pete was arrested for charging out onto the field after a big football game between St. Irene's and a black school, he was not particularly awed by the police. The police, for their part, reacted with the sort of force necessary to gain Pete's respect but not enough to inflict serious injury:

> The cop had pushed and shoved him along until they were off the field. Pete thought the whole thing was funny and he went along. But when they got under the stands, the cop began hitting him. In Pete's words, "Of course I wasn't going to take that so I hit him back. I landed a couple of good punches, but then a couple more cops grabbed me and they started beating me." However, he added that they didn't hit him too hard and didn't hurt much. He was charged with disorderly conduct and resisting arrest.

Later, in court, Pete was given twelve months' supervision for this incident. On the whole, the local police treat these youths with a certain amount of familiarity and familial discipline: tough but usually not severe. And one of the ploys they always use to keep youth under control is to point out how often they give them "breaks": of not treating them with full vigor of the law. As a result of good knowledge of police procedures, most of these youths are fairly skilled at getting out of borderline situations, and they have some contempt for those who handle themselves ineptly:

> One time, Tim had to spend a night in the jail of a nearby county for a traffic offense. While he was there, they brought in a very freaky-looking guy who was obviously high, and they found a pound of grass and about forty downers on him. They asked him where he had gotten the stuff, and he told them, "Fuck you," and answered a couple more questions in similar fashion. And Tim saw them just beat the hell out of this kid in the station. Pete had been talking about how he is always polite to cops, except that one time at the football game. He said that it was wrong for the cops to beat up the kid but that the kid was asking for a lesson, and he should have known better.

All of these youths had endless stories of run-ins with the police. Being out after curfew, drunken driving, buying liquor with false identification, smoking marijuana in the park, general rowdiness in public places—these were all regular occasions for "contact." Most of the time, they "got a pass." Yet they always referred to the police, in their absence, as "pigs," and this was in fact just a common noun without ideological connotations. The fieldworker tells a story that illustrates how a young person's family connections to the police force are representative of the community's sense of its power in the city:

> Mack's father is a captain in the city police force. Mack was at a dance recently at Sacred Heart where he had gone outside alone to smoke grass, and after that he put his grass in the trunk. As he was going back in, some cops grabbed him and said they were going to get him for dope because he smelled of marijuana.
>
> They searched his car, but they could not find the key to the trunk because he had gotten rid of it. He told these cops who his father was, but since they were county police they weren't impressed. They took him to the station and eventually released him. Afterward he told his father, and his father was mad and went with him to tell off the county cops. They were very respectful and said yes sir and apologized, and Mack obviously enjoyed the whole spectacle of their humbling themselves to his father.

Encounters with the police are frequently free of the tension and fear that youth sometimes associate with "drug busts." Many of the Mother of God girls accept these contacts with the police as a normal and not especially problematic part of their round of peer group activities:

> The girls were talking about dope and how the cops were hassling kids a lot. It turned out that Joan, Phyllis, and Ruta had been stopped by cops in Parsons Park Friday night before curfew for no other reason than to stick their noses in the car to see if they could smell dope. Phyllis told of three friends of hers who were sitting in a car smoking dope and were busted this weekend. The cop stopped them, had taken their dope, told them to beat it, and just kept the dope.

The sense of cultural commonality that is expressed in contacts between youth and police tempers any conclusion that youthful rebellion against authority is an unmistakable sign of cultural change. One might infer that some of the more rebellious youth were well on their way to a final rejection of the legitimacy of the moral authority of the church and community. And perhaps some are. But the tug-of-war between youth and authority, as we can see so clearly in case of relations with police, can be easily relegated to a phase of one's life. In other words, it is quite possible that, as adults, many of these youth will look back at their sexual experiments, their use of soft drugs, their jostling with the police as part of the normal process of growing up. They may be somewhat more tolerant of youthful deviance than their parents and more permissive when it comes to raising their own children. But that is a far cry from completely turning their backs on their past. The meaning of growing up as an urban, working-class youth and living in an ethnic, Catholic community is a powerful source of solidarity between these young people. This experience is so deeply embedded in their social identities that it seems unlikely that many will erase all traces of their cultural origins from their lives.

Continuity

When we first met Tom, he had his life all planned out. The fieldworker comments:

> The most impressive thing about Tom is the way he has planned his future. He says, "I'm going into law." He won a $1,200 state scholarship and will go either to State or Bergen College de-

pending on where he can get a better part-time job. After graduating, he will come back to the city, get a full-time job, and go to law school at night. As far as I could tell, there is no question in his mind. That is exactly how he intends to spend the next ten years or so.

Like many of the boys who go to urban parochial high schools, Tom is sophisticated in the ways of the city. He is purposeful in his commitment to getting ahead in the world and rather self-confident. Although most of these boys come from comparatively humble origins, they are not unaware that almost all the city politicians and powerful governmental figures had nearly identical backgrounds. The ambitions of boys like Tom are not empty dreams but are patterned after literally thousands of young men before them who transformed their credentials as bright, energetic, politically adept representatives of white ethnic communities into positions of respectability throughout the entire political and economic structure of the city.

During the next eighteen months of acquaintance with him, he did not deviate significantly from that plan. Tom was a varsity athlete at St. Irene's, and the group from Mother of God went to all the big football games, basketball games, and hockey games together. The boys at St. Irene's agreed with their teachers over the issue of discipline. The boyfriends of the Skunks generally admired their teachers and coaches for their "toughness." For example, Tom's coach told the basketball team that they did not have "any balls," and Tom's response was to come to the next game stoned. Yet this act of defiance is mixed with respect for the coach's dedication to winning and his willingness to use verbal or even physical coercion to make players bend to his will:

> Tom said that the coach said this at halftime when they were playing the number two ranked team in the state and were losing thirteen to fifteen. "These guys were really good, and the coach was telling us all this stuff. But, it's funny, you can't laugh or the coach would really kill us." Bob said that maybe the coach was trying to psyche the players out, that he knew you were doing your best but he was trying to put you down so you'd do better. Then Tom defended the coach a little and his voice trailed off and he began a new thought. He said the guys feel like laughing at him when he makes statements like that but "we did make a lot of mistakes in that game. He's always like that, once in awhile he hits guys." There was one player that the coach had gotten permission from his father to slap

whenever he wasn't playing well. The coach thought this made him play better, but Tom was ambivalent because he didn't think slapping a kid made him play better.

This little episode reveals a facet of the culture of Parsons Park we mentioned earlier. Men believe that life is tough and that young people have to learn how to compete against each other without worrying too much about the moral niceties of their public behavior. In one's home and community the traditional moral restraints apply without diminution. But the rough and tumble rules of the city dictate that the spoils go to the strong. While Tom is too young to have consciously adopted this philosophy, it is implicit in his reaction to the coach's behavior vis-à-vis the team. Tom recognized that this sort of treatment humiliated the players. It was not only being shoved around whenever the coach was frustrated that angered Tom, but it was being talked to as if he were someone who did not know the difference between a good and mediocre opponent. Tom is caught midstream between rebellion and respect—between subverting the coach's authority by using drugs and admiring his desire to win at all costs. This, incidentally, is a pose that youth in Parsons Park often find themselves in: flouting the authority of people they basically admire.

The social identities of working-class males in Parsons Park combine styles that are rigidly segregated in Cambridge. In Parsons Park, a young man does not feel forced to choose between presenting himself as a self-reliant, independent person who is willing to stand up to anyone who demeans him and a serious student and athlete who gets along reasonably well with adult authority and never steps too far out in line. The reason for this is that in Parsons Park teachers, coaches, and police conduct themselves in a way these male youth respect even though there is a good deal of friction between them. This emphasis on self-assertion, on not backing down in a dispute, are qualities encouraged by male authority figures. They are not shocked when these youth challenge their authority because they see this behavior as a confirmation of their own way of dealing with others. Conflict with authority does not destroy the underlying solidarity between the generations. As these young men look around them, they see older male authority figures who not only have made a name for themselves in the wider society but who are known to help their younger relatives and friends find similar places in the occupational system.

Although the St. Irene boys were quite diverse, they nonetheless managed to combine the classic working-class emphasis on personal toughness with the sort of discipline and surface respectability that give them an aura of considerable poise and maturity. Though these boys were polite and friendly, they boasted about their physical prowess and willingness to take chances:

At the party Tim told about an incident with a cop last night. Tim, Al, and Bob were drinking near a local hangout, and a single cop in a car came by. He was across the street with another group of guys, and these guys taunted him with shouts of "pig, pig." When the cop started chasing Tim, Al and Bob yelled, "Fuck you, pig, we're over here," and ran the opposite way. They did this sort of thing several times without being caught. Tim says he cannot remember anything after midnight when he passed out on the floor of a friend's house whose parents know his parents. He is afraid they will tell them what happened.

There is a fundamental difference between the emotional significance of the way these youth deal with authority and their counterparts in Cambridge. Despite the provocative language and behavior vis-à-vis the police, there is an almost brotherly quality to these encounters. This is not to say that these games of daring do not occasionally get out of hand and the participants on both sides may lose their tempers. Yet there is nothing remotely equivalent in Parsons Park to the unpredictable episodes of nearly uncontrollable violence that occurs between loosely knit groups of peers. Except for racial incidents at football games and in similar situations, it would be considered somewhat deviant for a group of young men to drive around the community looking for trouble or going to a party hoping to provoke a fight. It is not that the young working-class males in Parsons Park are all bluff and no fight. Although they occasionally get into some potentially dangerous physical altercations, they do not approach others with an almost explosive sense of personal honor. It is for this reason that the police tolerate what would be by any other standards construed as hostile and intolerable behavior by young people. They know that, while these young men give them some trouble and may even physically resist arrest on the usual disorderly conduct charge, they do not, unlike youth in the 32d Street community, rove around the neighborhood carrying deadly weapons and engage in a regular cycle of periodic homicide. By urban standards, these boys are relatively "good kids."

Yet they take offense when they feel that their personal honor has been impugned. At the party, a boy grabbed a girl's wrist, and Tim squared off and was ready to fight until some of the other guys grabbed him. It is noteworthy that in all incidents like this (except for those that were racially motivated) peers intervened and tried to prevent the situation from deteriorating. By way of contrast, it is not unusual in Cambridge for peers to exacerbate a tense situation. In Parsons Park, escalation of the risk of real violence is almost always a last line of defense and not of self-aggrandizement.

There is solidity to the essentially "straight" attitudes of many of the St. Irene boys. Yet some boys in this community gravitate toward a definite "hippy" style. Interestingly enough, these differences do not make communication between various cliques of Catholic high school boys difficult. Some of these boys experiment rather freely with soft drugs and are entraced by "counterculture" symbols of freedom from conventional mores. The fieldworker described a dinner to which he was invited:

> The occasion was obviously important to Mike. He had put up posters and mobiles all over the living and dining room. They were peace posters and mod posters, and there were candles all over, and incense was burning constantly. The dining room had a clean, fancy tablecoth and was set with his grandmother's fanciest crystal and china. Everything was ready-made but set up artistically, and he made hors d'oeuvres.
>
> Mike and Jason got into mescalin and acid lately. Mike said that while he was tripping the people in a Santana poster he has seemed to come out of the poster and play a concert for him. Mike told about a girl he knew who took three tabs of acid and wanted to jump out of the window, but the window kept moving away from her so she couldn't. He also told of tripping with Dan and another guy at the third guy's house. This guy's mother wanted them to go to sleep and made them undress. Of course, they couldn't so they were running around in their underwear. The boy's mother got so frustrated that she began beating her son which made Mike and Dan laugh uproariously.

There is a marvelous incongruity in this scene: psychedelic posters and fine linen are not ordinarily envisaged as going together. For these youth, the experimental, drug-oriented aspects of youth culture do not carry the same meanings that they do in more "conventional" freak social circles. For these boys, there is undoubtedly an element of rebellion against parental injunctions, the pleasure in partaking of forbidden fruits. Yet the primary significance of this exploration of "far-out" styles is disclosed by the conjunction of an appreciation for the accoutrements of social taste and the mind-expanding properties of drugs. Both are symbolic of avenues into the sophisticated, cosmopolitan world that lies beyond the cultural borders of Parsons Park. It would be premature to say whether this sort of activity will make a substantial difference in how these youth define their mature social identities. However, this sign that ideas and values that do not fit into the traditional social patterns of Parsons Park intrigue some youth suggests that they may find it difficult to remain firmly rooted in this community after they leave school.

Moe was one of Tom's group of friends. During the Christmas vacation of his first year away from home, he came back to Parsons Park and had a long talk with the fieldworker about his relationship with Mary:

> Until near the end of my senior year, I mostly just went along with the whole program. But, as I was getting out of high school, my thinking started to change. And I met Mary and that kind of influenced me too. Well, now that we've broken up [laughs] I thought a lot more. It just wasn't in terms of me and her, *now it's everything.* Not that I didn't when we were kind of serious, but it's more so now. Like everyday during the summer I saw her. And now that I look back on it, it wasn't that good. I saw her yesterday, and we can't even talk anymore because she's a little straighter than I am. We started talking about women's lib and my ideas about women, and government and a lot of other things. And she thinks a lot in terms of herself. Everything's a big game to her. It's just what she can get to make her happy. She knows I argue with my parents a lot, and she doesn't like that. She went to the big university and got into all the frats and sororities. When I came back, the break was even bigger, so it was really hard.

For Moe, Mary represents the taken-for-granted, unreflective attitude toward the past. It is not that Moe rejects the entire tradition of Parsons Park. Rather, as he is trying to orient himself in the world, he realizes that he has to think through his values and personal commitments in a new way. His growing self-consciousness of himself as an autonomous being involves the knowledge that he must make reasoned decisions about the direction he gives to his life. And he is discovering that he cannot do that unless he examines the reasons others give for the way they choose to lead their lives. In this respect, Moe's interest in women's issues is merely one sign of a much more universal concern with the implications of cultural pluralism. It is difficult indeed to find a firm place on which to stand that does not look flimsy from another seemingly legitimate point of view.

Moe, like many youth from communities like Parsons Park, is beginning to think about where he is going in terms of where he has come from. Since he cannot accept the past uncritically, he senses that his relationship to Parsons Park will not be one of either simple acceptance or blind rejection. Mary, on the other hand, seems oblivious of real discontinuities in Moe's eyes. She fuses two distinct orders of experiences into an experiential whole despite the fact that there are real differences between local traditions and college life. Moe recognizes that Mary is able to connect what appears to him as incongrous because she is devoted to conventional responses to the world. For her, the round of parties bridges the insular life of the parochial school and the security of fraternity and sorority world at a large university. Life for Mary is simply being played out on a bigger stage with a more glamorous cast of characters.

Moe's sensitivity to the subtle discontinuities between parish-oriented social life and the more impersonal and less fraternal patterns of mainstream America is not obscured by the pieties of authority. Though it is hard for Moe to put this into words, there is a sense of loss as well as gain that comes from moving out into this more competitive and uncaring part of American society. Mary's single-minded celebration of the present seems, to Moe, to miss the most poignant and, in some respects, precious moment of their lives.

Moe is beginning to see clearly things that he has seen all his life but missed because he had no alternative standpoint from which to view them. While this process is sometimes painful and confusing, it is infinitely more frustrating not to be able to share it with someone to whom he felt close at one time. It increases his sense of cultural dislocation and personal isolation. And Mary's refusal to recognize what Moe is talking about strikes him as particularly perverse because what is going on inside of him is happening to both of them. Moe is searching for a vocabulary in order to describe a wrenching change in a familiar landscape where one's reliable points of references such as family and friends no longer seem as stable as they did when he was younger. Moe, like many young people in his situation, feels that he is being forced to invent words for experiences that he has never heard anyone in Parsons Park allude to, let alone discuss openly.

Less introspective and cosmopolitan youth than Moe are not likely to accept everything authority proclaims. These young people

will not be an exact cultural reduplication of the older generation.
The fieldworker met Andy at a backyard party:

> Andy seemed kind of out of place. He's extremely straight look-
> ing: fairly short blond hair, a little older than the others. He had
> just finished his freshman year at college but said he was basi-
> cally going to college to waste a little time until he can take the
> test and become a fireman. He told the story of last Monday
> when the police superintendent spoke at Fisher. It was a police-
> community workshop. He made a lot of fun of the superinten-
> dent and the whole meeting talked about how the
> superintendent kept saying things like this district has the
> lowest crime rate in the city and we've got no dope problem
> here. Andy laughed and looked around him at the various joints
> being passed around, and the whole bunch of people who were
> obviously tripping. He didn't smoke any of the dope and was
> probably the only one at the party who didn't get drunk. He
> said that eventually the kids at the meeting got up and walked
> out, he among them.

Andy represents the cultural center of Parsons Park, even
though his behavior at the party was more constrained than his
peers. He is sensitive to official hypocrisy over social and moral
issues as his ironic comments on the "dope" problem in Parsons
Park indicates. He is less receptive than the older generation to
traditional pieties about the way one ought to live one's life, but his
own choices reflect traditional values. Deciding to become a fireman
moves him toward the cultural center of Parsons Park, and, in the
context of being in college, this choice has little of a forced quality.
It is something he wants to do because being a fireman or policeman
represents the core values that traditional male youth in Parsons
Park admire. And, in this respect, Andy is not much different than
the mobile St. Irene boys like Tom. They are striving for upward
mobility, but the route they are taking is understood, appreciated,
and sanctioned by the community. These youth are aware of their
somewhat elite status as students in an academic parochial school.
By hoping to become professionals they know that the political and
economic ties that gives this community its strength will stand them
in good stead in the future. Unlike Cambridge, moving upward does
not entail a leap of imagination into an unknown future where all one
knows is that one will be a vastly different kind of person than one's
parents.
While many of the straighter young people were tolerant of their

friends who experiment with soft drugs, they were not always as receptive to forms of behavior that violate the moral precepts of traditional Catholic family life. At a party where a number of young people were high on acid and mescaline, the fieldworker observed a young guy around sixteen involved in heavy necking with an older woman who was around thirty:

> These two were rolling around on the floor, and a group of us were noticing that this woman's husband was there. Lee was obviously freaked out by the whole thing and kept saying, "Look at what they are doing," and he started asking the husband, "Don't you mind. Aren't you jealous?"
>
> The husband was quite nonchalant about the whole thing. I asked Lee why he was upset if the husband didn't mind, and he said he believed that once you were married you ought to stay faithful. Mona was also freaked out and turned her back purposely to she wouldn't have to watch it.

On the other hand, the apparently incompatible values one might associate with traditional ethnic affiliations and sophisticated use of drugs and sex coexists in the lives of some of these girls:

> Joan and Ruta are graduates of the Lithuanian high school and both told of going to Lithuanian camp when they were young and about being in the Lithuanian girl scouts. When someone called, Joan started talking in Lithuanian even though she and Ruta say that they are not as nationalistic as the other girls, although they sat at the Lithuanian table in the lunchroom at school. They told a story about a party they had at Joan's house when her mother was away visiting relatives. Ruta said that she and Joan had both screwed the same guy in the same bed though I assume at different times. Ruta is sweet on Ernie and wanted Joan to go over with her to Parsons Park to get him because she did not want to appear too forward. How either Joan or Ruta can appear anything but forward is hard to figure because that's just the way they are.

Before one assumes that the behavior of these girls is aberrant for young people coming from such a conservative background, we must remember that culture is built on compromise and adaptation. Logical consistency is not as meaningful an element of the way people put their lives together as is the emotional compatibility of their everyday concerns and involvements. Girls like Joan and Ruta are different from many other girls in a subtle but important respect. Their identity is so firmly anchored in communal traditions that they are shielded from the impulse to continuously try to improve their position in the world.

In more concrete terms, they are happy with who they are. This does not mean, however, that they will be content to do things exactly as their parents have done. Rather, their secure identity provides a stability to the larger course of their lives. This gives them the emotional freedom to experiment and innovate in what seems like quite improbable ways. To put this another way, Joan and Ruta can go about shaping their personal worlds according to their own lights because they are protected, so to speak, by the obvious cultural differences between themselves and mainstream America.

Mainstream Americans appear to be able to recognize what they share with others only if these symbols of commonality are embodied in universal forms of sociability which are accessible to anyone who meets minimum criteria of social acceptability in the wider society. In these terms, community is a negotiable commodity that is singularly devoid of shared memories of particular times and places. Joan and Ruta experience relatively little internal pressure to conform to mainstream images of propriety because the cultural bond that unites them is, in some respects, itself a sign of unassimilatable difference. That is, the sort of cultural identity that gives these girls the inner strength to be as alike or as different from the surrounding culture as they choose has this power because it cannot be translated into symbolic currency that would have similar meanings elsewhere.

The youth of Parsons Park often talked about racial prejudice. Some of them admitted that prejudice was bad and criticized their parents' "racism." Some denied that they themselves were prejudiced, but many also claimed that the power of their upbringing was too strong to resist: "Well, I am racist, because that's the way my parents raised me." It was mostly boys who said this. And this issue was a common cause for argument between girls and boys. Yet not all of the girls disagree with the racist tendencies of the local subculture. Jane was a classmate of Sally's, and she apparently identified fully with her father's feelings:

> Sally told me that Jane's father is always talking about "niggers" and how he will burn out or kill anyone who tried to move in. Sally said awhile back she was walking home from school with Jane and they passed a small black kid. Jane threw a snowball at the boy, and when he ducked she taunted him: "What's the matter, nigger? Afraid of a white snowball?" Sally said something to her, and she answered, "He's just a nigger."

Sally said the whole thing was "sickening" and that she won't walk home with her anymore if she can avoid it.

Change

For some the decision comes early, for some it comes later on, but there is a group of teenagers who decide to move out, not simply geographically but culturally. The girls take the lead in this. Jill and Nellie were, in the fieldworker's words, "the first really radical kids I have met from Parsons Park." Jill was nineteen, lived in Lakeside, was gay, "heavily into karate, which she teaches," got kicked out of Donahue. She worked at the Gemini coffeehouse. Jill did come to her parents' house to do her laundry from time to time but pointedly observed that it was their home not hers.

Sometimes the cultural out-migration is comfortably supported in the home, as with Sally. Sally's mother was recently divorced and was beginning to go to meetings of the city's women's liberation organization. She supported her daughter against the older son, and approved of her daughter's self-reliance and readiness to question traditional ideas about appropriate behavior for young women.

The prospect of leaving home, neighborhood, and host culture is for many youths attractive yet threatening. One reason is economics. Many of them said, after a long complaining harangue about their family, that they knew they couldn't make it on their own. For many the fear is centered on just being alone and unsupported in a social and cultural sense. Lyn was one girl for whom this issue was a continual dilemma. She wanted to go to college in the East, but her parents wouldn't give her any money, although they did support her brothers who went away to school. She went to the local community junior college, lived at home, and talked about moving into an apartment with two friends. But that didn't work out. What she really wants to do is to work with handicapped children, but she takes accounting and business courses to be sure she gets a job. After one evening's conversation with Lyn and her two close friends, the fieldworker observed the following:

> All of these women would be considered fairly liberal by neighborhood standards, but none of them certainly could be called radical. And there was this whole aura of not knowing what to do. All of these kids had strongly considered moving out of the neighborhood. None of them really wanted to; they still had a lot of friends here, and yet they found the neighborhood inhibiting and stifling.

There is a tender point in the culture of Parsons Park. The authority of the school and church is experienced as unreasonable by the more articulate, ambitious, and resourceful girls. Youth recognize and value the rational basis of the school's authority: it prepares them well for college and the occupational world. And, almost without exception, they accept the rational basis of some aspects of family authority. Very few of these youth denigrated working hard in school, and just about all of them took it for granted that they would have to work at jobs after school and during the summer. But what they cannot accept is the idea that authority does not respect their maturity and acknowledge their own powers of judgment and discretion. It is on this point of the unreasonableness of authority that the culture of Parsons Park is locked into a serious dispute with some of its most energetic and talented youth.

Conclusion

The dilemma of staying or leaving the community is not unique to Parsons Park. What is characteristic of this community is the degree to which most youth experience a strong desire to escape the narrowness of local culture and an almost equally strong desire to remain within the protective confines of the very institutions that create this feeling. They are torn between contradictory values, and there is no easy way to resolve the tension between them. For many their educational and occupational choices will decide the issue for them. Some will move into the professional middle-class and may eventually move into communities that are congruent with their occupational identities. Others will opt for jobs that make living in Parsons Park a realistic option.

However, what is not so easily resolved by the economic and social movement into adulthood is the underlying significance of the absence of a public forum for discussion of the problems of personal freedom and self-determination. The culture of Parsons Park, especially its emphasis on the preeminence of traditional moral precepts, inhibits intergenerational dialogues about these matters. At an even more elementary level, there is no shared language, no body of images and ideas, that would enable young people to express their personal doubts and fears about the future to the older generation. The latter assumes that a road map to a secure place in the adult world has been carefully laid out. Youth discover that the road markings are, in many cases, hopelessly out-of-date.

It would be a mistake to stress the fragility of the culture of Parsons Park. Demographic and political changes in the city could alter the racial composition of the area. The possibility that existing institutions would preserve many local traditions but assimilate newcomers with different cultural backgrounds is slim indeed. One of the continuing strengths of the community as far as youth are concerned is that growing up in Parsons Park gives them a clear sense of where they come from culturally and socially. Equally important, Parsons Park is a place to which a young person can return without feeling that moving back means that one is a failure.

Despite a rigid public morality, Parsons Park gives youthful exuberance reasonable leeway inasmuch as a young person would have to commit a serious crime before he or she would be shunned in the neighborhood. The open patterns of peer sociability gives the community a warmth that is easily missed by a superficial glance at its culture. While the morality of the parish church and school is confining and inflexible, there nevertheless is a strong measure of comfort in the thought that one never forfeits one's place among those people with whom one grows up. The unreasonableness of official authority, then, is tempered by this spirit of mutual acceptance of a common destiny as working-class, ethnic Catholics.

In contrast to Cambridge, ambitions to rise in the world are much more definitely focused on realistic goals of becoming integrated into the political and economic structure of the city. Put somewhat differently, youth are not confronted with images of success that do not show them very concretely how working-class people can get ahead without sacrificing their loyalty to their family or peers. In Parsons Park, the rationality of authority goes unquestioned because it is understood that the routes to success are paths along which many people like oneself have traveled.

Part III

An Affluent Suburb and an Inner-City Community

GLENBAR IS AN affluent suburb removed from the disorder of inner-city life. Although 32d Street is not the poorest or the most disorganized inner-city community, conflict is very much part of everyday life. Armed youth shoot and occasionally kill one another. Despite the magnitude of the differences in the wealth and power of these two communities, they are an instructive contrast for a number of reasons. The comparison between youth who take privilege for granted and youth who must struggle to get a decent education or job reveals a good deal about how class and ethnicity shape the lives of young people in urban America. Yet this comparison also discloses continuities between youth cultures that might otherwise go unnoticed. In both communities, young people accept conventional images of success. In other words, these youth believe that an affluent way of living is highly desirable and that education is the primary route to getting the kinds of jobs that support such a mode of living. Both groups of youth accord the means to this end—education—only instrumental significance. That is, education is useful to the extent that it helps one get ahead in the world. Where they differ is the way in which they work out the expressive component of their peer cultures.

Glenbar is virtually surrounded by a green belt of exclusive golf courses that meander around spacious and expensive homes. It is a commuter suburb where the professional business concerns of its residents is segregated from their domestic lives. These successful and ambitious people move to Glenbar in order to provide their families with a peaceful, secure, and comfortable environment. They choose to live in a community like Glenbar because they want their children to have an education that will give them a decisive advantage in the competition for places in good colleges and universities. Some families moved to Glenbar to escape racially mixed neighborhoods. Glenbar is as close as one might imagine to a community that is free from the ethnic and racial diversity that most of these adults associate with the less desirable aspects of city life.

32d Street maintains its distinctive Mexican identity without resistance to the values of the larger society. Most youth on 32d Street speak English with the same facility as young people elsewhere but are completely at home with Mexican customs and values. This bicultural orientation seems to entail little in the way of normative strain. Although these youth believe that education can pay dividends on the job market, their involvement in school is for the most part limited. They go when it seems possible for them to get by without sacrificing too much in the way of safety or boredom. Yet, despite the nearly universal desire to make out in the terms set by conventional society, very few of these youth devote much of their energies to studying. Instead, they are oriented to the street world and to the standards of personal honor that form the core of the local identity of youth on 32d Street.

As we have seen, young men in working-class communities are sensitive to insults that affront their manhood and personal dignity. On 32d Street, this concern is raised to an exponential power. Here honor is a group as well as individual attribute. Those who promote or defend their honor respond to insult with violence. Domination, precedence, and personal aggrandizement through armed conflict is a central preoccupation of gangs, in particular, and street life in general. By contrast, the youth of Glenbar seem to live in another universe. They are very much concerned with academics and grades, and the worst sort of deviance is the use of soft drugs and alcohol. Yet both groups are very much involved in the expressive rather than the instrumental side of youth culture.

Both groups accept the rationality of conventional adult values, but in Glenbar youth conform because the payoff is so tangible that it would be foolish to do otherwise. In 32d Street youth do not conform to conventional norms with much consistency because the payoff is so remote and problematic. Yet both groups question the reasonableness of certain adult values. In 32d Street, the compelling qualities of an identity based upon honor far outshadows the pallid rewards of not breaking the law. In Glenbar, investing all those qualities of self that one values most about oneself in intimacy, friendship, and activities that remove one from civic or public institutions (such as the school) compensates for adult emphasis on future success. For these youth, the emphasis on striving and competition are devoid of personal value, and one tolerates but does not endorse any activity (such as learning) that is infused with such instrumental meanings.

6

32d Street

Community Setting[1]

32d Street is located a few minutes from the center of the city and is surrounded by railroad tracks and heavy industry. The people who live here are largely of Mexican heritage. This area is bordered on the north by an extremely deteriorated black area. Empty lots are filled with refuse. Burnt-out buildings and rundown apartment buildings give the impression that only the survivors of a long siege remain, too demoralized by the depravations of a ruthless army of invaders to leave the community. 32d Street is separated from this area by huge railroad yards and, in comparison, shows relatively little of the massive urban blight that is associated with the image of an inner-city slum.

Yet someone passing through 32d Street would probably see it as an ethnic ghetto. The weathered frame homes and dark apartment buildings, the old and, in some cases, physically decaying elementary schools, gang slogans on walls, and dirty streets make it appear that this is a place where people live because they cannot afford to move to a more desirable neighborhood.

Much of American middle-class life is predicated upon assumptions about the relationship between physical settings and the moral properties of the self. It is thought one can infer a good deal about the kind of persons that inhabit a place from the physical appearance of the place itself. Looking at the less than sparkling exteriors of the buildings on 32d Street, one might assume that the interiors of these buildings were dingy and drab at best, and unsanitary and unlivable at worst. While not elegant, most of these homes are well-cared for and comfortable, although sometimes cramped because of the size of families by contemporary standards.

1. See Horowitz (1983) for a complete analysis of this material.

While 32d Street is a major port of entry for migrants from Mexico, and its apartments rent for considerably less than in comparable sections of the city, the great majority of residents feel that this is a place where they choose to live rather than are forced to live. The Latin flavor of the neighborhood has been increasing as the last remnants of the Eastern European population move out. Local institutions recognize that their constituents represent a Spanish-speaking population, and churches have been responsive to this change in the ethnicity of their constituency. Equally important, the gangs or clubs, as they are called locally, are completely comprised of youth who identify themselves as persons of Mexican origin. While there are some Eastern European families in the area, their children are socially invisible because they lack the mass to contest the "right" of Mexican youth to make their presence conspicuous in public places. Although at the time of this study political power was almost entirely in the hands of non-Latin groups, Mexican dominance of the community was so complete that it never occured to anyone that youth from other ethnic groups would challenge their appropriation of public space.

Shops, restaurants, dress, and music combine Mexican and Anglo styles and language. Garbage cans are overflowing in the alleys, but the sidewalks are clear. Some homes are freshly painted, and the front steps are places where people of all ages gather to visit and watch the arrivals and departures of their neighbors. In the summer children play outdoors until late at night, while groups of youth gather in parks and on street corners, "rapping," waiting for something to happen.

32d Street is a community in many senses of the word. Its residents participate in social networks that make it possible for someone to know a good deal about another person even if they do not know one another personally. The rich and active street life, which goes on in front of homes, in parks, bars, and street corners, brings people into constant face-to-face contact. Gossip is as much a part of the life of this community as it is in the peasant villages from which some of the residents have recently migrated. The anonymous urban dweller who does not know and is not known by his neighbors is foreign to the spirit of 32d street.

32d Street is a poor but by no means a poverty-stricken community. In 1970, the median family income in 32d Street was $8,560. Though low when compared to other communities in the city, 32d Street is not the lowest (18 percent rank lower); 17.7 percent of the people are below the poverty level, and over 12 percent have incomes over $15,000. The unemployment rate for adults according to the 1970 census is 4.5 percent; most people have unskilled or semi-skilled jobs. The unemployment rate in the city of a Latin male (ages 16–21) without a high school diploma is 27.9 percent while for non-Latin males it is 46.8 percent. According to estimates by the public high school, the dropout rate is close to 70 percent for Chicano students in the area. The level of education is the lowest in the city; 21 percent of those over twenty-five have graduated from high school.

The vast majority of men do not enjoy the benefits of well-paid industrial work and union representation. Because of the older generation's difficulties with English, minimal formal education, and lack of connections in the highly paid craft unions, most men must find work in the less attractive manual occupations. Although they are subject to fluctuations in the labor market and forced to seek marginal jobs, there is almost no cultural support in the community for avoiding work whenever it is available. On the other hand, work is regarded as one of life's necessities, which no reasonable person questions but which no person invests more of himself than is essential to bring home a paycheck. Although many wives and unmarried daughters find low-paying jobs in small factories, two incomes do not appreciably change the economic situation of most families. It is quite usual to have many children, and it is considered in very bad taste to withhold money when relatives request it.

In the 1970s, the community was split into two wards, which meant that the Mexican community was deprived of direct political representation in local affairs. Mexican-Americans were a minority in each ward at the time, and many residents could not vote because they were not citizens. There is little doubt that the community had been gerrymandered by the groups that controlled city hall. Representation on the city council means jobs and access to funds that are channeled through city agencies. It also means essential neighborhood services and attention to local facilities and streets. Yet 32d Street is not a politically passive or unsophisticated community. Many community leaders were aware of the fact that many ethnic groups have used the political system as a stepping-stone to improving their position in the socioeconomic system.

Community leaders lobbied successfully for programs from state and federal agencies concerned with social services and immigration issues. They successfully used popular support to pressure local bureaucracies for change. One group of parents removed an elementary school principal they felt was insensitive to the needs of their children by petitioning, picketing, and finally "sitting in" the school for several days. The struggle with the citywide school board over the construction of a new high school in the community involved many residents. A year of negotiations, writing proposals, and demonstrating peacefully had little impact on the school board. Then community members took over the ninth-grade extension of the high school which was located in a building that had been condemned for more than ten years. Violence erupted when no one from the district office or the Board of Education listened to their proposals. After people were hurt, the Board of Education decided to build a new high school in the community.

Close ties with shopkeepers, visiting with friends and relatives who live in the area, and church-centered activities create a powerful sense of community vitality. Many of the traditions of Mexico, including the language, food, and the *compadrazco* system are part of everyday life. While adults are frightened by the fighting between clubs and are discouraged by the school system, they do not dream of moving away. A mother of nine refused the offer of her husband and oldest son to buy her a house in the suburbs. Both she and her husband were born in the United States. Yet she feels that it is important to bring up their children in a Mexican community. Often those who have moved out to the suburbs return regularly for shopping and socializing. One youth who regularly returned from the suburbs for weekends felt that "everything was happening" in 32d Street. One young married woman discussed "moving back" from a residence ten blocks away from her parents:

> I've always lived close to my family. My married sister lives around the corner, my parents live on the next block. I have six aunts and uncles within five blocks, and my husband's family mostly lives around here. It was nice over there. I got to know a different place, but it's better over here.

There has been some discussion about whether the normative order of an inner-city ethnic community such as 32d Street is an adaptation to socioeconomic marginality in the larger society (see Gans 1969). This question is difficult to answer unless two issues that are often confounded are disentangled. Subordinate groups must adapt many of their traditional social patterns to the demands that the institutions of the larger society make upon their lives. Thus, the culture of 32d Street will reflect the economic pressures and institutional constraints that arise out of its residents' position in the class structure of the wider society. However, it is not legitimate to infer from this fact that the residents of 32d Street organize their lives in terms of a secondhand version of the larger culture which is spiced with enough retentions from their ethnic past to give a loose sense of coherence to an otherwise fragmented existence. People in 32d Street experience their cultural activities and communal relations as integral wholes even though they are a mixture of indigenous beliefs, situational responses to local circumstances, and ethnic traditions that reflect the new opportunities in an urban environment.

One way to judge whether the culture of 32d Street is a direct reflection of the socioeconomic situation of its residents is to examine the role that instrumental concerns play in their lives. To do this, we must remember that American culture endorses instrumental values. Consequently, it is easy to assume that groups that seem intent on improving their material welfare also give instrumental modes of thought and action priority in their lives. Thus, we must ask whether the members of a group are ready to question the validity of traditional values and forsake the comfort of communal relationships in order to maximize their chances of raising their socioeconomic position.

There are many ways in which this shift in consciousness is marked. We can see a new orientation toward mobility in the manner in which a person uses his time, acknowledges the claims of relatives on his resources as legitimate, the way he presents himself in face-to-face contacts, the place that informal sociability occupies in his life, and so on. All of these observable changes in behavior derive from a basic shift in the way a person thinks about his relations with others: he calculates the relative costs and benefits of particular kinds of social involvements with others.

Of course, the residents of 32d Street are capable of looking at their relations with each other in these terms. Not being able to do so would jeopardize their survival. Yet, when it comes to the specific meaning of the norms and values that regulate communal relations, instrumental considerations are usually secondary issues. In an honor-based culture such as 32d Street, the expressive integrity of the self (as it is symbolized by the purity of the virgin daughter and the dutiful wife and mother and the dominant and protective father) is of the utmost importance.

In 32d Street, the kind of person a man sees himself as being depends upon his resolve to demand deference from those persons he recognizes as his social equals. This sense of honor, which is grounded in signs of respect in face-to-face relations, is an unsurpassable value because it cannot be bracketed by pragmatic concerns. There is an all-or-nothing quality to honor-based cultures. A man feels that he must insist upon being treated properly or else he loses face in the community and is shamed in his own eyes. The inability to stand one's own ground in the face of an insult is tanta-mount to a loss of one's manhood. The perception that a man is weak or passive undermines his capacity to protect the reputation of his family and exposes the purity of his female relatives to the sexual predations of men who will boast about these conquests. Without going into further detail at this point, it is obvious that the dif-ference between the culture of 32d Street and mainstream Ameri-can society cannot be understood solely as a collective response to blocked or incomplete upward mobility on the part of Mexican Americans.

The norms that govern the allocation of social prestige in 32d Street are not congruent with mainstream conceptions of respect-able public behavior. It would be misleading to characterize the lo-cal status system as "deviant" inasmuch as these people are aware of the implications of legal sanctions against the use of force in per-sonal disputes. The norms of the larger society, however, are set aside when issues revolving around dominance and subordination arises among young men. The norms of the larger society are ig-nored rather than rejected. The reality of one's honor and reputa-tion supercedes the authority of the state and, in some circumstances, concern for one's physical safety. Armed clashes be-tween clubs and occasional homicides are not the result of an aimless predatory instinct or an irrational streak of destructive aggression. What is the most "deviant" form of youthful activity from the per-spective of the larger society is experienced as something that is congruent with a taken-for-granted conception of manhood on 32d Street.

The Family

The social worth of a family in 32d Street is based on financial independence, helping other members of the expanded family unit, and maintaining the honor of the family. Honor, in turn, is main-tained through protection of the virginity of daughters, having chil-dren, and protection of one's "face."

The major principles underlying family relationships—male dom-ination, respect for elders, and reciprocity between family mem-bers—are learned within the context of the expanded family. *Compadres* and relatives make up the expanded family network. They are generally the only people invited over for meals, whose homes are always open without an invitation, and who provide fi-nancial support when necessary. Women move freely back and forth between homes—cooking together, talking, taking care of each other's children, shopping, and going out together.

Although the church, community organizations, corner groups, and similar institutions knit the community together, the family is the preeminent institution in 32d Street. The family includes many more persons than the mainstream, urban nuclear family with its weak ties to collateral relatives. However, the bonds of solidarity between relatives and *compadres* are not as intense or durable as those between children and parents, especially mothers and children, and between siblings. It is within the household that the fundamental values of 32d Street are exemplified. Ideally, the father is the source of authority to whom deference and respect is owed as a matter of course. Loyalty to one's family is taken very seriously. This means that one avoids doing things that would bring shame on one's family and that one does not allow a slur on one's family's name to pass uncontested.

Judgments about families are not based on "social problems": alcoholism, interpersonal violence, lack of money, or having only one parent. Nor is it possible to distinguish families in terms of what their children do in school or on the streets. For example, Amelia's family remains close-knit though the family is beset with "social problems"—the mother drinks heavily, and there is little communication between the parents. Her mother was elected president of an elementary school PTA and went to Washington for a conference. It was the first time she had ever been away from home overnight except to give birth to her children. That night they all sat around and talked about missing her. Amelia considers her family to be a "together" family. They constantly help each other, including brothers fighting anyone who expresses doubt about the virtue of their sisters.

Daniel's family was considered a "not together family." His parents did not get support from the expanded network (Daniel often had nowhere to go for dinner while others had choices), and the members of the family failed to maintain their honor. The key factor seems to have been the behavior of Daniel's father. Daniel's mother commented:

> My children have no respect for him and don't do what he says. All they see is a lazy bum who works for a while and quits to lay his women. I guess we got married too young and he needs a chance to run around. I keep telling the kids not to get married too young but to make something better for themselves and get an education. Some are turning out OK, but I don't know . . .

Daniel was a member of the Lions club. The Lions thought Daniel's father was "cool" for being sexually active, but they condemned the blatant aspect of his sexual liasons as disrespect for Daniel's mother. His sisters were not regarded with respect. At eighteen, Daniel shot and killed his father after finding him with a young woman.

What makes the crucial difference between Amelia's family and Daniel's family is a value that is not apparent from the perspective of mainstream culture. Both of these families would be seen as deviant in terms of the norms of conventional society. But, in Amelia's family, the feeling of unity and mutual support, despite occasional conflict, gives its members a sense of self-respect and dignity when dealing with other members of the community. In Daniel's case, his family was dishonored. Not only did his father publicly cast contempt on his mother, but his sisters had also lost their standing in the eyes of the community. While Amelia's family might seem disorganized and chaotic, its members had not lost the most precious and, in some respects, the only value that matters: their honor was intact.

The expanded family network, while a major source of support, creates other tensions. Some young people want more privacy than the network affords. Tina observed:

> I hate living around the corner from my mother-in-law. She always wants to know what's happening over here. It's my family, and I'll run it as I choose. I like some of my relatives but having them all over here asking for things constantly is too much.

Youth often complain of surveillance by relatives. *Compadres* have been known to report a girl's activities to her parents, sometimes embellishing the details. In one such case Tanya, age fifteen, was allegedly seen with her boyfriend while walking down the street. That evening her mother was told that her daughter had been seen doing "many bad things" with her boyfriend. Tanya was restricted for over a month and vowed not to speak with her uncle again.

Public events that demonstrate a family's worth—cotillions, baptisms, weddings—are expensive, require much time, cooperation, and effort, and do not always come off well. The cotillion is an affair that symbolizes a fifteen-year-old girl's entrance into adulthood and attests to the family's financial capability, solidarity, and the virginity of the daughter. Rules of etiquette are strictly observed at these events. Chairs are held for women, youth address adults deferentially, and doors are opened for women and elders. Club members attend these events regularly and are carefully observant of all the rules. After the church service when the girl prays to the virgin, there is a party for 200–400 guests in a rented hall, often with two bands, a dinner, and an open bar. The girl usually has fourteen couples standing up with her, the girls wearing bridal dresses and she a wedding dress.

Young women begin to learn the duties of wife and mother at a very young age and often take on many of the responsibilities within the home, though not always with enthusiasm. Young males are served by the women whenever they come home. This pattern of sex-role differentiation reinforces an asymetrical relationship between males and females. Women are dependent on men for financial support and their position in society while the men are dependent on women for bearing children and for domestic services. However, a husband's mother can perform the latter function weakening the wife's role and strengthening the role of mother.

Confirmation of a woman's worth as a person is closely tied to motherhood. Few young women were so emancipated from the culture of 32d Street that they could imagine foregoing having children or insisting upon an egalitarian relationship with their husband. In fact, most young women thought the suggestion that a father might care for young children was humorous since that sort of nurturance on the part of a man is culturally inconceivable. While there is considerable consensus on the need for strictness in raising children and physical discipline is thought of as necessary for young children, there is great variability in the way these ideas are put into practice. Some children are indulged by relatives, only to be held to much less permissive standards by their parents. Other parents fight about the children in front of them whereas others act in concert. In some families, the father may be the disciplinarian whereas the mother assumes that role in others.

What is important in the culture of 32d Street is that a family ought to be able to maintain order without exposing its internal conflicts to the world at large. Moreover, parents who are genuinely concerned about the behavior of their children and willing to take a consistent stand on how to raise their family are regarded favorably. Many families could not meet this standard and personal chaos in the family sometimes breeds excessive physical punishment. In the final analysis, what really matters in 32d Street is whether family members are willing to stand by each other. There is considerable contempt for families that throw their children on the street or turn their back on them when they get into trouble.

Teenaged girls are often subject to coercive forms of control. Since the virginity of girls is the principal symbol of family honor, parents believe their activities outside the home ought to be closely supervised. Young women often feel that they are being unfairly restricted. Fathers assert their authority vis-à-vis their daughters in a preemptory manner. On 32d Street, male authority in family relations is unilateral and nonnegotiable. While the kind of paternal authority that speaks for the family as a corporate unit fits smoothly into a traditional society, the father's authoritarian injunctions lose some of their legitimacy in an urban context. There is some variation in family regulations for unmarried daughters with respect to independence outside the home. Moreover, it strikes young women as less than reasonable to obey their fathers' dictums without explanations for excessive restrictions on their freedom to move about the community. There is a good deal of deception and evasion of parental restrictions among young women, but the direct rejection of family authority is rare indeed.

Fathers are particularly sensitive to what they see as their daughters' vulnerability to seduction. Women are thought of as susceptible to the predatory machinations of men because it is, paradoxically, men's responsibility to protect and to undermine their sexual purity. As fathers, men know that all nonrelatives have one purpose in mind. And they know this because manhood on 32d Street is exemplified by one's capacity to make one's sexual conquest a matter of public record. A father typically remarks:

> You know what all men are after. It's natural for them [the men] to go out and get "it" anyway they can. I don't trust any of the young punks around here. They take it and run. There are too many unmarried pregnant girls around here. The young girls don't know how to handle themselves.

Except to eat, sleep, and occasionally to watch television, men are expected to spend their time outside the home. Parents rarely seem to know what their sons are doing. The male's world outside the home is largely closed off to females, though today young women are spending more time in the streets away from home. Jim's parents did not know he was in a club (the Lions), and when the fieldworker went to meet them he told the fieldworker to tell them she had met him at a "settlement house." Even if the parents are aware that their son is in a club, they rarely know his "street name" (the name by which he is known by his age group). Most parents feel they they can do little to control their son's behavior outside the home. One father says:

I know my son [age sixteen] is real smart; his teachers told me
that many times, but he and his friends leave school everyday
before they finish. He says it's boring. He's a good artist—I
told him he could go to art school, but he says the teachers are
all "fags." He has to finish school to get anywhere, but I can't
force him. He's a man.

This father's comment that his son is a man should be interpreted
literally. In 32d Street, adolescents are not treated as if they were
part children, part adult. Adolescent boys, in particular, but girls as
well, are seen as mature persons who can act autonomously. Girls
may need to be protected and guarded by their families until they
get married, but they are not viewed as childish and impulsive people. This status of social maturity is especially important because it
brings youth into conflict with school authorities who treat them as
if they were errant children who can be scolded and embarrassed
without regard for their dignity as adult persons.

Reputation

Male youth clubs feel safe in the community if they are not at
"war" with any of the other clubs in the area. Though each of the
clubs has its own location in a park where many youth "hang out,"
there were no fixed territorial boundaries within 32d Street. If a
"war" is declared between clubs within the 32d Street community,
then boundaries form around "their hood" (neighborhood). These
youth make statements such as, "We can't let those Nobles come
around here. They'll think they own this territory." As soon as the
altercation is settled, the Nobles (a club) again move freely in and
out of the park where the Lions spend much of their time.

For a young man, honor not only sensitizes him to aspersions cast
on his person or family but the public maintenance of honor forms
the basis of who he is in the eyes of others. The public manner of
making, interpreting, and reacting to aspersions on his honor is the
basis of his orientation toward his *reputation*.

The code of honor is handled in three different ways by young
men on 32d Street. These are the styles we call (see Toch 1969) the
"image promoter" who actively seeks to enhance his reputation; the
"image defender" who is very sensitive to aspersions cast on his
honor and yet does not provoke incidents to enhance his reputation,
and the "rep avoider" who stays out of the status system as much as
possible. Such a person might be provoked when someone tampers
with the honor of a female relative.

"Rep" in the streets is demonsrated by a variety of skills: fighting, "rapping," "styling," "cool," knowledge of the streets, and leadership. Fighting ability includes courage in the face of danger as well as ability to demolish an opponent. Rapping refers to a smooth verbal facility in talking to women. Styling refers to dress, and cool refers to the ability to make intelligent decisions under duress. Knowledge of the streets covers such things as where to purchase guns and how to deal with the police and courts. Leadership is shown in one's judgment about the advisibility of seeking retribution in a particular situation, and how one handles differences between the members of one's group.

Reputation is both an individual and collective property. Clubs have their collective reputation to uphold and, if possible, to promote. In the street world, youth must take both group and personal reputations into account when dealing with each other. There is one constant element in the ebb and flow of personal and group status on 32d Street. It is taken for granted that anyone who is oriented to this world will seize the opportunity to increase his reputation at the expense of another person's. In this zero-sum game, trust in interpersonal relationships with peers is rare. Even if one does not look for opportunities to demonstrate one's power over others, it is an article of faith that others will act this way if they are given a chance to get away with it.

Thus, anyone sensitive to imputations that they lack honor must be on guard for actions that place him in a demeaning position. On the one hand, refusal to grant another's claim to precedence is likely to be interpreted as an insult. On the other hand, unchallenged acceptance of his claim to superiority is tantamount to humiliation. If a youth confronts the person who attempts to demean him, there are few viable options other than fighting. Despite the fact that these youth value verbal acuity and can talk their way out of ticklish situations, honor impels one to become totally involved and to take an unequivocal stand. One must choose decisively between divergent courses of action and enforce one's claim to deference as a nonnegotiable right. Violence, then, symbolizes one's total commitment to rejecting imputations against one's honor.

Since the late 1960s the number of guns on 32d Street have been increasing. The ever-present possibility of a challenge to honor makes access to a gun very important. Sam claimed, "I never go anywhere without my "heat" (gun), you aren't anyone without one. It's dangerous." Elaborate preparations are made to carry them secretly, for example, portable radios are often fitted to carry the weapons. Club members lose or misplace guns with some regularity. "The pigs were after me so when I came around the alley I threw it in the garbage. I really looked for it after the pigs cut out, but it wasn't there. Now what am I going to do without a 'piece' (gun) I got dudes after my ass?" Len told his fellow club members.

Interpersonal Etiquette

Not every interaction between peers is seen as a potential challenge to one's honor because all youths in the 32d Street community are well schooled in rules of interpersonal etiquette. For example, not staring at someone or avoiding bumping into someone on the street or even in a crowded hallway in school can avoid a confrontation. There is, however, one rule of standard etiquette that places a man in a demeaning situation, apologizing profusely for an act already accomplished. This is called "gripping." !f an individual puts another person in a demeaning position, he should accept responsibility for it. For example, if a Lion shouts, "the Nobles suck," thinking there are none around but a Noble is within hearing distance, the Noble will interpret the act as demeaning and react in the defense of his club's honor. If the Lion apologizes, he is "gripping" and places himself beneath the other.

Rep

Dress is a reliable sign of a youth's identity as a club member. In winter, club members wear dark, silk-like slacks, Italian knit shirts, high-heeled black shoes, and black "cashmere" coats. In summer, they wear dark pants and "Italian t-shirts." Street youth wear their hair greased and combed straight back. Long hair was "out" until the end of 1973 when many youths let it grow out and began to wear more casual clothing. The most important insignia of club affiliation is the sweater, with its distinctive colors.

A youth's identity as a club member reveals little about the magnitude of his reputation. His status within the group and on the streets depends on the way he plays out his role as a fighter, a leader, a "styler," a lady's man, and a man who "knows the streets and how to keep his cool."

The Image Promoter

Image promoters put themselves in a position to challenge or to be challenged by others. They are ready to see the slightest gesture of indifference to their reputation as an insult and to transform a demand for deference into a fight. If a youth wants the reputation associated with an image promoter and does not want to fight continually, he must avoid situations in which he does not want his behavior to be interpreted as provocative. He can do this by using his best manners and acting politely. Those who have extensive reputations receive the deference they perceive as their due from less ambitious, fearless, and combative participants in the status system. However, anyone who has risen to prominence has enemies who are "out to get them" for past conflicts which have yet to be settled. No image promoter can ever rest securely on his laurels.

Some youth make their reputation in a club and others do it on their own. Although making a reputation in a club is easier for many, it also has its liabilities. An image promoter in a club must compete with other image promoters in the group, and he must defend not only his own reputation but that of the group. Image promoters usually have only one fully trusted male friend, the "partner." Partners' loyalty to each other goes as far as going to jail in defense of each other. In one case a youth refused to implicate his partner in a murder charge even when offered a reduced charge in the case. Partners have been known to suffer serious beatings when coming to the defense of each other.

The most respected reputations on 32d Street are those of image promoters who have not relied on a group. They are responsible only to their partners. Mick observed, "I don't need a club. If I get into trouble, it's my trouble, but in a club you're responsible for the trouble everyone gets into." The next group of individuals have a rep that is more important than their club affiliation, yet have obtained it within a club. They are referred to as "bad dudes." It is "Ray of the Greeks," not "he's a Greek." These men have all committed their share of violent acts which are talked about throughout the community's youth world.

Slightly lower on the hierarchy are those who have almost reached the level of the men just described. For example, Gilberto and Dennis of the Lions are higher in status than those who are known only as a "Lion." Gilberto, nineteen, and leader of the Lions, is the "man" with the biggest "rep" and known throughout the community by young people. Dennis, a member of the Lions, fights "when necessary":

> You got your pride, don't you. You can't let anyone step on you. We know when we do wrong, we really do, but sometimes you have to do things. Like five dudes came towards you and do something to you—we fight back, man, we really fight 'em. You

know even if we're outnumbered and you know you're going to
get killed. You do anyways. You have to protect yourself, you
know we got pride and there's some things we have to do. I
know other people will say "excuse me" or "it must be a mistake" and walk off. We can't do that. It's not in us. I know the
consequences when I do something wrong.

His reputation is built on his ability to negotiate with other
groups. When there is an altercation with another club that the
Lions would prefer to settle verbally rather than by force, Dennis is
called upon. He said he rarely fought before he joined the club and
does relatively little fighting now. Yet he does not want to leave the
club. "They know me whether or not I wear a sweater. I'd get shot
as soon as I'd drop out. These are my friends anyway and who else
do I have?"

As much as physical prowess is valued by these groups, the ability to inflict serious damage upon one's opponents in a fight is only
one aspect of a young man's street reputation. As we mentioned
before, these young men are sensitive to the way in which various
social attributes such as the ability to impress women or negotiate
with a warring group are fused into an attractive personal style. It
is the overall impression one makes as a socially competent person
that makes the difference in one's status in the group. Peers lose
points for starting fights they can't win or for involving the club in a
conflict that is ill-timed. Flagrant violations of the code of honor
such as choosing a much weaker opponent or using violence in a
situation where it is not called for (e.g., "rolling" drunks) reduces a
young man's stature among his fellows. Inability to survive in the
conventional world which is indicated by continuous arrests also
creates a negative impression. Although gang members engage in
what the larger society regards as extremely serious deviant activity, they share many of the larger society's judgments about
what makes a person worthy of esteem, and they do not hesitate to
find fault with their peers who slip into what they see as a dis-
reputable way of life. It is one thing, as Dennis remarks, to defend
one's honor and to stand by one's friends; it is quite another thing to
lose one's self-respect by failing to manage many of the tasks of
everyday life with grace and style.

The Club's Reputation and Honor

The club has few rules, few formal offices, and a flexible pattern
of leadership. The least flexible aspect of club structure is age: clubs

have miniatures (ages 11–12), midgets (ages 13–14), littles (ages 15–17), juniors (ages 18–21), and seniors who are over 21. In 1971 the Lions were one group. Then they decided that it would be better if they became the Littles and the Juniors. "It just happened, we didn't hassle about it, the older dudes became the Juniors and the rest Littles. "We [Juniors] don't have any real officers, we're friends and we can have meetings when we want," said Dennis.

Although club rules are not rigidly defined, members do not allow individuals to disregard the group's authority. Whenever the members of a group see a member as insufficiently committed to it, they are likely to make their feelings known to the person whose interest or loyalty is flagging. On some occasions, the issue is serious enough or the person marginal enough so that he is subjected to what they call "walking the line." The club members make two lines facing each other, and as the victim runs through the center each club member hits him, sometimes with a stick.

Entering and leaving a club is regulated in the same loose, almost haphazard fashion. Sometimes a prospective member must fight several club members so that he can prove his toughness. But if a person comes with a rep already established, he may not be required to prove it. There are also several ways a youth can leave the club. Some just drift away, others are beaten up if they try to leave, and some buy their way out.

Within the club, the youth support each others' reps. Rarely is anyone completely dishonored in the eyes of the club by losing a fight. Although an individual's rep is closely tied to rep of the group, the group does not feel responsible for protecting the rep of someone who foolishly precipitates an incident or who has low status in the group. On one occasion Ken, a midget Lion, came running to the park yelling that the Nobles told him that he could "fuck himself," and he wanted help to protect the name of the club. Jim slowly turned toward the others and said that he had seen Ken trying to provoke the Nobles and he ought to be able to handle the situation himself.

On other occasions the entire group must fight to maintain their reputation. According to the Lions, they were taunted by the Junior Greeks when they were walking along minding their own business. Ronnie [a Lion] struck one of the Greeks and the fight began. Some Aces spotted them from a car and joined them on the side of the Junior Greeks. Ronnie was struck forcefully on the head with a crowbar but continued fighting. Rat Man stabbed one of the Aces, who had to be taken to the hospital. Later that afternoon the Lions argued about whether the Ace had been stabbed two or three times.

They left again to find the Greeks. About eight that evening all the Lions returned to the park. The Greeks had fired several shotgun blasts at them but missed, and the Lions had retreated because they were not armed at the time. Some Greeks were arrested by the police. The following Saturday night Ronnie was alone and was stabbed in the back by the Ace who previously hit him with a crowbar. The Senior Greeks disowned the Junior Greeks and told the Lions that they would not take the Junior's side in future fights between the Junior Greeks and the Lions.

When Pierre failed to go with the others when they went after the Junior Greeks, Amos, then president of the Little Lions, cursed Pierre for his failure to support the group and hit him across the face in front of the group. Amos then pulled out a knife and lunged at Pierre who was quickly moved out of Amos's reach by several other club members. Amos missed and tripped, and Pierre left quickly. Nen also did not fight on this occasion. His absence was no threat to the solidarity of the group because he fought frequently with the group and had previously sustained two serious bullet wounds (both bullets are still inside him).

The war between the Lions and Aces continued over three years. Expectations of possible affronts and small skirmishes kept up its momentum. Rat Man thought he saw some Aces riding in a car so he shot at them, but the .38 did not go off. "That is what you are supposed to do when you see an Ace," he said, "because we are at war." Gilberto received several telephone calls from the Aces stating that "blood would return blood." An Ace threw a brick through Amos's mother's window in early February of 1972. Amos and two other Lions ran into this Ace late in April. Amos beat the Ace unconscious with the butt of his gun, but he regained consciousness a few days later and identified Amos as his assailant. Amos claimed that he should have killed him but did not have ammunition for the gun at that time.

The ferocity with which these young men defend and promote their sense of honor often leads to serious injury and occasional homicide. These are not wars over territory in the strict sense of the word (see Keiser 1969). There is an individualistic bias to these collective efforts to dominate other groups. The intent here is to not keep them out of the neighborhood but rather to have them serve as both the audience and the object of one's power and indominability. To be respected on the streets of 32d Street is to be feared by opponents who are worthy of this attention.

The authority of the state and civil society seem largely irrelevant to the status system of clubs on 32d Street. Yet these youth are fully aware of the moral significance of legal proscriptions on armed violence. None of them will say that violence against others, *outside of this context,* is justifiable. Nor should we assume that their respect for conventional norms is nullified by what looks like unremitting deviance. From the perspective of 32d Street club members, fighting has a rationale that makes sense when one is challenged by others who recognize no external constraints on the use of force. Under these circumstances, they argue, it would be foolhardy to back away from a potentially dangerous encounter. What they fail to say, of course, is that their investment in the pursuit of status gives fighting its singularly imperative quality on 32d Street. Failure to recognize the power of conventional society's authority is, in effect, an admission that it also cannot bestow the sense of personal potency that these young men believe is the essence of individual merit.

Image Defenders and Rep Avoiders

Image defenders do not provoke others to demonstrate their superiority. Most youths with this orientation try to maintain a "good rep." Some have been in clubs and dropped out, and others "belong" to certain corners where they regularly hang out with friends. When asked if they fight, the most common response is, "Only if I have to." Carlos quit the Lions when he was fourteen. He still manages to get into fights over what he often admits afterward are "mistakes." One night when he was walking home he saw a Lion who could barely walk. He went over to him to see if he could help and leaned over. The Lion must have interpreted his move as threatening and hit him in the face. Carlos would not tolerate that insult and proceeded to fight with the Lion.

Some youth rarely fight. But there is scarcely a single individual who had not been in at least one fight or feels that he would never feel called upon to protect his honor or that of a female relative. Sometimes their "I would rather fight them . . ." is more of a threat than a reality. The tension between the maintenance of the honor of the family and the desire to stay out of trouble on the part of mobility-oriented youth makes decisions difficult in some situation for youth who feel strongly about both. However, reputation as it is assessed by other youths has little significance for rep avoiders. Their personal identities are created through their *lack* of reputation in the street.

Roberto, an "Ivy League" college sophomore, rarely fought, but when he found out that some of the Nobles were "messing with my sister," he went off after them without thinking, he claimed. Later he "regained his senses" as he put it, when his brother grabbed him and made him think—the Nobles had guns and there were more of them. "I guess," he said reflecting afterward, "that we all cannot be pushed beyond a certain point. We [Mexicans] all have 'hot blood' so we explode at one point."

Rep and the Life Cycle

Most youth drift slowly away from their street reps in their late teens and early twenties. For instance, after Dennis had a brush with the law which affected other plans he considered important, he started spending less time with his club. Yet Dennis often carries a gun and has been involved in several shootings. In 1971 he was stopped by two plainclothes detectives, frisked, and charged with carrying an unregistered gun. At the time, there had been several altercations with the Junior Greeks, and the Lions were prepared for trouble. Three months before this incident he started a white-collar job in a downtown bank and had a perfect attendance record. He enjoyed his work and was proud of his progress. Though he had no prior criminal convictions, Dennis was fired unceremoniously after his employers discovered that he was being tried on a felony charge. After this, Dennis enrolled in a high school equivalency program. He had previously completed the eleventh grade, but he said that things were too "hot" to return to school for his senior year.

Once a youth has decided to leave his club, the path is not alway clear: others still identify him by his past rep. Rick attempted to indicate the change in his social identity by growing his hair, wearing jeans and old army jackets instead of the "pressed look" of club members, hanging around the community less often, and attending a junior college:

It's difficult when dudes are chasing you with a gun to turn around and say, "Hey, wait a minute, I'm not into that shit anymore, would you lay off please?" You tell dudes to cool it but they ain't going to believe you just like that. They think you're just saying it to put some shit over on them.

Police and Youth

As one might imagine, relations between youth and police are tense and unpredictable. Many youth have had some contact with the juvenile justice system. Being picked up, arrested, and brought to court is not an experience that is exclusively restricted to gang members. Youth report stopping police for legitimate reasons such as wanting to prevent an old man from being beaten on the streets, only to find themselves embroiled in a dispute with the police over respect. The police are sensitive to the provocative and, at times, hostile attitudes of many of the young people to their authority. At times, they approach these youth expecting to be tested. Moreover, these encounters not infrequently lead to physical clashes between youth and police. Resisting arrest is as common as stripping cars or assault and battery.

Some officers mildly harass youth who congregate in the park but seem to avoid confrontations that might lead to serious conflict. There is an element of play in these encounters over drinking in a public place or swimming in the local pool after hours. But there is always the possibility that what begins as reasonably good-natured teasing can turn into physical violence. The pattern of police patrol in the park and similar areas where club members congregate fluctuates between surveillance at a distance and forceful intrusion into the space where youth hang out. Police, for example, will drive around the park in cars and simply observe what is going on even when the aroma of marijuana smoke lies heavily over the place, or they will get out of the cars and search youth for weapons. Part of the reason for marked differences in the pattern of police/youth contacts depends upon media and community concern with gang violence. As youths experience it, police sometimes are reluctant to pursue some of the club members who "have a price on their head" but who are known to be willing to resist arrest with deadly force. If this is true, it accounts for the polarity in police youth contacts. Police either approach youth in a very truculent manner and are prepared to react to the slightest indication of resistance with force. Or police keep their distance and intervene only when circumstances force them to become involved.

The usual pattern of contact with the courts creates the feeling that justice is a lottery, and that luck, and not the seriousness of the charge, determines whether one will be punished for an offense. This extends to first-degree murder and attempted murder as well as to lesser violations of the law. Everyone knows who is in or out of jail, what the bail situation is with respect to a particular case, and what lawyers cost for various kinds of cases. There is considerable knowledge about how to appear before judges and how to create the most favorable impression before the court. Not all club members have criminal records, and many go to some lengths to avoid having one.

The irrationality of the justice system is its most salient quality. One club member claims that he spends his weekends in jail because, whatever he does during the week, he seems to end up in jail over the weekend. Or police will come in the park and tell club members to run, and if one is armed that is one way to avoid being charged with an offense. It is not uncommon that for an offense as serious as shooting and wounding another club member a youth will be taken to jail and held for a few weeks and then be released without being tried and sentenced for this crime. Other youth will spend considerable time in jail or juvenile detention centers for less serious matters.

In general, the authority of the state and the power of civil society is remote and weak. It is almost as if the law itself represents an erratic alien country whose troops occasionally force their way into the community, harass the local population, but more often than not leave little in the way of permanent damage behind them. The justice system, as it represents the moral power of civil society, is administered in such an inconsistent and unpredictable manner that the disapproval of the larger society is dissipated by its inability to respond in an evenhanded way to similar offenses. It is misleading to speak of rebellion against or rejection of the authority of the larger society on 32d Street, at least as far as youth who are oriented to the streets are concerned. Except for the purely coercive aspects of the law, the sanctions of the larger society against violence have little force because these youth live in a world where one's self-respect is based on principles that do not accept peaceful resolutions of personal disputes as valid.

While youth may have little respect for the formal appartus of criminal justice, they have great regard for the larger society's image of a socially competent person. The paradox of 32d Street culture is that although these youth are the most serious violators of the most important legal norms of the larger society, they do not conduct their activities in a spirit of opposition to the culture of mainstream society. In other words, these youth are nothing like violent motorcycle gangs who cultivate their reputation as "outlaws" who go out of their way to defy the norms of respectable society. Other than their deviant activities per se, most gang youth on 32d Street try to conform to the image of a person who has the social skills to move throughout society.

Though these youth may create serious problems for their families, very few reject their ties to their elders or ridicule the older generation. Nor do they have any doubt about the value of being able to present oneself as a proper person in formal social situations.

Even though, at times, these youth make decisions that appear diametrically opposed to the norms of the larger culture, all of these young men would prefer to be seen as persons who are polite and who know how to conduct themselves with some sophistication when they are not on the streets with their peers. Since this image of an admirable person incorporates personal qualities that are incompatible in a particular situation, it is easier to give lip service to this ideal than to actually live up to it. Yet there are some youth who achieve some success on the streets and within the institutional framework of the larger society.

Women and Their Reps

A woman's honor is assessed in terms of her virginity before marriage and motherhood afterward. Her honor, moreover, is linked closely to that of her family. Moreover, hers is a passive and reactive sense of honor; she can only protect her reputation. Since many women lose their virginity prior to marriage, the critical issue for a woman's identity in the community is whether, if she becomes pregnant, she accepts the role of motherhood. By doing so, she must subjugate her sexuality to the norms governing married women, that is, she must be chaste in the eyes of anyone who is not her husband.

The use of birth control is highly problematic for all girls except those who admit they "have been around." To use birth control indicates prior intent to violate the norm of remaining a virgin until marriage and may result in a woman's rep as an "easy lay." The process of building up an intimate relationship is complicated by dual expectations: that a woman will guard her reputation and is vulnerable to passion when she falls in love with a boy.

Falling in Love

The first stage of a relationship involves mutual glances and a little casual conversation. The "seeing" stage occurs when both agree to meet in the usual "hang out." "Going out" is often said to be a girl's downfall. One afternoon the fieldworker was walking with Alicia, Ramona, Raquel, Gayle, and Lydia, when Harry, Ramona's boyfriend (who she was "going out with"), approached the group. He twisted Ramona's arm demanding to know where she was going. She replied that we were going to listen to records. He pulled her around and told her she was going with him. She did not resist and none of the other girls paid attention to this incident. The fieldworker asked her sister, Raquel, why she did not put up with that kind of behavior from Dennis as she had seen her walk away from him several times, telling him to get lost. Her sister replied that she was not in love with Dennis and, therefore, did not have to do everything he wanted. Ramona was in love with Harry and so she had to do his bidding. Alicia said that women lose all their control over men when they fall in love and that was very dangerous but unavoidable. All the girls agreed it was "just a fact of life."

Once the young women feel committed to a relationship, most of their boyfriends ask them to engage in intercourse. They must make a decision to remain a virgin or anticipate becoming involved sexually and guard against pregnancy or wait until an emotionally charged situation and explain that in a "moment of passion" she gave into her boyfriend's demands. Before she was nineteen, Alicia bore two children out of wedlock.

> I never believed I would get pregnant because I messed around for almost a year before I got pregnant. I thought maybe I couldn't have kids. I really didn't think I was pregnant 'til I was six months gone and started getting hives. My parents took me to a doctor. I really couldn't believe it.

Alicia and her friends all knew about birth control. Her married sister was on the pill, and her mother thought that birth control was valid if a woman was married. Alicia said she could not use it because she was not married.

Virginity

Girls who have maintained their virginity are rarely seen at parties or dances and spend most of their time after school around the house. Clara, at seventeen, is still closely watched and permitted very few dates, but had been going out and seeing young men from the age of thirteen. Many young men follow her around, and she has had as many opportunities to become committed to a relationship and engage in sex as others. She is very attractive and is not afraid of men, yet keeps her distance. "I'm not ready for marriage yet," she says.

Loss of Honor

Some girls decide not to marry the father of their child and some men will not or cannot marry them. Unmarried mothers have to be careful about how they conduct themselves. These women must strike a delicate balance between "a woman who had been through it" and a nice girl who realizes her mistake and would like to settle down now. If a girl gets pregnant by the first man she sleeps with, she has a better chance of "catching" him. He must also be old enough to get married and support her or one set of parents must be willing to let the young couple live with them.

Ivy is an example of the girls who do not marry the fathers of their children. She had her first child at fifteen but decided that she did not like the father of her son and refused to marry him. She lived at home with her mother and went back to Tudor High. However, she took primary responsibility for her child, taking him everywhere with her. Pierre, Leonard, Nen (Lions), and the fieldworker passed by Ivy's house one evening. The three of them agreed that it was time Ivy got married because her reputation was getting pretty bad from fooling around with so many different men. Pierre said, "She's already got one kid now and she'll probably have another if she doesn't get married soon. People are beginning to talk."

Violation of Virginity and Motherhood

Young women who refuse to publicly admit they are really *not* virgins anymore are typified by both men and other women as "losers." They are seen as trying to be what they obviously are not. They account for their motherhood by justifying it in terms of their naiveté and, in the eyes of others, thereby denigrate its importance.

Alicia failed to portray the image of a good mother and tried to cover her loss of shame in public by blaming her youthfulness and her love of Gilberto for the *error* (her son) in her life. Other girls described her as a "flirtatious bitch" who caused most of her own troubles. They saw Alicia throwing herself on men and trying to "capture" one of them. They expressed disgust for her "two faces." Many of the men viewed her pathetically. One of the Lions remarked, "She's OK, she helps us carry the 'heats,' sneaks them into dances, and she'll take them off you if the cops are coming. Remember the time she hid that .45 in her kid's carriage with him asleep?"

The issue here is not simply one of hypocrisy: showing one side of one's character to one audience and an entirely different side to another audience or pretending to be someone one is not. Alicia makes a major cultural blunder because she refuses to take responsibility for her misdeed in a way that restores the honor of women and respect for their femininity. It is culturally acceptable to depict one's moment of passion as a "mistake." But one must never put the resultant state of motherhood in disrepute by denying its power to restrain one's sexuality. Of course, one ought not to pretend to be virginal when one is not. But one cannot advertise one's sexual availability after having a child because motherhood is itself a form of chaste sexuality. That is, an unmarried young girl who gets pregnant can show respect for the ideal state of feminine virtue by keeping her sexuality under control until such time as she becomes a mother and wife. By throwing herself at men, Alicia was ruining her chances for getting married because no man likes to marry a woman who regards infidelity merely as an indiscretion. There are women who have effectively severed their ties to the local culture by treating their sexuality as a matter of purely personal inclination. What is much worse in the eyes of traditionalists, these women make their feelings public knowledge.

The young women who use contraceptives and do what they want with their bodies are often typified as sluts or free whores. They intentionally violate both the norms of virginity and motherhood. Sally, June, Allison, Peony, and several other girls spent one summer hanging around the park with the Lions. They each "went out with" one or two club members during the summer and spent most of the time sitting around drinking and listening to love songs on the radio just like the other girls. They were not completely immune to talk and were upset to find that the Lions had smeared their names all over the community. After that they had their own parties and tried to keep the Lions out who were "babies" and "didn't appreciate us at all." "The dudes from the north side are finer anyhow. We go up Fridays and Saturdays and look for some fine-looking dudes."

Independence as Counternormative

By focusing their activities outside the community, some young women have struggled to develop their identities outside of the culture of 32d Street. Several have fought for and won their independence, but not without some extremely painful conflicts with their families. Their idea of having an equalitarian relationship with men is not understood. One young man who knew several of these women said, "It's all very confusing to me. They [women] go off on their own, don't want any help from us. I don't get where they are coming from."

Marianne joined local political groups in high school and became increasingly involved in a number of university-wide groups in college. Her friends came from all over the city and from different ethnic groups. Her struggle with her family had been long and difficult. Her father had thrown her out several times and seemed more willing to help her younger pregnant sister than her. For long periods she was cut off from her family and struggled on her own.

One might argue that these culturally independent women in 32d Street were ahead of the rest of their generation. When the majority of their peers become acculturated to mainstream culture they will be more receptive to a companionate image of heteroxexual relations. This view, however, depicts as a deficiency something the culture forcefully negates. That is, the idea of intimacy between a man and a woman which makes them into an emotionally self-sufficient "couple" apart from their relations to their children and their ties to a wider kin network is culturally inconceivable. It destroys the rationale for the institution of marriage which delineates the man's role as the dominant figure because he is responsible for the welfare of the entire family. By elevating women to the status of equals, the role of the man as head of the family evaporates. In the eyes of traditional culture, he would be no more than a paying boarder and occasional sexual partner. This attempt to breach the division between the sexes implicitly rejects the notion that one seeks emotional comfort and understanding from same-sex relatives and peers, and adventure and excitement in relations with the opposite sex. In this culture, women are potential conquests or wives and mothers, but they are not, and never can be, friends.

Thus, it is not a lack of compassion that makes Marianne's family so resistant to her cosmopolitan, urban values. From her family's point of view, she has intentionally abandoned those beliefs and roles that sustain the culture of 32d Street. By symbolically casting off her role as a dutiful daughter and potential wife and mother, she undercuts the viability of the communal culture by elevating the value of personal autonomy and self-definition over familial obligation and conventional sex-role identities. This is more than a situation where different generational perspectives create familial conflict. From her family's point of view, Marianne is insisting on moving into a social world that has no clear points of orientation or standards for the evaluation of one's worth. Marianne stands at a boundary beyond which traditional culture on 32d Street cannot exist as a coherent whole.

Tudor High School

Tudor High School is disorganized and dangerous. Fighting in and around the school is commonplace. The city police, not school officials, are called to restore order or to prevent many of the dropouts who hang around the school from breaking in and wreaking havoc on an already overcrowded and physically decrepit building. Students report that teachers spend much of their time trying to keep a semblance of order and that noise and confusion in the classroom are part of the routine experience of going to school.

Going to a public school is doubly difficult for club members. A confrontation with members of other groups in the halls is always possible. There are black as well as Latin groups in the school which adds fuel to an already volatile situation. In fact, many club members say that it is simply too dangerous to go to school. They often contrast this situation with that of parochial schools where club sweaters are not allowed and serious violations of the rules result in expulsion.

In Tudor High, the tacit norm is to ignore all but the most outrageous and persistent challenges to the authority of the school and to push students through the academic system regardless of whether they meet minimal academic standards. The basic policy of Tudor High is of an educational warehouse where teachers babysit for students until they drop out of school or cause so many problems that the administration is forced to take action against them.

The attitude of many young people toward school is that it is a place to be when there is nothing better to do than kill time and, of course, to get together with friends. The academic standards of the school are mystifying to most students. One girl remarked that she missed seventy-one days of school last year and got all C's whereas some of her friends with similar attendance records flunked. Another girl commented in a matter of fact way that she flunked all her courses last year, and although she planned to go back she was not sure whether the school would accept her. It is an open secret that getting through school is no guarantee of having basic literacy skills. Getting through school is more of a test of survival skills than mastery over the subject matter we ordinarily associate with education.

Even when classroom decorum is reasonable and teachers are trying to convey information to students, much of the interchange is incomprehensible to both parties. In one class, an English teacher reads poetry for forty minutes to a classroom whose reading skills are, for the large part, primitive. In another class, a math teacher tries to teach geometry to a class whose members do not have the faintest idea of what he is talking about. There is almost no provision for the fact that the learning deficits of most students are so great that the ordinary academic curriculum is totally inappropriate.

Relations between students and teachers range from impersonal neutrality to open antagonism. If a class is noisy and unruly, a teacher may declare that everyone will fail the day's assignment, or a teacher will routinely mark students absent when they come in late. Perhaps the most sensitive issue is the feeling that many teachers have little respect for students. One girl commented at length about how teachers talk down to her. She described going up to a teacher who she admired but who never smiled and asked her why. The teacher replied that it was none of her business.

While many students complain of being bored or confused by school and while girls as well as boys must constantly be on guard against being attacked or drawn into fights, many youth have ambitions that involve getting an education. The problem is that the authority of the school as it is experienced in the classroom has little connection with the larger society's goals and values. These youth recognize that doing well in school is necessary in order to get ahead in the world. But the rewards for conformity to the rules are so slight that this institution commands almost no allegiance from the vast majority of students. Tudor High comes as close to being a pure case of a nonrational and unreasonable urban institution as one could imagine.

Graduating from High School

Though most youth agree with their parents on the importance of graduating from high school in order to obtain a well-paying job, only approximately 30 percent graduate. Most of those who graduate do not go on to college. In general, education is seen as having little meaning beyond having the diploma which opens doors to some jobs that might be closed otherwise.

Peers generally support those who remain in school. For example, when four of their members graduated from eighth grade, thirty of the Lions attended the graduation wearing their club sweaters. When each club member walked up on stage to receive his diploma the entire group clapped and cheered. One member who failed to graduate for the second time did not appear at the club's meeting place for two weeks. When Ronnie graduated from parochial high school they all congratulated him and spoke of him as an example for the younger members to follow. On the other hand, most youth are not criticized by their peers for dropping out, though many felt that it was strange that Nen, the president of the Lions, had dropped out of school in his junior year at a parochial school where he was an honor student.

It may seem strange that some gang youth give much more than verbal allegiance to societal values at various points in their lives. If the circumstances are reasonably supportive or safe they are willing to invest considerable energy in school or in a comparatively prestigious and well-paying job. Failing at what the larger society defines as basic social competence is not something most of these youths take lightly. It is no badge of honor to get thrown out of school or to flunk all of one's courses. That may happen, and it may be unavoidable. But no one has any illusions about its effect on one's options in the job market.

Commitment to instrumental values is contingent upon circumstances that allow one to give them greater or lesser prominence in one's life depending upon the state of relations with one's peers and one's involvement in the status system of the streets. As we indicated earlier, there are mobility-oriented youth who stay out of trouble and remain in school. But they tend to remain in the background and do not participate in any meaningful way in the activities of the peer group world of this inner-city neighborhood.

Most gang youth know that getting into trouble with the law may be counterproductive in the long run. Yet this sort of abstract knowledge cannot become much more than that unless there were substantial rewards for risking what would be a lonely and arduous task of trying to get ahead on one's own. Despite the risk of being shot or injured in a gang conflict, the rewards are much more palpable for remaining close to one's peers than trying to succeed in terms of conventional values in a community that lacks institutional support for that effort.

By institutional support, I do not mean approval for conventional behavior on the part of the older generation because that certainly is the case in 32d Street. No adult sanctions this kind of deadly conflict. What is missing in 32d Street is the kind of intergenerational alliance between nonfamilial authority figures that would support a redefinition of a youth's identity that could override the assessments of his peers. In other words, these adults would have to have the sort of respect among youth in the community that coaches, priests, teachers, politicians, and some policemen have in Parsons Park. Their perceived power and status in the larger world would have to counterbalance the attraction of the immediate satisfaction of acquiring a reputation in the street world. One gets the impression that some of the most energetic and clever youth are drawn to the streets because it is the one place where they can test their enterprise and daring.

Few graduate from the local comprehensive high school, but a number of youth have sought other means of obtaining a diploma. Some attempt to demonstrate to the school board that they live in other neighborhoods in order to attend schools in other districts. A few move in with relatives or friends in Texas or Mexico, and a few attend technical schools. Dennis claims:

> I did real well the year I was in Texas in school. I was always a good student. Once my family took me to Mexico when I was in the seventh grade and I missed too many days of school. They said I had to repeat, but me and my mother challenged them. They said that I couldn't pass the final tests, but finally they let me take them and I passed to eighth grade. But at Tudor it's different. There's too many other things happening. You've got to protect yourself. I just couldn't handle that last year and tried to transfer to another district but they wouldn't let me.

Some youth, especially young women, attend parochial schools. A school in which a student has few friends from the streets may be an advantage as they cannot persuade one to leave in the middle of the day. Club members may not be identified so that they are less likely to be challenged by fellow students. In addition, in a parochial school one does not have to protect one's claim to precedence with a priest as one might feel one has to with a public school teacher.

Alfredo, now twenty-two, was expelled on his sixteenth birthday by the counselor at Tudor. He called his mother and the counselor, overhearing the conversation, laughed. Alfredo perceived the laugh as an insult and punched the counselor in the mouth. From Alfredo's perspective, the counselor was laughing at him for having a close tie with his mother and that could not go unchallenged: Alfredo is artic-ulate and could have lashed out verbally. But he felt that the only way he could regain any dignity was to hit the teacher.

One of the most interesting aspects of the culture of 32d Street is how young men segregate their commitment to honor on the local scene from a strategic orientation to more impersonal relationships in the wider society. For example, they do not respond to a felt lack of respect in a job situation as they would with a peer in their neigh-borhood, although these young men are incapable of overlooking a direct insult wherever it occurs. There are, however, certain sym-bols that touch the center of a young person's identity. Family honor and devotion to one's mother are the ultimate values of 32d Street. Mothers have a special role in the lives of sons. While fa-thers are remote and often authoritarian, mothers are the emotional bedrock from which a son draws nurturance and understanding as long as he lives.

To have laughed when Alfredo was talking on the phone *to* his mother was a grievous mistake on the part of the counselor. To laugh *at* Alfredo and his mother was an unforgivable insult. Alfredo could not do otherwise than to strike the counselor without being profoundly ashamed of himself and without sacrificing his family's honor.

From the point of view of the dominant culture, this sort of irrational behavior is a sign of social disability. It would be interpreted as an indication that Alfredo could not defend himself verbally and was forced by his own lack of social skills to resort to a primitive mode of defense. This sort of analysis smuggles in a conception of how young people ought to react to unreasonable treatment at the hands of authority. Regardless of the justice of their case, it counsels young people to tread lightly before powerful figures who can act on one's behalf rather than forcing a confrontation over a presumably trivial matter. And that is precisely where the issue arises.

When authority recognizes a narrow sort of rationality as the legitimate basis for its dealings with youth, it creates the conditions for a struggle over the issue of reasonableness. The symbolic exclusion of the expressive integrity of the self in personal relationships is part of a powerful dialectic of adolescent rebellion against authority. The negation of the identity of a young person leads to a negation of the authority who impugns the dignity of adolescence. Tragically, in the case of the culture of 32d Street and the bureaucracy of urban society, there are very few mediating symbols either party can draw upon to resolve the conflict between them.

In Alfredo's eyes, the counselor was acting as a surrogate for the society as a whole by treating people like himself as inferiors whose feelings can be ignored or ridiculed. Thus, there is cultural significance to Alfredo's apparent impulsiveness. By striking out, he not only transforms the relationship between cultural superiors and inferiors, but he also refuses to accept the imputation of inferiority passively. Alfredo thereby leaves the scene a man rather than as a schoolboy.

Youth who finish school have varying reps on the street. A number of Lions have graduated from both public and parochial high schools, and many of the "good kids" who are not members of gangs fail to graduate. Involvement in deviant activity is not a reliable indicator of a youth's academic standing. Felice said, "My boyfriend Rick got all A's and B's. I hope they let him back to school [parochial] when he gets out of jail [attempting to shoot an officer— the gun did not go off] because he would graduate in June." He graduated a year later.

Work and Money

Financial success is valued in 32d Street. Nen is admired by everyone as someone who has succeeded because of his job as a computer operator at the bank. He also maintains his status as the best fighter and as the president of the Lions. He attended a special training program for "disadvantaged youth" at a downtown bank. He was the top student in the class and became a full-time employee on the night shift. Nen is rarely absent from work. Also he rarely misses an evening with the Lions at the park or in the club house. Intermittently, Nen finds the night job detrimental to his relationships with the group. A year after he started he did not go to work for several days telling the other club members that he was quitting since he could not get on the day shift. He finally decided that he could never get a better job and returned to it two weeks later.

As far as work is concerned, most youth prefer blue-collar jobs, but some prefer the "rip-off" white-collar "rap" jobs. Many youth feel that white-collar jobs are just "talk" jobs where no one is really "doing" anything. Those kinds of jobs are all right for women but men need physical labor to be "really men."

For women, a good job pays well enough to buy the things they want. An office job has other advantages such as being able to "style" and pleasant working conditions. Some parents encourage their daughters to work in downtown offices in hopes they will meet someone "nice" to marry. "My father wants me to meet a doctor or lawyer to marry. But none of those men are going to be interested in me," a nineteen-year-old girl told the fieldworker. Many young women, however, never go much beyond the ninth grade in school and do not qualify for anything but factory jobs which are rarely held for very long. The women, like the men, find them dull, dirty, and devoid of any merit except the money they bring in.

Having money to entertain friends is very important to many young people in the community. Everyone, it is assumed, will return favors. If a person does not reciprocate and does not have a job for an extended period of time, relations may become strained. Saving is almost precluded by the constant exchange of loans and the expectation that the person with money buys for those who don't. Not everyone participates, and some save or buy a car or house. But most youth feel free to spend money on a "good time." This means that an individual can get financial support if he does not have a job and, conversely, that an individual needs a ready supply of cash to maintain his position as someone who can return a favor.

The system of reciprocity of financial and similar favors between relatives and friends is not as inclusive or as normatively supported as it is in peasant communities. Nevertheless, this pattern of giving sociability and amicable relations priority over saving for the future is a fundamental aspect of the culture of 32d Street. If an individual drew a careful line between his own economic interests and the needs of relatives and friends, it would be difficult to maintain the network of communal relationships which, in turn, reinforce the distinctive values and beliefs of the Mexican-American community.

This is not to say that Mexican-Americans are unaware of the utility of capital accumulation or that they dissipate all of their resources by acceding to requests of friends and relatives. Some families own their own homes, and most purchase items for which saving is required. The important point is symbolic rather than economic. The pattern of reciprocity affirms the importance of personal relations over the impersonal and more objectified material signs of self that are valued by the mainstream culture. Put simply, Mexican-Americans are much more concerned with the good opinion of their neighbors, relatives, and friends than they are with how their material possessions represent the sort of persons they are in the eyes of the world at large. Generosity, then, confirms one's sense of oneself as a strong and reliable person who can be depended upon to do what is right and proper by local standards. It will take the opportunity to accumulate a good deal of money before the residents of 32d Street are ready to relinquish the satisfaction of being recognized as a person worthy of respect.

Most youths work with some regularity. However, the prestige gained within the group and the money earned are the only positive supports for working. There is little feeling of satisfaction from the work itself. Those who do not obtain jobs or go into the service when they are eighteen are the exception rather than the rule. Almost any other job is acceptable as long as an individual is not degraded on the job. Leonard explains:

> You know, I've been working for more than six months and I only missed two days. Now I'm making $2.65 an hour. It's beginning to look pretty good. When my girl comes back from Texas [she was finishing school] we can get together. It feels good working cause I don't have to go jackrolling with the dudes to get money to get high.

On the job, freedom from close supervision is highly valued. This allows youth to avoid conflict with those in authority. Ten Pin at twenty was going to be a father soon and was very concerned about getting a job. "I want a talk job—you know, bullshitting with people. I don't want to be closed in with some dude hanging by my head." Pick agreed with him about supervision:

> I'm a truck driver out by myself, no one breathing down my neck. I do my job—earn around $13,000. I like driving. Had other jobs. I never had any trouble finding a job. Once I got laid off and went to collect unemployment. I refuse to stand in line waiting for some hand-out. I walked out and found a good-paying job.

Jock (about twenty-six years old) has set up his own contracting business and is doing well, making good money, and as he says:

> I'm my own boss and work my own hours and employ other men to help me but I don't stand over them. I'd like to go back to school now. I have a couple of college credits. It's really my first goal, but to leave this business would be really difficult. I really can't make a windfall profit or support my family while I go to school, but I really want to be a lawyer.

As we can see from the remarks of both gang and nongang youth, there is little evidence that they lack the ambition or motivation to succeed in the terms set by the larger society. They understand the value of obtaining and holding on to a good job, and they are willing to spend the time and energy to find one. But for everyone who finds a situation that meets his or her expectations about a well-paying job with reasonable working conditions, many others have to be satisfied with much less. This is a clear case where the opportunity structure determines attitudes toward work. The greater the reward, the greater the commitment on the part of youth. That is simply an affirmation of the basic principle of rationality of our culture.

Conclusion

Unlike any of the other communities in this book, there is a nearly complete separation between the norms of family and peer group and the values that support the school and other public institutions. The authority of the latter is so weak in the day-to-day relations of youth on 32d Street because it is experienced as fundamentally irrelevant to the concerns that make a difference in their lives. The local high school offers little more than a place to meet one's friends and to watch out for the members of other clubs with whom one is at war. Few youth ever mention teachers or classes as significant aspects of their lives. The dedicated, serious student who is deeply involved in academics is as rare on 32d Street as a youth who was involved in fighting would be in the upper-middle-class suburb of Glenbar.

Youth on 32d Street neither deprecate the value of education for getting ahead in the world nor reject the conventional means of obtaining good jobs. As we have seen, some of these youth are capable of finding employment in relatively well-paying white-collar occupations. What they do reject, however, is that the authority of the school, and the culture it represents, can prescribe an authoritative model for living one's life as a social person. Here the fundamental roles of manhood and womanhood, of sociability and interpersonal competence, are defined by the traditional values of family life and the strenuous and often dangerous norms of street life.

The lives of young people are not marked by major social disabilities. The community places considerable emphasis on polite manners and decorum in public places. Club members are well-schooled in the subtleties of respectable behavior such as seating a lady in a good restaurant or negotiating flexibly with bureaucrats in public agencies. They are attentive to the clues that identify a person as capable of managing to get along in conventional society and do not suffer from feelings of inferiority, in this respect, in comparison to socially dominant groups. Youth on 32d Street, therefore, do not deny, in deed as well as word, the standards of the larger society, and they are willing to conform to them as long as those standards do not infringe on their sense of honor. It is when honor becomes an explicit issue in face-to-face relationships that the authority of the larger society diminishes, and "deviance" becomes, from the perspective of the culture of 32d Street, a matter of acting in a culturally intelligible and viable manner. Cowardice, shame, and humiliation are infinitely stronger incentives to live up to the code of honor of the streets than are the sanctions of the state or the disapproval of mainstream society.

One can grant all of this and still ask the obvious question, Why in a community that has comparatively strong ties between the generations do adults exercise so little control over the deviant activities of youth? This is a particularly compelling question because gang conflicts cause great suffering for families who lose a child in the unpredictable warfare in the streets. As we mentioned before, fathers see their sons as no longer subject to their authority *outside* of the home. However, even if the cultural definition of social maturity and personal autonomy was changed so that fathers felt they had the right to set limits on their adolescent sons' activities on the street, that alone would not substantially alter the situation.

There is a disjunction between the domestic authority of the older generation on the local scene and their lack of political and economic power in the city. In other words, in the eyes of youth their parents' generation represents cultural continuity and viable models of interpersonal behavior. But their elders do not have the collective power to enforce their will on the way in which the younger generation seeks status in the community. There is not disagreement over cultural fundamentals: honor, respect, and direct response to insult are valued by both parties. It is the limits on the way in which youth can pursue and accumulate status at the expense of their peers that is at issue between the generations. Gang youth are practicing a version of untamed cultural capitalism where each "corporation" plays the game by its own rules and recognizes no other end than taking as much as it can regardless of the consequences for its members or other players.

Thus, the problem is one in which authority is missing in a vital sphere of community life. If adults had the political power to extrude those from the community who persistently and flagrantly violated the rules against homicidal violence, gang conflict would be less likely to escalate into protracted warfare. In actual practice, the adults cannot mobilize the political support necesary to keep youth under control that is evident in older and more established inner-city ethnic communities.

For instance, in an established Italian neighborhood a relatively short distance from 32d Street youth are, in general, no more disposed to follow the law than their counterparts on 32d Street. Male adolescent groups in this area participate in a wide range of deviant activities, but they do not engage in open warfare on the streets of their community (see Kobrin, Puntil, and Peluso 1967). If the behavior of adolescent males becomes a public nuisance or danger to the community, influential adults let those who are behaving in this manner know that their presence will not be tolerated on the streets if they continue to act this way. But as Clifford Shaw and Henry McKay observed many years ago, powerful adults in these communities are effective agents of social control because they are perceived as having the sort of connections that will be of great value to enterprising young men who want to get ahead in either the legitimate or illegitimate opportunity structure of the city. When adults have this kind of power, it would be foolish as well as foolhardy to show disrespect by ignoring the admonitions of their elders to stop from wreaking havoc in their neighborhood.

7

Glenbar

Community Setting

Glenbar was incorporated in 1920. At the time it had 200 permanent residents for whom it served as a weekend retreat in the country. The town, which is about thirty miles from the city, is encircled by green belts which separated it from the surrounding prairie and farmland. Glenbar soon became a place where wealthy city residents moved in order to be near their country clubs. It was accessible to a small number of people, and the residents wanted to keep it that way, discouraging any industrial or commercial development in the area. The town grew slowly. The population in 1930 was 808; 1940—1,270; and 1950—1,800. Glenbar's population surged to 4,624 by 1960 and grew to 8,247 by 1970 at which time most of the land area had been filled in.

According to 1960 census, its residents' income, years of education, and percentage of the labor force in professional occupations put Glenbar at the top of the metropolitan region's suburban communities. Although the 1970 figures (median family was $25,000 and mean home value was $50,000) show that Glenbar remains wealthy, both objective indicators and the feelings of the residents of the community disclose a decline in the prestige of the community. From 1960 to 1970 the only suburb in the entire metropolitan region to decline in median family income was Glenbar. Glenbar was jolted by this diminution of its "exclusive" suburban tone. Many older residents blamed the newcomers for tarnishing the community's image:

> Mrs. Clark told me the people who used to live in Glenbar were here because they liked the type of life you could live here, the gardens and open space. Now the people who come are either escaping the city or are coming here because of the status of living in Glenbar, even though this status is not as great as it once was.

While the differences in the class of the original settlers and the new residents is not great, the meaning of living in Glenbar differs markedly for these groups. For the former, moving to Glenbar was a sign of having the wealth to pursue life at a slower pace. Glenbar removed one from the press of business in the city, but those who moved to the town did not do so because they felt that the city was becoming uninhabitable. If the older residents led an upper-class existence, the newer residents represent the business and professional segments of the upper middle class. They are people who have substantial incomes but who, for the most part, have neither the leisure nor the financial resources to retire from making a living. As the demographic character of the city changed over time, Glenbar has become a different kind of retreat for some people. Newcomers are seeking to escape from what they see as deteriorating neighborhoods. These new families are not as wealthy as the older and more established segments of the upper middle class. As a school administrator remarks, this is reflected in funding for the high school:

> Wilson, an administrator, talked about the physical plant of the high school and related this to the change in the community. The new addition, although an excellent one, was not of the caliber of the present complex, and this said much about what was happening in the community. When the high school was originally built nothing was skimped on and the intention was to build a school that might be the best in the country. But now the people who are coming here are doing so for another reason: they are escaping the city. They are tightfisted, and the new high school building reflects this shift in the community. Money is now a problem.

The Midwest Railroad makes it possible for people to live in Glenbar and commute to work in the city. Glenbar has always been an island of affluence which contrasts sharply with neighboring communities. While neighboring middle-class suburbs became racially integrated and poorer suburbs became almost all black, Glenbar remained almost entirely white. In 1970 less than 1 percent of Glenbar's population was black, although it was located in the suburban sector with the greatest concentration of blacks. For many new residents who have business or professional ties in the surrounding areas, the move to Glenbar allowed them to remain in the area without staying in racially mixed communities.

There are fewer children in Glenbar under five and old people over sixty than in the wider population, but the glaring difference is the absence of young people between the ages of twenty and thirty. Adults who are at or near the peak of their earning capacity and who have school-age children are attracted to Glenbar. The age group between the school-age children and their parents is missing. This skewed age distribution has become a demographic fact of life; the young continually leave and rarely return to Glenbar.

Unlike other suburban belts in the metropolitan region where neighboring towns are very much alike, Glenbar sticks out like a sore thumb. It is as if an accident of history—the extension of the railroad and the development of country clubs around the turn of the century—has withstood the general tendency of the towns in this area to reflect the industrial character of its economy. Glenbar, in contrast to the surrounding area, is a preserve of the most successful strata of the white-collar world: people in managerial, entrepreneurial, and professional occupations. Their business and professional lives are completely detached from their domestic concerns. The separation between home and work identifies Glenbar as a prototypical suburban dormitory community.

Nowhere in American life is the opposition between disparate meanings of the idea of community so acute as in Glenbar. In terms of its cultural homogeneity, physical boundedness, and class composition, there are few places that look more like a community than Glenbar. However, in terms of communal relations and cultural traditions that unite the generations and link members of nuclear families into larger and more enduring forms of associations, none of the places we have studied is less of a community. We must take the notion that Glenbar is a place to live quite literally. By moving to Glenbar, these upper-middle-class people have chosen an area that is consistent with their ambitions for their children and their status in the larger society. Such a choice has either detached or liberated them, depending upon one's point of view, from the relations that arise out of propinquity and residential stability.

These upper-middle-class families have a highly developed sense of the separateness of the nuclear family. Where they live is less important than the kind of community in which they live. Living in a place where socioeconomic likeness creates institutions that will sustain the upward mobility of their children does not, by itself, translate into either strong civic consciousness or a corporate identity.

These people believe that each family must acquire the cultural resources that constitute an investment in its childrens' future. The metaphor of acquisition may be a little heavy-handed since the process also involves knowledge of how to monitor the social and academic progress of one's children rather than merely the purchase of certain kinds of educational services. Since the socioeconomic hierarchy of the larger society is so clearly etched in the minds of most parents, they are sensitive to one aspect of individualism in American life. They know that despite the almost pastoral tranquillity of the community a run of bad fortune or a slip in a family's resolve to stay ahead of the competition could result in the disappearance of this magical aura for them.

These families are neither so wealthy nor so successful that they cannot envisage what it would feel like to fall back into the great mass of people who struggle to make ends meet. As they remind their children, they don't want to go back to what they have worked so hard to escape: a life with limited horizons and without the sense of ease, superiority, and invulnerability of a place like Glenbar.

Many families move to Glenbar because they see it as an ideal place to raise their children. Not only will the carefully designed schools give their children a substantial advantage in the competition for places in good colleges and universities, but it also is a very protected environment. Glenbar lacks the distractions and dangers of the city. In Glenbar, young people are raised with peers who come from similar homes and whose parents have similar aspirations. There is no conflict of cultural styles and social backgrounds. It is assumed that everyone appreciates the safety and security of living in a community that does not foreclose enjoying the pleasures of the city. Glenbar is something of a hothouse where young people can be nurtured and their abilities cultivated without having to weather the storms that afflict less-sheltered environments.

One of the most prominent features of the culture of Glenbar is its faith in the ability of professional educators to supplement whatever understanding of the world that families cannot communicate to their children. Without a rich neighborhood life and without a network of youth-serving institutions, Glenbar relies on school to provide their children with whatever is needed to develop a sense of themselves as persons who occupy a particular niche in the wider society. While teachers recognize that the community places a very high value on education, teachers are hired because of their expertise and have little connection to the community outside of formal school activities. The fieldworker reports a conversation with a young teacher in the high school:

Rich lives in the city and doesn't know much about the social lives of the kids in the community. He sees them only in the classroom or after class and rarely in any role other than the teacher-student relationship. Rich feels that a problem that many of the kids have is that they have no contacts with any adults other than their family and the professionals they meet in very structured situations. That is one reason he thinks many of them don't know what they want to do when they get out of high school. They don't know what they could possibly do if they didn't go to college—there are not other models around who aren't teachers, doctors, or dentists.

The culture of Glenbar lacks a viable model of intergenerational relationships. Parents represent the adult world in general to their children. This so skews young peoples' perception of the older generation that they often respond to nonfamilial adults as if they could play no significant role in their lives. That is, they unconsciously react to many adults as if, outside of the specific service they provide, they are merely *non*parents. Youth in Glenbar are almost uniformly polite when approaching their elders. For this reason many adults have trouble locating the source of emotional distance they experience when dealing with young people in Glenbar.

What this teacher is talking about involves more than the absence of a broad and enriching range of contacts between youth and adults outside of specific functional contexts (e.g., coaching or teaching dance). The culture of Glenbar lacks a clear image or set of images of what makes a man or woman worthy of a young person's respect above and beyond the talents by which he or she makes a living. The parents of the youth of Glenbar invest so much energy in their business and professional careers that their occupational identity determines their sense of what is most meaningful about themselves. Yet, the occupational world is so detached from the day-to-day experience of Glenbar that most youth can only assimilate vague images of what kind of human being engages in specific professional or business activities.

By putting the most valuable part of themselves in another world, the adults of Glenbar have denuded its landscape of people who they see as having a significant bearing on the course of their lives. Consequently, their evaluations of neighbors, friends, and other local adults do not have that fateful quality one finds in most communities. In turn, this makes it difficult for youth to distinguish

between the moral standing of an adult in the community and his or
her professional identity in the wider society.

Parents and Children

Youth in Glenbar are aware of the variation in parental concern
with deviant activities and with the importance parents place on
supervision of their children's activities. Yet there is consensus on
one point: all parents stress the importance of doing well in school.
One young man says:

> Some parents don't care what their kids do [whereas] other
> parents are super dominating [with respect] to control. The only
> common thing about living in this town is that there are certain
> expectations you have to live up to—that you have to work
> hard in school and [eventually] make some money. My parents
> want me to make good grades and want me to be a professional.
> They don't care what [I am] as long as I'm happy.

This pressure to succeed in occupations that require many years
of schooling is usually muted by the refrain, "but all my parents
want is for me to be happy." The contradiction is more apparent
than real because both youth and parents assume that a reasonable
degree of material affluence is a prerequisite for personal happiness. Yet the deeper ambiguity in the culture of Glenbar that concerns the degree to which parents are willing to allow young people
to make their own choices is not so easily resolved.

When parents sense that their control over their adolescent children is waning, they use the combination of the carrot and stick.
One young man says that now that he drives, his parents "hold [it]
over my head." What is at issue here is not only the youth's compliance with his parents' rules but their sense of his lessening enthusiasm for sticking to the path they have set out for him. This young
man discusses the fine line he must walk between self-assertion and
compliance to parental wishes. He associates this mild resentment
of having to deal diplomatically with his parents with a sense of
diminishing investment in anything outside of friendship:

> I've just cut about two feet of hair. I have to talk [to his par-
> ents] with respect which doesn't bother me a heck of a lot.
> When I got mad I didn't restrain myself. I said what I felt
> whereas now I'm going to play their game with them to some
> extent. I hate living up to expectations or having to do some-

thing. If they asked me if I would do this, I'd probably do it, but if they tell me to do it I'll do it but be mad about it . . . I don't give a damn about all the institutions I once felt tied to. Except for my close friends, I don't feel that anything is important.

To a certain extent, this has the ring of the complaints of privileged youth. Showing one's parents some respect and living in accord with ambitions one privately has for oneself cannot be too onerous. However, there is more here than an attempt to define oneself in a situation where all struggles seem a little ridiculous since the worst one can do if one fails is to skin one's knee. Yet, this youth is not so self-centered that he does not appreciate the effort it took for his parents to provide him with this sort of environment. What is hidden behind this seemingly weak sort of rebelliousness (i.e., "if they tell me to do it I'll do it but be mad about it") is a feeling of incompleteness that is somehow redressed by the intimacy of friendship. Note, however, that while this young man claims to have an emotional antidote to the enervating task of "playing their game," he is not about to seriously try to change the rules of the game.

Authority in the family is a mix between parental injunctions, negotiation, and compromise. Parents tolerate a good deal of discussion over the rationality of their rules. But there is a reserve clause in this appeal to the good sense of their children. Parents often say that as long as their children are economically dependent, parental wisdom is the final voice in disputed matters:

They won't let me do [certain] things like buy a motorcycle, go hitchhiking, have women in my bedroom. They can't say why [he shouldn't do these things]. They just say it's my house and [you'll] do it the way I want you to, that as long as I am living with them I'll have to accept it whether I want to or not.

At the same time, this young man said that his parents know he uses marijuana with some regularity and occasionally does "mood changers." While they accept the former and disapprove of the latter, he remarks that after he was caught using pills he was watched closely and grounded for a month but that his parents know "there was nothing they could do about it." In Glenbar, both youths and parents are keenly aware of the fact that proscriptions on deviant behavior are only partially effective. Consequently, there is a heavy investment in the idea that young people must develop the powers of discernment that prevent them from doing anything that would be self-destructive or foolhardy.

Deviance in Glenbar does not center so much on doing the wrong thing in a public situation or getting into trouble with the law. Rather, deviance involves a failure of personal and familial ambitions. It raises, for adolescents, the specter of the cessation of emotional support on the part of one's parents. That is why friendship is so vital since peers can reassure each other that they are the last line of defense against the loss of nurturance. And they can assure each other that nurturance cum intimacy has nothing to do with their parents' insistence on success.

Mutual closeness and understanding between friends is experienced as the antithesis of the vague yet encompassing expectations of one's parents not to do anything that forecloses the possibility of doing well later in life. Incidentally, what attracts these youth to mild forms of deviance such as doing drugs and protects them against involvement in serious violations of the law is something that escapes hedonistic or utilitarian theories of adolescent motivation. These young people are drawn to activities that make them feel as if their relations with friends fills in what is otherwise absent in their lives: the sensation of an expressive wholeness that is, in some ways, stimulated by the culture of Glenbar only to be withheld in the service of instrumental goals.

There is little in the way of harsh punishment, authoritarian control, or humiliating surveillance in this community. Yet many parents fear the expressive spontaneity of youth even though they do not attempt to repress it. They realize that rigid controls over youthful behavior would defeat their primary goal: making youth capable of dealing effectively with situations that require fine judgment. One cannot expect young people to show considerable initiative with respect to a demanding academic environment and ask that they mechanically conform to the rules.

By way of contrast, we should note that working-class communities like Cambridge and Parsons Park would regard this faith in the judgment of adolescents as misplaced. It is the responsibility of the older generation to inculcate moral precepts into the mind of adolescents. Authority figures in working-class communities can point to evidence that young people do not necessarily gravitate toward the good. At the same time, this apparent moral rigidity supplies something that is missing in Glenbar. It outlines the boundaries of the moral community. In Cambridge and Parsons Park there is very little doubt about what sorts of things will put young people beyond the pale of respectable society. In Glenbar, adults are so used to thinking of adolescent behavior in terms of its psychological, social, educational, and legal consequences for a youth's personal development that they are almost incapable of defining modes of conduct that are intrinsically right and wrong. While youth in Glenbar cannot quite put their finger on it, they sense that adults do not operate with a consistent moral vocabulary. Thus, just about anything can be either good or bad depending upon how, where, and with whom it is done.

The cost for this concession to the autonomy of youth is the fear of their being pulled into deviance that destroys the very qualities of the culture Glenbar nurtures. One young man speaks about parental reactions to the presence of drugs:

> They're scared. They're afraid of everything—of long hairs, of hippiedom, of their kid jumping out of the window and killing themselves. They're afraid that one joint will lead to going on hard things like acid. Parents want to see the kids around here in homecoming, proms, football games, sports; good clean American fun.

While this young man sees other parents as being overly concerned with conventional activities, his own parents are tolerant of his own efforts to find a path between rejection of the value of success and mindlessly going along with the program.

> Socially [my parents] have always been radicals, somewhat liberal to say the least. I don't know why but they haven't had such vast amounts of money [as other people in Glenbar]. My parents used to have some expectations, like they weren't too sure because I didn't perform as well as they might have liked me to in high school. My whole refusal to conform has made my parents think a lot more, to accept the fact that I smoke marijuana, that I did participate in antiwar demonstrations, that I was questioning the system. My parents have always made an effort that we be on truthful terms. If you sort of lay it on them slowly you get to where you have him understand that you smoke dope, show him why you're experimenting with this, and the potentials of it. Then they're more ready to accept [it]. They have to know more about it.

Despite the somewhat sanctimonious tone of the way this young man describes how he educates his parents, there is a reference to an ambiguity in the culture of Glenbar. In ordinary usage, we tend to think of achievement and performance as near synonyms. Achievement refers to the completed process of striving after a goal whereas performance refers to the activity by which such a goal is attained. However, in upper-middle-class culture, achievement and performance can be quite different.

Performance is inherently hierarchical. It ranks persons in terms of how well they do at tasks that are defined as indicators of individual skill, ability, or worth. Performance does not involve assessments of the inherent value of whatever is sought after. Its justification is that it serves as a universally applicable standard according to which individuals are judged as better or worse than one another. A good example of performance are school entrance examinations that rank individuals on national standards but have no demonstrable connection to anything other than the sort of intellectual acuity that performs well under pressure, solves problems in ways that are congruent with conventional images of intellectual competence, and can pick up clues from highly generalized questions. Achievement is more content oriented and may have little or nothing to do with skills or abilities that can be translated into universally measurable units of performance. Writing a perceptive paper or constructing an interesting argument are good examples of an achievement.

This young man seems to confuse achievement and performance. In this respect he is like many of his peers in Glenbar. Achievement, whose primary meaning is a job or task that is well done, can have a value or significance that is defined by the self regardless of the evaluations of others. Performance invariably involves an audience-oriented element which makes it impossible to conceive of a solitary accomplishment whose meaning is incapable of being translated into terms that are highly negotiable currency in the wider society. This young man seems to have convinced his parents that their expectations for his work in school were a matter of performance and not of achievement.

This desire to throw out the intellectual baby with the academic bathwater is common among youth in Glenbar. Many youth in Glenbar try to avoid unthinking conformity to externally imposed expectations. What this young man fails to see is that he is caught in a sterile opposition between working hard at school for instrumental rewards and self-exploration through the emotional revelations of drugs and friendship. He has not found an activity that is valued precisely because it transcends the opposition between the economic payoff of succeeding academically or losing oneself in the pleasures of the moment.

This has little to do with deviance per se but rather replicates an opposition that we encounter frequently in Glenbar. Youth experience a disjunction between the rationality of the goals authority holds out and the reasonableness of the means to attain them. This protest at having to labor in the academic fields to reap the benefits of admission to a good college falls a little flat unless we realize that the omnipresent pressure to do well obscures the distinction between those who define their own image of achievement and those who succumb to the power of performance to determine one's social destiny.

What is apparent in this youth's discussion of how he tells his parents about his deviant activities is that his ability to calmly discuss the advantages and dangers of dope must be reassuring to his parents. Parental authority depends upon the hope that adolescents will be conscious of what they are doing and will see the negative side of deviant involvements. In this sense, then, this youth satisfies one of the normative principles of Glenbar: if one accepts what he says, his behavior is guided by knowledge of what he is getting into.

The Adolescents' Perspective

The dominant motif of adolescence in Glenbar is the feeling of a gentle yet nevertheless pervasive constraint of control without much overt conflict between the generations. This is experienced as living in a world where the crucial decisions have already been made by other people.

> This place never seemed like the real world. I always had a fear about being run down a certain chute. I never had much control over what was going on. Of course, when I was younger, I just took things as they are and keep on going along. And now things are changing for me. I can alter my life a little bit. More things are open to me now than they were before, and maybe when my brother goes to college things will change for him, too.

While the passage to college can be liberating, the absolute certainty that one is going to go to college goes to the heart of the way these young people experience adult control. They feel that their whole lives have been organized to get them to college. Even if that prospect is attractive, their desire for independence is confounded by the realization that they are being processed through a system set up by adults. A high school senior, Cindy, says:

> While things like the courses at school can be stimulating, kids around here just want to get through school—they don't care

about learning. The school is a place to go through and graduate from and go to college. Around here it's not "Are you going to college"—it's "Where are you going to college?" I know you don't have to go to college, but kids just assume they're going because they've heard it so often. At school they call in all the juniors and ask them about their plans, and if a kid says he's not going to college the counselor will ask him why he's decided on such a dramatic decision.

There is little in the way of deep resentment about the expectation that everyone must go to college. What many youth feel is missing from their lives is more ambiguous. Though it is difficult for them to say exactly what bothers them about being given these privileges, they feel they lack the power to make genuinely consequential decisions about their own lives. And what they do not say, but nonetheless feel, is that they lack enough experience in the real world to know how to make a fateful choice that goes directly against the grain of conventional wisdom. At best, they can see that they can make minor, correctable mistakes but are almost never in a position where they could irreversibly set the pattern for their lives without at least the tacit approval of their parents.

While many would be afraid to take a chance with their prospect of ending up a part of the affluent middle classes, even those who would go off in their own direction have almost no knowledge of how they might do that. Despite their cosmopolitan values, they have yet to encounter a situation where they cannot fall back upon their families for aid and advice. While that is comforting, these young people also know, since their parents never tire of telling them, that the "outside" world is a hard place and that they will have to struggle for what they get. But, for now, any sign of what that struggle will be like is absent, save for the routine of academic testing and grading. Some youth suspect that college will be little different than high school and that they will slide smoothly throughout life without ever having stopped to figure out whether where they are going is consistent with what sort of person they hope to become.

Mert, a high school senior, is uneasy about taking the path that has been laid out for him:

> I feel I should to to college when I'm completely ready for it. If I feel ready for it the first day next year it will be only because I've been completely programmed in that direction since I was about age zero. It's never really occurred to me to not go to college; it has, now, but not as a distinct possibility. I may go to college, smoke a lot of dope, and not get anything done for the

first year which would waste my parents' money, whereas at the same time I could be out working at whatever I could do to support myself. Then, when I was ready for college and wanted the knowledge, I could go. [Why don't you do this?] I really don't know why I don't do that. Something's wrong. I keep having these ideas that everyone is scheming, everyone has these things they know and are hiding from me. It's just that I see certain capabilities in myself that I could try to fulfill, but it's like my parents are putting value judgments on different professions. You can never accuse a parent of saying that being a lawyer is better than an actor, because they probably never said that. It's just what they've been saying for the whole seventeen years of your life that has sort of been ingrained into you.

The message, as Mert observes, that parents deliver to youth is subtle. Parents almost never take an authoritarian posture and say, in effect, "You have to do what I want you to because I know best." Parental authority, moreover, is predicated upon respect for their children's individuality. As Mert says, they would never come right out and tell him what or who to be. Yet the communication between parents and children in Glenbar is hardly neutral on such a culturally significant topic as a young person's education. In many ways, parents let children know two facts about their situation in the world. Most parents are salaried professionals and businessmen whose income does not come from inherited wealth and who cannot pass their positions on to their children. What they can give them, however, is an educational head start, a jump on the competition, so to speak. Their adolescent children know that education does not mean the pursuit of knowledge for knowledge's sake. The communication from parents to children is heavily loaded with the message that one has to make the "right" career choices or one is likely to be left out in the cold economically. The second is that everything one does now must be evaluated in terms of its possible effect on the future. Whether something feels right or wrong in terms of one's personal sensibilities matters far less than whether it looks rationally useful as far as one's success in the adult world is concerned. The present is something that should, according to the culture of Glenbar, be sacrificed for the future because where one ends up in the socioeconomic system is infinitely more important than how it feels at any given moment to get there.

Adults believe that a young person ought to develop according to his or her own innate potential and that parents ought to intervene if a young person begins to move in the "wrong" direction. At a more general level, the culture of Glenbar is sensitive to variable patterns of adolescent development and is equally committed to the normal as that which is socially acceptable and psychologically useful in the course of a young person's career. The message from adults is to be responsive to one's own inclinations and interests while never losing sight of the fact that one's talents must be harnessed to goals that have instrumental value in the long run.

These articulate and self-conscious youth have been encouraged to develop a sense of personal initiative that will give them the inner resources to mark out a special place for themselves in the world. And, of course, with the right backing these youth are ready to do just that. Yet, beneath Mert's complaint that his parents would want him to choose the more conventional career of a lawyer than an actor is his ambivalent feeling about his uniqueness. Mert would like to see himself as someone who has whatever it takes to distinguish himself in the world. Since specialness for Mert resides in the desire to be different without a compelling sense of what would make him stand out from the crowd, it is easier for him to symbolically recast his doubts about himself in the form of a complaint about his parents.

It would be wrong to dismiss Mert's complaint simply as the angst of growing up in a mildly elitist environment. There is a note of real passivity that informs these complaints about excessive support and overzealous but not crudely intrusive parental guidance. It is as if many of these youth are embarrassed to admit that their parents are right. That is, authority tells youth that prudence, conventionality, and economic security form a package. It is very difficult to have one without the others. And youth believe that but are unhappy with themselves for accepting it with so little real struggle. After all, actors can make as much or more money than lawyers. It is the fact that trying to become an actor involves real risk and uncertainty and the possibility of genuine failure that unnerves Mert. What bothers Mert is not so much that he will not have as much material security if he decides to become an actor but that he might discover that he is not as talented as he hopes he is.

The following passage shows how strongly formal and informal pressures bear on the adolescent who is thinking about stepping outside the path that has been set up for them. Amy, a college sophomore, tells her story:

My whole senior year in high school I didn't want to go to
college. This teacher, Mr. Moore, said that college was the most

unreal atmosphere, that you're stuck in this little community for four years, and you don't know what's going on—you're suckers. Well, I believed this and said I wasn't going to college. I had all these applications and I wouldn't apply. Finally I applied to State U because I said if I decided to go to school it's the cheapest. But I didn't get in. I missed the cut-off by half an ACT point or something really absurd. I just didn't know what to do after that. I remember getting really upset about it. I decided I wouldn't go, but then I went to talk to my counselor who decided I would.

I didn't know what else to do, because everybody around me was going to college. I guess I had to. I really don't think I believed in the end that I would go, but I applied anyway just in case. That's how I operate. My life is "just in case," and earning money "just in case." My father is really bad about this—he pushed you thinking about college long before you really should think about it. I was away on a trip one summer and at the end of one of my mother's letters he wrote, "I hope you're thinking about college."

This young woman's teacher challenged her to do something about the complaints about the insularity of the community and the unreality of life in it. He touched the sore point in these young peoples' image of themselves: that they know nothing of what it is like to make out on your own in a world in which no one is watching out for your best interests. For a moment, she was tempted to break out of the mold that had been laid out for her life. But, as she reveals, she could not make such a drastic move without a second opinion. She asked her counselor for advice. This was akin to asking a banker whether it is a good idea to save money. In essence, what this young woman did was to take the safety clause she complained about having been thrust upon her by her parents. She chose to do something that did not feel completely right for her at this time but which is guaranteed to offer her at least a modicum of security. This is not so much financial security but simply knowing what to expect by going away to school rather than having to start at the beginning. What she sacrifices, however, is the very value that she sees the adult community taking away from her: control over the course of her life.

The High School

Built in the 1950s to hold 2,000 students, Glenbar High School has expanded to meet its present enrollment of almost double that amount by extending classroom wings into the flat land surrounding the school. The school buildings are modern and functional, attractive but without flair or ostentation. The school houses impressive laboratory and athletic facilities, work areas and practice rooms for the practical and fine arts, and an auditorium capable of handling professional level theatrical productions. The teaching staff is well-paid, energetic, and concerned with the quality of their instruction. The range of courses rivals that of many small colleges. Besides the traditional high school subjects, students may select courses such as existential literature, Shakespearean tragedy, economics, anthropology, human relations, political science, international relations, sculpture, filmmaking, architecture, environmental science, and child development.

Besides basic courses, the college preparatory curriculum of the high school is divided into honors, advanced, and intermediate levels. While the administration points out that this is not a tracking system inasmuch as students can seek whatever levels they are comfortable with in a particular subject, it does reinforce the idea that intellectual activity is hierarchically structured. It is no accident that the most intellectually demanding courses are called "honors" courses. Since this school has such a good academic reputation, students who make reasonable academic progress can ordinarily get into a four-year college.

Counselors encourage students to take courses appropriate to their academic level, which is determined by test scores, teacher recommendations, parental aspirations, and student ambitions. What usually happens is that a student ends up taking courses at one level, and his or her associations with peers are determined by the academic stratification system of the school. Eventually, presumably neutral indicators of intellectual ability become signs of more general competence and talent. Those on top of the academic hierarchy tend to look down on those below them. The fieldworker describes a conversation with two girls about academic levels:

> Nora and Sue both felt that there is a big tension between the
> intermediates and the honors kids. They said these two groups
> have almost no contact with one another . . . Nora said you
> don't feel right when you are in another level. She had picked
> an honors class when she was a freshman and just by the way
> the kids treated her she knew that she didn't belong in
> there . . . Sue mostly takes advanced classes. She said she
> doesn't care enough about history to take honors in that and
> she's not good enough to take honors in math or science. She

doesn't take intermediate classes because there is "sort of a stereotype" about intermediate classes: "they are filled with kids who goof off, and greasers, and strugglers—kids who just get by."

Disinterest in the academic side of school is nothing new. At one time, studies of upper-middle-class suburbs like Glenbar (see Coleman 1961) attributed this anomolous state of affairs to the influence of the youth culture. Young people whose lives were supposed to center around their academic prowess were drawn to images of the gifted athlete and the pretty, popular cheerleader. Social competence and personal attractiveness rather than an inquiring mind and a studious orientation held sway in the youth culture of the 1950s. In the 1970s there is no indication that this disinterest in the academic side of school is due to a pervasive concern with popularity and athletic stardom, although the "jock" and "socialite" are still very much in evidence.

In this light, the apathetic response of these young people to the intellectual content of school is puzzling. There are generally a curious and analytical group of young people. But, in school, this openness to the world seems to disappear. The fieldworker describes a literature class:

> Ted [a senior planning on attending an elite college] told me about his course in Protest Literature. They are reading *Johnny Got His Gun* by Dalton Trumbo. Ted went into detail about how horrible it is as Johnny gradually discovers that he has no arms and then no legs, and then no face. He is just a mass that doctors want to keep hidden from the public because if anyone saw him they would be so sickened that they would stop fighting. Ted said that the book is gory, but it's really good.
>
> [One week later in Ted's class] Ted introduced me to the teacher—a harried-looking man in his twenties—and he welcomed me to sit in on the class. They were discussing *Johnny Got His Gun.* The teacher lectured on points in the book, but no one seemed very interested in what he was saying. Ted who had cornered me to talk about the book now sat sullenly slumped down in his chair and didn't say anything. Other kids had their heads on their desks and seemed to be asleep. There was a constant undertone of murmuring and side comments along with the teacher's lecture.

At first glance, this lack of response to the book in class may look like a classic case of peer pressure. Ted is afraid to reveal his intellectual enthusiasms in front of the other students. But Ted does not stand out from the crowd in this respect. Many of the other students are equally articulate about this kind of material. Ted, in other words, is not afraid to look like a "brain" in front of other students because he knows that his ability to handle this material is little different from theirs. Nor is Ted communicating his dislike of the teacher as a person or of his teaching style. This response occurs so often in different classrooms that many students are aware of the curiously tepid atmosphere of the classroom. A withdrawn, low-key, and circumspect involvement in classroom discussions and activities is the norm around the college-oriented students in this school.

Ted, like the majority of academically sophisticated students in this school, makes a radical separation between his private enthusiasms which are communicated to friends and his public involvements in the formal culture of the school. Moreover, there is little, if any, disrespect for the teacher or contempt for learning in this lukewarm attitude toward the classroom. It is, ironically, that for Ted the classroom is not the appropriate place to share one's insights in the world with one's peers. That is too precious, in the culture of Glenbar, to disclose in what is experienced as the impersonal environs of the classroom. The fieldworker comments on another class:

> In a middle level American history class the teacher, Mr. Moore, is trying to lead a discussion on the difference between a strict and a loose interpretation of the Constitution. Moore is pacing back and forth, waving his arms, gesturing, speaking loudly, and filling his remarks with anecdotes and references to current affairs. He talks about the Bank of America, Jefferson, whether or not certain political parties have their base in the states, and the kinds of judges Nixon now wants. I think that Moore is a fascinating lecturer, but the students around me are distracted and bored. Moore now says, "We come to the most famous law case in the country's history." This doesn't seem to get anyone too interested, and Moore, pausing a moment, says, "This case will be especially important for those of you who will be taking college entrance exams or special social science achievement test." At this, several kids look a little more alert and carefully note down the essentials of the *Marbury vs. Madison* decision.

Moore understands the culture of Glenbar even though his classroom presentation is not predicated upon treating knowledge as something whose value is purely pragmatic. Nevertheless, in Glenbar, young people, teachers, and parents know that it is how well one does on standardized achievement tests that is the crucial factor in shaping one's future career. There is little dissent among students about the pervasive concern with test scores and with cognitive skills necessary to do well in this kind of academic competition. What is not clearly recognized in Glenbar is that this emphasis on keeping ahead of the competition and on learning whatever is necessary to do well on tests removes a good deal of the personal significance of education. These students are willing to grant to their parents what their parents' values dictate: getting ahead and future career are the preeminent concerns of schooling. Yet they are not willing to invest this process with expressive meanings that involve what they experience as the most vital parts of themselves. Consequently, they hold back, almost without thinking about it, those feelings, perceptions, and ideas that reveal their sense of who they are from the educational process.

The decision several years ago not to build a second four-year high school but to expand one facility has led to rules and procedures that both teachers and students experience as burdensome. Yet the authority system of the school is set up to encourage individuality, growth, and initiative. Teachers try to minimize the sort of routine make-work that many students find so boring. They are reluctant to impose the kind of form following—spending a good part of the class period taking attendance for example—that dissipates the relaxed atmosphere they believe is conducive to learning. The teacher's authority is based on expert knowledge, and many teachers communicate their own distaste for bureaucratic regimentation to the students.

This message that individuality cannot be mechanically programmed is aimed at a receptive audience. One might assume that this common value on individuality might constitute the basis for a strong alliance between teachers and students. But teachers report incidents where they have gone out of their way to increase the freedom given to students without any acknowledgment of that act on the part of students. The fieldworker describes a typical incident:

Mr. Williams said to the class that he had something to say to them before they began today. "Five years ago I was working with some students who were making films and they had gotten permission to film in the tunnels that go underneath the school—a fascinating place. But once they decided to go down there without telling me and they were caught and the problems landed on my shoulders. Two years later on a beautiful spring day the class met outside, and I told them to keep it quiet so we could continue it. But someone blabbed it around, and I received a call from the administration saying that from now on in order to leave the school building a teacher needs to fill out a special field trip form. [Laughter.] Last year we decided to make things more comfortable in one of the classes, so we brought in a coffee maker and a little goodies. This lasted two weeks, until some big mouth talked to another teacher about it and she decided to cook her breakfast at the school and the smell was all over. Three days later a 'no cooking' order was received by the administration. Yesterday, five students from this class walked off and got into trouble." Williams paused and then he proceeded in a weary, slow voice. "Now, I have no control over what you do in the halls, nor do I have a great concern over it, because it's your life. But if you do it again, the whole program that I have been trying to set up will be jeopardized. If one person gets in trouble, that's ok, but when there are five this comes back on me. I hope you all understand. OK, let's start today's assignment."

One's first response to a story like this is to say that these students are spoiled. They do not appreciate teachers who really go out of their way to make things more comfortable and interesting for them. Yet, as the teacher realizes, something more is involved here than the narcissism of adolescence. The lack of responsiveness to the teacher's kind gestures reveals the absence of moral bonds between the generations in Glenbar. Most youth are genuinely attached to their parents, but they are incapable of seeing those qualities in nonfamilial adults that they value in their friends. These youth speak eloquently about the importance of sensitivity to the feelings of friends. But they seem nearly blind to the same attributes they admire in their peers when they are manifest in their relations with adults.

On Mr. Williams's part, the feeling is less of irritation than a resigned acceptance of the fact that an opportunity for mutual confirmation of each other as vital and interesting people has been lost. He is neither shocked nor angry about what otherwise looks like a negation of his identity as a teacher because this sort of response, as he notes, is so deeply ingrained in the culture of Glenbar. On each occasion, Mr. Williams observes, he has taken the position of an adult who respects the character and judgment of the younger generation. And, on each occasion, students have found some way to avoid engaging him in a way that transcends the ordinary routine of the classroom.

There is a rather passive sort of resistance to the belief that all youth must move along the same path to a successful career. These students complain about being processed impersonally by the school. The fieldworker reports a conversation with a student:

> One student had just completed the computerized registration process and said to me: "I don't want to go back at all. If I could go on my own time and learn, then it would be good, but look at this [showing me a bundle of cards]! I went to register and I ended up with a pink card, and a schedule." "It's really official," I replied, "like . . ." I was going to say a college, she interrupted me and said, "Yes, like a prison."

There is more than a little irony in the not infrequent complaint that school is like a prison. Of all the high schools one might encounter, Glenbar High is least confining, restrictive, and arbitrary in its day-to-day routine. Moreover, its authority structure is collegial. Teachers go out of their way to involve the class in deciding how to proceed with class projects, and class discussions are organized to elicit as much spontaneous material from the students as possible. It would be seen as bizarre for a teacher to lecture to a class in a rigid and authoritarian manner without any respect for student interests and opinions. Disciplinary matters are handled in a low-key fashion and lack harsh overtones. In short, it is hard to conceive of a school less like a prison than Glenbar High except, perhaps, a school without teachers, classrooms, or grades.

Yet we ought not dismiss this complaint merely as adolescent exaggeration. As these students use the word, prison is a metaphor for a dilemma they experience as externally imposed upon them, but which, in actuality, is one in which they are complicit. At the cultural level, Glenbar encourages personal autonomy and intellectual creativity, and yet channels these inherently pluralistic interests into a narrow mold. Sensing this, the students resent this double message to be themselves and to explore their talents as long as that leads to the proper destination. But the pressure not to stray from the straight and narrow path to success is as much self-imposed as it is externally mandated. Rather than face what might be described as a failure of nerve, students pretend that the world has conspired to force them to see education as a goal-directed activity which can only be measured by practical results. In fact, many teachers spend a good deal of time trying to broaden their view of learning with little success because these students are so concerned with not falling off the track to a professional career.

There are perhaps few schools where the faculty tries so hard to create an environment that makes young people feel comfortable. The fieldworker remarks:

> Ms. Campbell's classroom is a double-sized room with pictures, posters, and maps covering the walls, models of log cabins and crafts on desks, chairs arranged helter-skelter and in groups, encyclopedia volumes lying in different places. In world history the class has decided that some wanted to work on their own and others in a seminar. Today the individual study group was listening to reports from each other on assigned topics because Ms. Campbell felt each should have some common background before going off on their own. The seminar group had divided up topics for each to present to the rest of the group, but today they had nothing planned and were sitting on their desks and talking.

It would be difficult to imagine a school of this size with a more consensual authority structure. Even in more conventional classroom settings where teaching methods follow traditional forms, there is a serious effort to dispense with extraneous coercion. Everything is arranged so that students are not forced to adjust to the teacher's rhythms and idiosyncracies but rather can go about their work without anyone looking over their shoulder.

> I went to algebra class with Paula and sat in the back with her and a friend. Kids took out their homework, exchanged them, and graded them as the teacher went over the problems on the board. There was a friendly and relaxed air to the class—there was fooling around and talking without anything being too noisy. Everyone was working and listening to the teacher who joked with the kids and let them work on their assignments. When he wanted to explain something to the whole class, he easily got their attention.

Despite the freedom from the intrusive modes of authority, students seem to almost perversely deny that this is the situation at Glenbar. Instead, they often claim that the reverse is the case. That they are being manipulated, controlled, and standardized by impersonal authorities who could not care less about them as individuals. In the following exchange between an egalitarian teacher and students, some of the latter seem to insist that the freedom he allows them to express their opinions and to structure class projects is illusory. Rather, these students charged that instead of being treated as equals, they were intentionally kept in the role of infants.

Mr. Slater ran his U.S. history class so that one day a week the class could discuss anything it wanted. Today June raised the question, "Why can't teachers treat students like equals and learn from them, too?" Patty said, "It's hard for teachers and students to be equals because the teachers know more, but it's possible to learn from the students." June replied that things are so formal and uncomfortable in here—"Why can't we call you [Mr. Slater] by your first name? That would be a better way to share different things." Slater said that if June objected to him calling her by her first name he would call her Miss Smith. June said that was exactly what she didn't want—she wanted everyone to be equal and informal. Patty felt that calling someone "mister" because you had to is a false kind of respect. Slater agreed but didn't seem convinced. Stu pointed out that there are lots of ways that things are set up to cut down equality between the teacher and the students: "All the kids are here in rows, and maybe this is necessary for expediency, but we are just like cattle." June broke in and agreed— "We're herded in and out with the bells and then we get to another cattle station where we're fed and watered." [Laughter.] Slater said, "Some students will take advantage of the teacher if he becomes more familiar with them." June shouted out, "How can you generalize since you haven't tried it? You'll never know if you are taken advantage of until you try it. We're always treated like infants around here." Slater said he thought he didn't treat them like infants, and Patty responded that it is not him, it is the whole system that acts that way . . .

Earlier, we mentioned that the bonds between the generations are truly impoverished in Glenbar. This incident discloses how little these students understand intergenerational relationships where a certain amount of formality and distance creates openness and receptivity to the other person. For these youth, all difference, even that associated with age, status, and authority, is antiegalitarian, and what is not egalitarian and peer-like precludes mutual understanding and recognition. They are saying to the teacher that unless we are all alike in important respects our relationships must be mechanical and lifeless.

What these youth are doing, albeit unconsciously and unintentionally, is foreclosing the possibility of learning something from a teacher's greater experience of the world that would probably be of considerable interest to them. There is a child-like insistence on the part of these students for authority to be completely transparent. It is almost as if they want their teacher to confess that he knows no more than they and that his assessments of their work are merely a matter of personal opinion, of no greater consequence for their intellectual development than the judgment of a peer.

For all of their adherence to the value of equality, these young people seem not to understand that equality is not equivalent to uniformity. Equality is predicated upon the noninvidious recognition of real differences between persons. Respect for the other person arises out of this perception of the positive significance of difference rather than out of some homogenizing feeling of sameness.

This diffuse animus the students feel toward authority arises from their own inability to either fully accept or reject the idea that they have no other choice than to keep their noses to the academic grindstone. Getting good grades requires discipline and effort. It is emotionally safer for most of these students to complain that they are being pushed around by an impersonal institution than to refuse to do the work. In other words, these students are willing to critique the system but not to jeopardize their place in it. It is much safer to accuse Mr. Slater of pulling rank by using the title "Mr." than to turn their back on college achievement tests.

Yet it would be unfair to the students not to point out that they experience school as devoid of positive emotional significance. The students feel powerless to resist the depersonalization of the student role, as is evident in comments the fieldworker recorded over a semester in a human relations course:

> Nothing I would have to say would be interesting to the rest of the class. If I saw a movie, the kids who hadn't seen it wouldn't want to hear about it and the ones who had seen it would already know about it. And school itself isn't interesting to talk about because everyone would already know and agree with anything I could say.
>
> There's nothing to say because we're different as people but we're not different as students. And the thing is that in school we are not people but are students.

This apathy and withdrawal is apparent in this comment by Gwen, one of the people who altered her behavior when in the school:

I'm different in school. I really get squashed. I can't make contacts with most of the people. Nobody wants to be there. If I'm learning, it's O.K., but lots of the time you end up sitting and the teacher is just talking and it's sort of empty. And it isn't all the teachers' fault. The kids don't give them a hand.

Extracurricular activities are seen by students as a way of finding a congenial group of friends. In this context students assert their individuality that is absent in their formal student roles. A teacher points out:

Many of the activities here at the school will be four-year entries into a particular social pattern. You will see kids group around the drama and speech things, and they will do marvelously well in them because their friends are in it, and they have summer plays. There is a close bond between them and their teachers—you will find the drama-speech kids spending spare time up in the projection booth of the auditorium where their teachers hang out. And these kids couldn't give a damn about the other kids [and vice versa]. They are winners of state play and speech contests, but probably 80 percent of the kids in the school never see a play or a debate.

There is a chasm between school and friendship. School is the place where one arranges to get together with friends whenever possible, but school is not something that can replace or substitute for the satisfaction of being with people who know and understand what one is like in one's private life. In this respect, school is as public a place in the eyes of these students as the post office. One would no more expose one's most valued feelings, perceptions, and dreams to others in school anymore than one would remove one's clothes in a public place. It is simply unthinkable for many of these students to invest the most meaningful parts of themselves in school because that presupposes something that does not exist: that striving for academic success is a value that brings people together or binds friends to one another. At best, academics is seen as irrelevant to the pleasures and difficulties of genuine friendship.

Friendship

There is a certain degree of irony in these young peoples' commentary on the relationship between their family life and their involvements with friends. They are resigned to the fact that their parents have influenced the way they respond to the world, and yet they feel that the choices they make in personally consequential areas of their lives should reflect their own sense of who they are. A young man comments:

> Your whole personality is impressed upon you by your parents. And most of your values. A lot of kids are trying to break away from it. They try to do their best to reject their parents' values and discover their own. They act as if they're not accepting their parents' values. Yet, really, when it comes to picking your friends, they follow the norm that their parents have handed down to them. Most parents in Glenbar believe you should be a good student, intelligent, and, though its an exaggeration, they don't want your friends to be an alcoholic from Steeltown Heights [a working class area]. They want properly raised up-per-middle-class kids.

After his critique of his parents' ability to communicate precisely what sorts of people they want their children to associate with, this young man admits:

> I usually find out that in the end the person my parents don't approve of [as a friend], I don't really approve of. I eventually get bored or disgusted with them.

For this young man it is not the potential conflict between his judgment about a friend and his parents' feeling about that person but the feeling that he is not locked into intimate relations with others on the basis of conventional stereotypes or superficial interests that is most important:

> I really don't know how other people would classify the majority of my friends: some of them have short hair and some of them long hair. I guess I used to be classified as a freak but now I'm not. Like some of my friends say, "He's a jock and he's sort of athletic." But each of us is unique. Each of us has different interests, and we have a lot of common interests.
>
> I pick my friends very carefully. My friends usually are very intelligent people—someone I can talk to intelligently, who understands me. I've known all of my friends for years and we've gone through a lot of stages and transformations together. So its really hard to say [what sort of people they are in terms of conventional stereotypes] . . . They are very warm, human people . . . They're just the average kid in the hall.

The youth culture in Glenbar puts a premium on friendships that are based on genuine intimacy: sharing feelings and ideas that constitute the core of the self. Exactly how one identifies this kind of emotionally honest and self-revelatory communication is less definite. One of the reasons for this sensitivity to genuine as opposed to convenient friendships is the extreme self-consciousness of these youth about their own perceptions of their own individuality. As one young woman points out, the need to define some activity or talent as the fulcrum of one's present identity complicates the problem of letting others know who you are as a unique human being. This student remarks:

> It is much harder to define a path for yourself than not make a choice at all. And so people, because they can't make an honest choice, take the path where they're going to meet challenges because they're trying to prove themselves. And their need of self identity . . . a sense of self can only be gotten through action of any sort—be it artistic pursuit, intellectual pursuit of a companion—something where you are communicating, where you are exchanging data, live information. I feel there is a great deal of confusion and complexity and a lack of self.

While this is not a model of clarity, this young woman's statement reflects the cross-currents that create a very complex image of friendship. On one hand, she believes that people like herself should choose their identity autonomously and without a need to justify themselves in the eyes of the world. On the other hand, she sees that it is in activities that bring a person into sustained contact with the social world that self is defined, and that implies getting involved in other peoples' ideas and projects. The issue is one of allowing oneself to become close enough to others to truly appreciate differences in personal aspirations, talents, and sensibilities but not depending upon others for one's own sense of inner direction.

For this young woman, this task is far from resolved as we can see in her image of friendship as something that abolishes differences and is free from hard choices:

> So many people build themselves into money because it's an easy thing to build yourself into. I must confess I have material wants too, but if I were out in the woods and I ran up to you or David [a friend] and all the trees were ours . . . everything was all ours except our own minds and bodies . . . and we would see each other as so much more alike than [our individual] ourselves and [than] all our possessions as opposing one another.

Though this free-flowing discourse is hard to interpret, the implicit opposition this girl perceives between the desire for material goods that sets people apart and the security of friendship that lacks competition and conflict plays a critical role in making intimacy such a powerful value in the youth culture of Glenbar. It is with friends that one experiences relief from the pressures that define individual striving for success or failure in terms of conventional values and rewards. And yet this kind of undifferentiated being together in some sort of retreat from the uncertainties of moving ahead in the world has an unreal quality.

Despite protestations to the contrary, we can see how deeply these youth have internalized their community culture. This girl is haunted by a feeling that she must strive relentlessly to become the sort of person she dreams she might become, although precisely who that person is and what that person does is left vague. She is affected by the feeling that the self must define itself through distinctions from others. Yet she resists this feeling because she fears that distinctions are invidious at base and build barriers to genuine understanding between friends.

This only partially conscious desire to be special fits nicely into a culture where hierarchy, performance, and individualism are core values. The ordinary solidarities between friends in which a young person feels neither attracted to absolute difference nor the desire for fusion through undifferentiated sameness is remote from the experience of many of these young people. It would be difficult for them to imagine living in a place like Ribley where both differences and similarities were largely taken for granted, and where very few youth felt any pressure to reach some position of preeminence among their peers. In Ribley, what made one special was the same thing that made one like others: each person's unique personality was woven into the collective history of their generation in the life of the town. More simply, just being recognized as the person one, in fact, was made a person special in Ribley.

This interest in friendship and intimacy is a masculine as well as feminine concern in Glenbar. Boys are equally absorbed by the subtle possibilities of self-disclosure and emotional openness to others that are part of their conception of genuine friendship. A young man describes a trip with a friend:

> You know we would sit out on the beach for five or six hours
> and we talked straight through the night. If anyone knows him,
> I do; no one could know him better. We could almost tell what
> each other wanted to do at a certain time . . . just from the

habit of the thing. It was the first time that I'd ever gotten that close to a guy. I'd gotten that close to girls like that. That's how Jennie and I were before she moved. But it was really cool to me that I could finally do that with a guy.

Another young man describes an experience with friends in the woods when they were "tripping" on acid:

We were singing and it was this whole spirit, like Ted started sword fighting with this stick. He called it younder stick and was leading an expedition somewhere. And we were feeling a closeness, I mean I knew exactly what was in everybody else's head, what they were thinking and going to do next, and they knew the same [about me]. It just seemed so perfect, everything fit together.

This feeling of being close, of really knowing how the other person experiences a situation, of being able to anticipate his response to an event, is one of the most valued aspects of friendship. Intimacy, in this respect, contrasts markedly with simple good fellowship and fun. It consists of the perception of having revealed an important aspect of the self to others and having that person reciprocate this gesture of trust.

It is not unusual for middle-class youth to look to friendship for the expressive meanings that lend some excitement and intrigue to the otherwise bland routine of going to school. Yet friendship has additional meanings in Glenbar. In Glenbar, friendship stands for all of the personal, intimate, and solidary aspects of human relationships as opposed to the abstract, impersonal, and instrumental demands of adult culture. This is often stated in the community as the conflict between immediate satisfactions and future success. But, for many youth, the issue goes to the core of their sense of self: do they stake their hopes to discover an enduring feeling of wholeness and individuality upon a promise of a future career, or do they invest their energies in their current friendships, knowing all the while that they are likely to be transitory?

Lisa talks about the pressure her father puts on her to think first and foremost of her future economic security and how this concern with the conventional path to a career interferes with her sense of the importance of the quality of present relationships:

My father wants his children to be happy which is typical of fathers, but at the same time he seems incapable of letting his children be themselves. He wants to make sure that his children don't get too far out of what's happening in the society in gener-

al so that they don't destroy themselves. My point of view is
just the opposite. I don't believe in adjusting; either you change
your environment or you go someplace else, but you don't
change yourself. My father used to say he didn't think you
should give up a permanent kind of happiness for a present kind
of happiness, but you have to be happy all the time or you're
never going to be happy.

Lisa recognizes the rational basis of her father's advice. It is a
difficult and impersonal world and without the proper educational
credentials it is not easy to survive economically. There is little bitterness in her awareness that he wants her to live a safe and conventional life, one where all risks are minimized. Lisa is not interested in a hedonistic mode of life where gratification of sensual im-
pulses contrasts with a stern devotion to academic progress.
Rather, her image of self-realization is embodied in the expressive
significance of a human encounter, and immersion in that kind of
relationship cannot be deferred or moderated in the interest of some
long-term goal:

I tried to tell him that I knew exactly what I wanted from my
life . . . and to me a good life at that moment was just one
where exciting things happened. He wanted me to be more
specific. He wanted me to say I want to be a teacher. To me the
idea of what you do or be, like a teacher or doctor, has so little
to do with my life it's incredible. The focus on my life was school
and friends, and in school it had a lot to do with the teachers
and people who were there. The main things in my life have to
do with my relationships with other people, because they have
to do with the fact that I want to know other people and I want
to love them and I want them to love and know me.

Underlying this dialogue between youth and parents about the
priority that should be put on friendship versus career, there are
antithetical images of the meaning of self-confirmation. Parents see
an atomistic and competitive world where the self is confirmed by
the economic and social resources it commands in a struggle with
others for limited goods. Youth do not deny that this is a true picture of the world but try to find trust, mutuality, and cooperation in
genuine, as opposed to convenient, friendships. In a class discussion, one young man remarks that the reasons people treat each
other in a "utilitarian" fashion is that:

because we are culturally trained to act in this way. Parents tell
you that you have to go to college in order to get ahead of the

next guy. In order to stop this kind of thing it would be necessary to skip a whole generation.

Social Identities

There is a remarkable degree of sociological sophistication among
these young people. They make a point of being able to grasp the
social criteria that divide people into groups and to conceptualize
the system of social relations of the peer world so that it can be
inspected dispassionately. For this reason, any social identity that
is ascribed to a young person on the basis of his or her group affiliation must be qualified by the culture of Glenbar itself. Here the
overriding principle is that individuality precedes all collective iden-
tifications. One's allegiance is, as far as cultural representations are
concerned, to one's inner light and not to "blind" social forces. In
Glenbar, then, individuality in the youth culture begins with an articulate recognition of the grounds upon which the peer society is
ordered, and individuality is realized by fashioning a personal identity that transcends that system. In other words, a young person
must be able to manage these social distinctions so that they do not
interfere with his or her friendships and activities.

Despite this emphasis on personal identity that is free from popular stereotypes, these students see freaks, greasers, jocks, socialites, and straights as salient social identities. Jocks and socialites
are, respectively, boys and girls who invest themselves in school
activities. They have a smooth, ingratiating presentation of self and
cultivate the sort of social self-confidence that merits approval from
adults. Freaks dress in a very casual manner, disdain involvement
in extracurricular activities, use drugs a little more openly, and,
generally, hold themselves back from showing any investment in
adult culture. Straights are neither conformists nor dissenters but
move, as far as possible, into their own friendship circles. They neither endorse or oppose adult authority but simply accommodate
themselves to it in order to pursue whatever interests or activities
resonate with their personal inclinations and tastes. Greasers are a
residual identity that appeals to the relatively few working-class
youth who attend this school.

There is a strong element of cultural continuity with the youth
culture of the 1960s which is reflected in the limited reality of any
categorical identity. Consciousness of the status markers in the adolescent social system of the high school provide real freedom from
being submerged in its internal distinctions and divisions. Looking
back at the early 1970s from the perspective of the mid 1980s, one

wonders if this ability to see oneself reflexively has been largely dissipated by the intense academic competitiveness and vocational orientation of upper-middle-class communities. In any event, awareness that others see one in a different light than one views oneself and that their perceptions may reveal some truth about one's conduct or character links these youth to the previous generation of self-critical youth.

In fact, a good deal of this generation's sensitivity to the meaning of intimacy and trust was generated by the previous generation's insistence that the authenticity of personal relationships were the standard by which social commitments and institutional policies were to be evaluated. If social arrangements diminished the possibilities of mutual exploration and personal discovery, then, whatever their other advantages or virtues, they were judged as humanly deficient. This is an ethic that is in keeping with the sensibilities of many youth in Glenbar, although the formal ideological tenets of the counterculture have disappeared.

Some social scientists (Schwendinger and Schwendinger 1985), on the other hand, credit popular stereotypes with profound social reality. Upper-middle-class youth are depicted as shallow conformists, much like the characters in "teen" movies where insensitive and opportunistic upper-middle-class "sophisticates" are bent upon their own pleasure and the humiliation of less fortunate peers. The "socialite" style in Glenbar lacks both the glamour and the notoriety that such descriptions are meant to convey.

Socialites

Socialites and *Jocks* are sex-specific terms for the same general social identity. Socialites do little that would cause trouble with their parents, teachers, or other adults. The socialites personify the way of life that is in keeping with the upper-middle-class, career-oriented nature of the adult community. In public, socialites are friendly and polite. This is often viewed as hypocritical by members of other groups who feel that this is a pretense because socialites back away if someone tries to move close to them. The congeniality of the socialites is a sign of social confidence, not an invitation to intimacy.

Socialites are more concerned with their public image than are the members of other groups. A long-haired senior boy remarks:

The only person who ever came up with a classification of me in a way that I came close to agreeing with was someone who

called me a long-hair socialite, a hippy socialite. It partly comes
from that I like talking to people. And it partly comes because
she said if I wasn't a socialite I wouldn't be worried about what
people think of me. Socialites are supposedly more worried
about what other people think about them. The kids that I
consider socialites do things just so that people will notice. It
doesn't matter if the normal kid walking down the hall sees him,
but that people in their group see them. So that they can sit
there and brag about it. "Wow, did you see what we did, man?
Was that ever cool!"

When this youth says that socialites are concered about what
other people think of them we should not infer that he was thinking
about how peers react to self-revelatory acts. He is not referring to
the fear that one may expose something about oneself that one
would rather keep from public view, which makes the thought of
finding oneself in an embarrassing situation quite painful. This reference to how other people think about oneself indicates the socialite's sensitivity to hierarchy.

On the surface, Glenbar High School was not a stratified society,
and people payed relatively little attention to status distinctions. In
fact, the fieldworker noted that there was disinterest in "popularity" and "social climbing" which had traditionally been staple features of middle-class adolescent social systems. However, because
the most obvious signs of social striving seemed to be missing from
Glenbar High School does not mean that all youth evaluated their
peers in egalitarian terms.

The socialite style emphasizes a person's presentation of self because it is grounded in the notion that one's public appearance and
demeanor reveals important properties about the self. When this
young man speaks of "coolness" as something that might not be
noticed or appreciated by the "normal kid walking down the hall,"
he discloses the core of the socialite ideology. Socialites stick together because they feel that they exemplify the qualities they admire. Coolness, as a certain kind of social self-confidence, poise, and
grace are attributes that elevate individuals above the ordinary
mass of their peers.

Thus, the observation that socialites are friendly but insincere
because they are amicable and polite on the surface misses the point
of this style. Socialites are not trying to hide their true feelings.
Rather, the very act of recognizing peers with whom one has little
or nothing in common and whose company they would disdain is
symbolic of a kind of social dominance and power. The socialite says,

in effect, to his or her peers that you may choose to recognize my
existence or not, and that will have no effect on my sense of innate
superiority. But when I recognize you, you will notice my regard
even though you may dislike me and prefer to look past me. Much
like the struggle for recognition that Hegel describes between the
master and slave, the socialite has a certain fearlessness and willingness to engage in psychological combat that most adolescents
prefer to pretend does not exist. It is more gratifying to accuse
socialites of being hypocrites than to admit that they dare whoever
thinks they are phony to challenge their public claim to preeminence. In the 1970s at Glenbar High School, there were no exclusive
social circles or social pyramid. But the instinct for social ascendan-
cy is so much a part of this style that it had a cold and impersonal
aura in the eyes of many other youth.

Freaks

Freaks publicly disparage the values of adult society and ridicule
the conventional world. Freaks disdain "school spirit," look un-
kempt to adults, and are often involved in drugs and rock music.
The freaks' public rejection of adult authority is usually only tenta-
tively voiced in private. Rarely do freaks do anything that would
prevent them from stepping back into the conventional world if they
so wished—rarely do they leave school, get in trouble with the police, or get so involved with drugs that the drugs dominate their
lives. They hold themselves above those who think that money is all
that matters, but they do not do anything that would cut themselves
off from a secure economic future.

Neither a life devoted to the mindless accumulation of money nor
a life of holy poverty is the issue here. Like socialites, freaks avoid
confronting whether they are going to allow their life to be orches-
trated by a performance-dominated culture. Looking scruffy and
making ironic comments about social conformity hardly addresses
the question of what sorts of personal sacrifices and emotional discipline one is willing to accept in order to insure success in the long
run. If the socialites seem oblivious to the fact that there is a choice,
freaks are adept at deferring it to some indefinite later date. Both
are conscious of the limited, provisional and contingent nature of
their high school identities. It would not surprise anyone to find that
they had more in common than a surface inspection of their appearance suggests. Though, theoretically, the freak and socialite
styles are the antithesis of one another, there is little antagonism
between adherents of these styles. Their differences are more over

how they deal with parental expectations instead of a statement
about whether they accept or reject adult values.

Straights

Straights are the largest group in Glenbar. The term "straight"
is not used in the sense of being conventional. What is conventional
in the adult world is characterized in the youth culture by the socialites who do *not* occupy the center of the youth world. The center
of the youth community is much "freakier," and straights occupy
that center. Straights dabbled in drugs and drinking, did satisfacto-
ry or well in school, planned on going to college, and were dissatisfied with life in the suburbs but not sure what to do about it.

What was distinctive about the youth culture of the 1970s in
places like Glenbar was that youth could describe themselves as
straight without feeling that they were cultural conservatives or
social conformists. Quite often, straight youth in the past comprised
the numerical majority but felt that they were a strangely residual
or submerged social category. It was as if their social persona had
little luster in the eyes of peers who did not know them personally.
This feeling of not being as socially attractive as peers with more
determinate social identities was not present at Glenbar High
School. No one felt inferior because they saw themselves as part of
the heterogeneous straight group. In fact, some youth commented
on the fact that since socialites were cliquish, they closed themselves off from developing friendships with people who were only
superficially not like themselves. And since friendship penetrated
beyond surface appearances into the "real" selves of intimates, it
was seen as constricting to limit oneself to contact with a relatively
closed circle of people.

Because straights were students who did not devote themselves
to "extreme" representations of shared sentiments, it was hard to
characterize them in positive terms. For instance, if socialites place
great value on maintaining a certain image in public, then that fact
can be used to characterize their relations with others. But since no
similar vice or virtue characterizes the straights, descriptions of
what they have in common are likely to be a hodgepodge of characteristics. For example, a seventeen-year-old male tries to describe
them to the fieldworker:

> There are all kinds of mixtures in between [the main groups].
> Kids who are combinations of these. You can't put them in one
> category. They're the straights—average kids. They don't do

drugs . . . but they may at least have tried grass—average student, average intelligence, has about five or six good friends . . . wears blue jeans. They may be interested in football, but they're not just totally athletic. They're not really towards one direction.

The fieldworker, however, did discern a strand running through the straight identity that he described as fatalism in the sense that these youth saw no way around the dichotomy between keeping their eye on the ultimate goal of success and being unable to invest any part of themselves that they valued in the process of reaching it. The value these young people give to intimacy and friendship is itself a form of compliant resistance. In other words, it is prudent not to fight the realization that one will have to make a living and that one would prefer to make a better rather than a poorer living. But, as we saw earlier, one withholds as much of oneself as one can from doing what is necessary not to fall off the track to success.

It is very difficult for these young people to imagine that this dilemma need not be experienced in an either/or fashion. Other generations have believed themselves capable of reshaping a stultifying moral order and of imposing their own values on the social arrangements that restricted their freedom. But to do so these youth would have to overcome this privatization of the self. They would have to experience forms of solidarity through collective action that are presently remote from their consciousness.

It is difficult to document this acute sensitivity to how the self appears to others in private contexts and near total disinterest in how humane values are related to action in public contexts. It is as if these youth were trying to invent a moral code that somehow could be detached from practical action. In the following discussion with the fieldworker, a perceptive young girl tries with the skill of a scholastic philosopher to distinguish between the meanings of being "nice":

> Nora had often used the terms "nice" and "nice" girls in pejorative contexts while at other times voicing her concern that she wasn't "nice." I asked her to explain what the word meant to her and her friends. She said that kind of nice that they made fun of and didn't want to be was the conforming kind of nice. That's what they mean when they talk about the nice little girls. Nora said she used to be this kind of nice. But now she is nearer a second kind of nice—the niceness that is convenient. You behave in a certain way, and you avoid hassles, and it helps you

get the things you want. But that isn't the kind of nice she
wants to be either. Nora is closer to the convenient nice than to
the conforming nice because related to the convenient nice is
the third kind of nice, the way she would like to be. This is the
caring nice. The nice you are when you care about other people.

Without pushing the interpretation of this passage too far, it re-
sembles an attitude that Hegel once termed the "law of the heart,"
where subjectivity and individuality are fused into a privatized morality. Whatever its philosophical grounding, this sort of response is
compliant, in the final analysis, with parental expectations because
it seeks no objective grounds upon which it can critique the limitations of instrumental authority. In other words, youth accept adult
authority as rational because they do not conceptually impose
bounds beyond which it loses its validity in the everyday world.
Rather, like Nora, they retreat to a charming world where they are
protected from the ravages of an untamed instrumental view of
human relationships. But, as so many of them commented, this
world of intimacy and trust was as transitory as adolescence itself.

Greasers

Greasers are a numerically small group. While the socialites expect to end up like their parents and accept the norms of Glenbar
society, and the freaks and straights expect to head toward upper-
middle-class culture but do not accept those values without reservations, the greasers neither value the culture of Glenbar nor expect
to become part of it. The greasers are on the periphery—culturally,
economically, ecologically—of Glenbar. They come from working-
class homes and most live in a visibly distinct neighborhood.

Socialites, freaks, and straights have contact with each other
through their personal networks, but the networks of the greasers
are more closely defined by the limits of their identity. Greasers
usually make up the basic sections of courses intended to supply the
minimal instruction necessary to get through high school and are
thereby academically segregated from the rest of the college-bound
students. Greasers feel that they get nothing out of school. This
becomes part of their identity, as illustrated by these remarks from
a nongreaser:

Greasers dress real sloppy and don't care about schoolwork.
They cause about 80 percent of the trouble. They're the kids
who don't study. They do a lot of drugs; they bully other people.

Drugs: Learning to Be Cool

A straight girl's comments about her parents' anxieties reveals how pervasive the fear of drugs is in the adult community. The fieldworker describes a request for advice on dealing with suspicious parents:

> Wendy broke the silence by suddenly asking, "As a sociologist, what do you think you should do when your parents don't believe you when you tell them that you aren't using drugs?" She said her parents were worried even though she has told them that she doesn't do that, she thinks they don't believe her. I asked her if she does use them and she said no. I then asked if she tells her parents the truth about things and she said yes. Then if she leveled with her parents and told them that she is telling the truth like she does about other things, wouldn't they believe her? She thought that this approach probably would work, but she did not like the whole idea of having to convince them she wasn't doing anything. Why can't they just believe her right away?

Although Wendy's parents were clearly worried about drugs, they are also afraid that some mistake in judgment or transient impulse might have permanent and damaging effects upon her development. In Glenbar, parents are not very worried about what the neighbors would think if their children's deviant activities became public knowledge. Instead, parents are afraid that involvement in drugs may be a sign of a potentially debilitating psychological problem. In a culture that gives priority to self-motivation and direction, authority is sensitive to anything that threatens to undermine a person's capacity to handle the complex cognitive and social skills that are requisite for making out in the larger world. In other words, Wendy's parents were not accusing her of doing evil things but rather were warning her against flirting with danger.

The Surveillance of the Park

Glenbar Park is the only public open space in the community. In the early seventies the long-haired youth congregating in the park symbolized the town's drug problem. The park attained this notoriety because drug transactions were rumored to occur there. The result of increasing public concern was that the Park District formally closed the park at dusk, and the police enforced this rule. This is how Officer Neff saw the situation:

Neff feels that every group that plans activities or works with the kids around here has to be very vigilant about the activity not becoming a place for drug traffic and problems. What happens when things get out of hand is illustrated by the case of "our little park." All these guys used to hang around there, and even with a loitering ordinance, the police would say to them, "Don't tear down the place and we'll leave you alone." But they started tearing down the bleachers and leaving six-packs everywhere, so it was the Park District, and not the police, that ordered the park closed at dusk. Just six or seven people ruined it for everyone. It was mostly younger kids that hung around there, and Neff thought that was a good place for them because they had no other place to go.

Officer Neff's response to the problems of the park illustrates the way in which adult authority deals with youthful deviance in Glenbar. The reaction is almost always nonpunitive. Adult authority communicates the idea that it is not what one does but how one does it that makes a difference.

Adults do not ignore youthful deviance or feel incapable of dealing with it. Rather, authority counsels moderation on everyone's part. This echoes the sentiments of youth ministers who commented on the drug situation in the park. Their attitude was that flagrantly deviant activity could not be overlooked but that authority ought not jump to the conclusion that young people who did such things were beyond social redemption. Instead, a gentle reminder that such behavior violates the tacit agreement not to intrude into the private affairs of young people if they show some respect for adults sensibilities is all that is needed to control the situation.

Coolness and the Coffeehouse

The coffeehouse of the Glenbar Community Church acted as a meeting place. There was a split between the "staff" and the "patrons" of the coffeehouse regarding its purpose. The church staff saw the coffeehouse as a focus for activities related to personal and spiritual growth. Most of the young people saw it as a place to hang out with their friends. Involvement in organized "activities" (banner making, poetry readings, organized discussions) was usually low. The youth staff mediated between the religious commitment of the professional church staff and the secular orientation of the majority of their clientele. Comments made at the youth staff's meeting on how to improve the coffeehouse shows how young people felt about being there:

Betty asked the rest of the group, "What is the reason for the coffee house?" "There's nothing to do on Saturday night"; "It's fun. It's a place to talk"; "It keeps people from roaming the streets at night" [laughter]; "It's more comfortable than a dance"; "You can have some good raps if you try"; "You can perform and meet people"; "It's good, clean fun" [laughter]; "You meet new people"; "It's a place to meet old friends, to get in touch with them again"; "It's a melting pot of talent and stuff. There's a real need for it here in this community—it's almost dead without it."

The laughter that punctuates certain comments reveals their ambivalence toward the community's perception of the coffeehouse: it is good, clean fun and it keeps them off the street. They know these are the things that are important to adults and allow them the leeway to run this coffeehouse. But many of the things that went on at the coffeehouse were not the sort of things that most parents would have termed "good, clean fun." The fieldworker comments:

I sat down with Kerry who told me she was coming down from some drugs and she really needed some speed. She was waiting here for some guy who told her he would bring some "crystal"; she said she really wanted that. Kerry told me this rambling, confused story having to do with a wild car ride out of state, crashing at somebody's house and getting picked up by the cops for disorderly conduct. I couldn't make sense out of it, her thoughts were disconnected and she looked ready to pass out. She used to deal in drugs at the high school but doesn't do that anymore because the small stuff that is transacted there is not worth the danger from the narcs. She said she doesn't sell around here, except that some of her sister's friends were begging her to get them some mescaline and so she did that for them, but that was all.

Kerry's contravention of the explicit norm of the coffeehouse against drug transactions was not experienced as a violation of trust by the young people who ran it. Many of these young people had some involvement with drugs, and the former youth manager was removed for dealing drugs on the premises. What offends these young people is when people do not handle their deviant activities in a "cool" way. This means more than doing something in a sophisticated manner: being covert enough to hide the activity from authority yet being smooth enough to impress peers that one knows how to handle oneself under pressure. Being cool is an analogue to the way adult authority treats youthful deviance. Authority does not lose control over a situation regardless of how much anxiety that situation creates in the adult community. Authority approaches youth in a manner that does not betray the emotions that might upset its capacity to examine the situation at hand in a dispassionate and rational fashion. The message adult authority seeks to communicate is that we care what happens to young people but we will not get upset by provocative or irrational behavior because that would reduce the efficacy of our intervention into the problem. In a similar situation manner, "coolness" in the youth community means being aware of all possibilities in a situation for creating trouble and thinking ahead so that one can extricate oneself gracefully from any potentially embarrassing situation. Coolness means that one appreciates the difference between creating a public image and one's private behavior with friends one trusts.

In the coffeehouse, there was considerable concern with coolness on the part of the youth staff because they knew that the youth ministers had sold the idea of the coffeehouse to a conservative and fearful congregation on the basis of the propriety of what was going on there. Any public scandal would not only compromise their alliance with the youth ministers and undermine the viability of the coffeehouse. It would also expose them as socially inept persons who are unable to keep up the appearances that give young people considerable freedom from adult control. Coolness, then, is a central value in the youth culture because it stresses the kind of social competence, self-control, and impression management that avoids painful confrontations with authority and the loss of privileges that make life pleasurable.

The youth minister explained how the staff of the coffeehouse dealt with the coffeehouse's image in the community:

> Tom says there has been no trouble with the police, even though a similar coffeehouse in the next town was busted by the cops. To prevent this, Tom had met with Glenbar officials, explained the program to them, and then discussed it with the kids. It was made clear that there was to be "no heavy traffic, this is a natural high." There have been two cases of kids being high on something and being asked to leave. They knew they couldn't come back if it happened again. One has left, the other has since been back regularly with no further trouble. Tom says as far as an occasional kid "popping a pill," nothing can be done about that, but the kids have been really good at self-policing.

Despite the overall success of the coffeehouse in keeping up a good front as far as drugs were concerned, the youth minister was uneasy about what he saw as the desire in the community to back away from unpleasant problems. In the following remarks, his criticism is aimed at the adult community. But it applies equally to the youth. Coolness is not peculiar to the adolescent culture. It is a pervasive value in Glenbar where the norm is that it is everyone's responsibility to make certain that they are not put in a vulnerable position in a public situation. This norm makes it nearly impossible to create a collective commitment to openly discuss troubling issues and to take common action in resolving them. One of the consequences of an ethic of coolness is that a person does not get personally involved in matters that do not touch his or her private life.

> People here aren't attacking problems, they just want to prevent things. They want to make it into a law and order place, no dope, no drugs. They won't talk about things. We had this first retreat to see if we could get the coffeehouse together, with the staff and members of the congregation, and there were certain things that they wouldn't talk about. Even Tony who is a professor at the university tried to ignore these things. You can't have a coffeehouse and pretend that things that are relevant to many people's lives aren't there.

What people in Glenbar want to pretend is that private problems are not public issues. There is a tacit agreement that each family will take care of its own children. Adults do not hold each other responsible for the well-being of the younger generation. This is something of an overstatement since this community does not recognize generational issues as such. It sees individuals who may need professional assistance with problems of one sort or another. It sees families that appear to have more than their share of troubles with adolescent children. And it sees institutions such as the school and church that are supposed to offer guidance and direction to youth. But it would be unimaginable for an adult in Glenbar to get up in a public gathering, like the one we described in Ribley, and say that these are *our* children and *we* are not going to let anything bad happen to them.

Adults in Glenbar are not less compassionate than in Ribley. Rather the ethos of Glenbar incorporates the individualism of the larger society in almost pristine form. It would be viewed as intolerable interference in the privacy of another family to take an active interest in the moral and emotional welfare of their children. So, when adolescents occasionally suffer from severe problems, the most many parents can do is say to themselves, "I'm glad it wasn't my child."

The inculcation of the ethic of "coolness" is shown in this meeting of the youth staff with Ray, a seminary intern working for the church:

> Ray told the group that the youth program is in transition and this leads to potential problems. Historically, the youth department has been under criticism, and the congregation brings up a lot of questions not only about the coffeehouse but about all the youth programs. Ray said, "I can justify things I know about, but other things, like there have been complaints about finding cigarette butts in the church sanctuary, and we have to be careful about this." Ray continued, "What I mean is that I don't feel comfortable because I don't know all that is going on. Any one person could blow the whole thing by not being cool. So the more people I know, the less uptight I am. For example, the thing about 'no heavy traffic' is necessary. Coffeehouses in Newton and other places have been closed down. The congregation feels all right that there's no heavy drug scene. But one freak-out could blow the whole thing. We must be cool and responsible for one another."

The conflict between responsibility and coolness is nicely illustrated by this young man's remarks. In the culture of Glenbar, responsibility does not extend beyond family and personal friends. Community, as the public order, is merely a facility, an instrumentality that has no intrinsic value. Consequently, one cannot ask young people to be responsible for something that goes beyond their personal concerns and private friendships. To say, in effect, that a young person ought to be responsible and cool means, in this culture, that a young person ought to exercise judgment and restraint in public. It does not mean that a young person ought to do something for the common good or that he or she ought to sacrifice something for the welfare of others. In this privatized and individualized world, responsibility means little more than the kind of prudence that keeps youthful deviance from injuring a young person's chances to move up the ladder to success. This is nicely illustrated by the youth officer's talk to the members of the coffee house.

> Neff talked a bit about specific drugs that were going around the community and then said that the legal responsibility of the coffeehouse is very limited. It is not responsible for the actions of the people in it, and so if a person gets nailed the doors of the

coffeehouse are not going to get locked. Neff said there are drugs there, but that isn't the coffeehouse's fault—wherever you get a group of people together there is going to be drugs present, like the high school. But the staff of the coffeehouse, in order to cover itself, should know what the stuff looks like so that you can get it out of the place, or so you can call us"—and then Neff laughed, "as if that would ever happen."

Ray broke in and said, but it still affects attitudes and community pressure. Sure, Neff said, parents are always asking him about the coffeehouse and he tells them it is safe there. He tells them there are some drugs there, but they are also at the high school and probably in your bedroom, and you can't expect the courts, police, school, and churches to raise your kids for you. Drug charges are an emotional thing for parents, Neff said, and they ask, "Where did we go wrong?" But not all parents are goofy—they're just more so with drugs than anything else. And this feeling could transfer to the coffeehouse, it would be an escape for them, they could vent all their anxiety for drugs on the coffeehouse. So watch out because you are in a fishbowl, and people are just waiting for something to happen. The police won't hassle you. Just cover yourself and then the enemies can yak all they want but can't do anything. I'll never close it down.

In this talk, Officer Neff referred to Glenbar as the "golden ghetto." This description captures the irony of the youth situation. Authority is dedicated to making certain that youthful deviance does not have harmful long-term consequences. Yet, at the same time, authority recognizes that this creates an unreal atmosphere when a young person's deviances are treated as little more than mistaken judgment, a sign of social immaturity. What is not said is that adult authority asks almost nothing from youth with respect to their ability to state the moral grounds for their own conduct. With all of this emphasis on the autonomy of youth, authority, in the final analysis, supports a public culture that merely approves of circumspection with respect to conventional norms.

Conclusion

In the early 1970s, youth in Glenbar were neither rebels nor conformists. They were aware of their privileged situation but were also conscious of the peculiar burdens that arise from feeling that they ought to replicate the socioeconomic circumstances into which they were born. Unlike the upper class whose station in society and property guarantees their children a similar position in life, these young people knew quite well that they had to translate a college education into a well-paying career or they would not be able to give their families the same advantages they had as children. It is a strange feeling to know that other people would give a lot to be where one is and, at the same time, wonder whether what one will have to give of oneself to retain that place in society is really worth the effort and sacrifice.

This contradiction between the expressive integrity of the self and the practical value of academic excellence was not resolved by the local youth culture. Rather than face the uncertainties and tensions of what appeared to be incommensurable modes of being, supreme value was given to intimacy and friendship. This sort of withdrawal to an emotionally safe place directed their attention away from the culture that stated this choice in an either/or form.

In other words, these youth were too quick to give to Caesar what is Caesar's. They were not ready to question whether adult authority had gotten the equation between work, career, and performance wrong. After all, only a few years earlier youth openly doubted that the performance standards of established economic and educational institutions were the only valid measures of a well-ordered and rational life. The idea at that time was that there were legitimate forms of human association that recognized forms of individual achievement grounded in cooperative and noncompetitive forms of sociability.

In one respect, then, these youth were very much like their parents. Neither seemed receptive to values that transcended the individualistic belief in the ultimate reality of each person's interests and needs. Like their parents, these youth went about constructing a personal world that satisfied their emotional desire for closeness and understanding but left the larger social and cultural worlds in which they lived the better part of their lives untouched.

This sort of nonideological resistance to any sort of idealism is probably due to the fact that Glenbar is a community that does not have much in the way of communal relationships. As we have seen, there is little in the way of contact between youth and adults that could embody the moral principles and social values that would sustain a local cultural tradition. In fact, the local culture of Glenbar is perhaps best described as individualism writ large where everyone accepts the idea that each person or family is responsible for its own social fate. And, of course, as long as youth accept that proposition, they will see no workable alternative than to adapt to increasingly impersonal and rigorous standards of adequate performance.

8

Conclusion

Comparisons between communities have illuminated aspects of their cultures that might have gone unnoticed. Yet ethnography creates the impression that each community is a singular individual that exists more or less on its own terms. The reader, however, may wonder whether this material can tell us anything that puts the problem of authority in a broader perspective.

This is not an innocent question. Can one find a common denominator in culturally variable circumstances when the differences between these situations are inextricably interwoven into their commonalities? We have seen that there is a dialectical relationship between youthful identities and styles and the ways in which local traditions assimilate and transform elements of the common culture. The particular and universal meaning of these phenomena seem to be indissolubly wedded together. Breaking them apart analytically would render them lifeless.

Although it is a discipline that is constrained by its concern with historically constituted events, ethnography is not tightly bound to concrete universals. It can extract more general implications from its research by extending the reach of its conceptual framework.

There is an inverse relationship between the cosmopolitanism of a community and its receptivity to the moral substance of intergenerational relations. At first glance, this may strike the reader as counterintuitive. Cosmopolitan youth are known for arguing the ethical merits of their positions on the social issues of the day. It will take further explication of the notion of authority to show that references to ethical issues in one's social discourse is a different matter than the sense that one's identity is intimately connected to the way in which one regards the moral judgment of one's elders.

There are two facts about cosmopolitan youth that we ought not forget in this context. The reader can refer to the chapter on Glenbar if he needs to refresh his memory on these points. Cosmopolitan youth and their elders have trouble feeling that their commitment to common values sustains communal relations between them. Remember, by the way, that authority relations were defined primarily in terms of contacts between youth and nonfamilial adults. Cosmopolitan youth and their elders also have difficulty thinking of communal relations as the medium that enables them to share perceptions of what it means to become the kind of person they mutually admire.

What makes authority figures appear virtuous in the eyes of youth is the perception that their social character exemplifies a "cultural and moral ideal" (MacIntyre 1981:28). They are someone a youth "looks up to" because they have the experience and resolve to make certain that the right things are done for the right reasons. When authority figures are questioned about their decisions or commands, they are able to communicate the feeling that what they want a young person to do is something that will ultimately enhance that person's sense of dignity or integrity, even though it may at the moment seem silly, distasteful, or onerous. In short, their judgment can trusted.

Authority is a communal phenomenon which becomes distorted when it is detached from the kinds of social relations that give it its proper significance. Authority involves personal knowledge of the other party, and, at some point, face-to-face contact between authority figures and youth who are subject to their decisions.

The idea of the communal should not be restricted to the physical places where young people live with their families. Any institution in which young people and adults relate to each other in terms of their commitment to common goals can be thought of as a community. Of course, this commitment must have a material bearing upon the social fate of a young person. There are probably many transitional cases such as membership in athletic clubs and the like. Colleges are communities in terms of this definition.

Consensus over the rules that facilitate the realization of shared ends does not create the communal aspect of authority. Communal relations cannot be legislated or simulated. They can evolve only in a milieu that enables youth and adults to interact with each other on a regular basis. The task or activity that brings them together must allow them to see each other's peculiarities, weaknesses, and strengths. The process by which authority figures organize routine activities reveals as much about their characters as their decisions about how to handle difficulties. The manner in which they applaud or rebuke youth for their behavior is as important as the fairness with which they reward accomplishment or dedication to the common objective.

There is a symmetrical quality to authority relationships that is overlooked by those who emphasize the differential power of command. The evaluative terms in which a person is judged by authority are the same as those by which the character of authority is judged by those subject to it. Authority asks whether a young person's behavior is clever or devious, foolhardy or courageous, impudent or respectful, and so on. Of course, the person whose conduct is scrutinized this way characterizes the decision of the judge with a similar moral vocabulary. There is a very real sense in which both parties have the symbolic power to confirm or disconfirm the other's sense of the appropriateness of their judgment. Adult authority figures often become angry about aspersions cast upon their judgment when they tolerate behavior that defies their edicts.

Thus, the expressive meanings of authority take priority over its instrumental functions. For this reason, young people cannot listen to the judgments of authority as if they were objective determinations of advisability or permissibility of certain courses of action. Instead, they sense that what they are being told about how they should act also communicates how the community sees them as moral agents. That is why youth sometimes become more aggravated when they are told that what they are doing is infantile or impulsive rather than wrong or immoral. Since authority is sensitive to whether young people feel that its judgments are fair, it cannot look at youth's response to its decisions solely in terms of compliance or resistance. It matters to authority that youth take what it has to say seriously, even if young people make the same "mistake" again.

Authority becomes noncommunal when it becomes impersonal. It is impersonal when it believes that its character as a moral agent is irrelevant to assessments of its competence. As long as its judgments are consistent with formal rules of procedures and written statutes, impersonal authority can remain aloof from moral issues. Exercised in this manner, authority is a legitimate expression of the power of the state.

We should add, however, that because impersonal authority does not thrive in communal settings, it is not, for that reason, devoid of ethical content. Impersonal authority may rely upon ideas of distributive justice that apply to entire categories of persons and groups. Its decisions are often seen as even-handed because it shows no respect for the persons to whom its decisions apply. What impersonal authority lacks is the ability to transform the moral status of those subject to its decisions by recognizing them as persons worthy of respect by those who share their ideals and values.

In sum, youth and adults can assess each other's conduct in terms of its moral significance when they participate in a cultural tradition that is invigorated by a vision of what makes some people worthy of praise and others of condemnation. MacIntyre (1981:119) sees the connection between moral judgment and communal authority when he describes the idea of virtue in ancient Greece:

> . . . first of all morality is always to some degree tied to the socially local and particular and that the aspirations of the morality of modernity to a universality freed from all particularity is an illusion; and secondly that there is no way to possess the virtues except as part of a tradition in which we inherit them and our understanding of them from a series of predecessors in which series heroic societies hold first place.

This enriched concept of authority will show why cosmopolitan youth are less receptive to communal forms of authority than their provincial counterparts. First we must define cosmopolitanism and provincialism a little more precisely. In brief, cosmopolitanism will stand for being located near the center of mainstream cultural values and provincialism at the periphery of those values.

In our study of Glenbar, we saw that the community's attachment to the symbols of hierarchy, performance, and individualism replicated the values of the larger society.[1] It is as if these values are reflected directly in its culture without being distorted or diluted by other local concerns or traditions. All that cosmopolitan means in this context is that young people incorporate pristine representations of these values into their perceptions of adult authority.

---

1. Hierarchy, in this context, does not refer to a fixed order of social ranks or to a rigid social structure grounded in invidious distinctions and inherited privileges. Rather, it refers to a pervasive cultural tendency to transform perceptions of relative difference into dichotomous qualitative judgments. Paradoxically, hierarchy, in this sense, follows from an ethos of egalitarianism that allows one to make judgments about the personal worth of others only if that judgment focuses solely on the properties of a highly objectified performance and relies completely on universalistic criteria. Instead of looking at looking at the abilities of others in ways that take account of context and allow for change, hierarchy disposes one to think in terms of categorical oppositions that implicitly deny the historical or developmental aspect of all human action and endeavor. For example, heirarchy leads Americans who subscribe to the current ethos of egalitarianism to judge their peers in such terms as "winners and losers," "successes and failures," "competents and incompetents," etc.

Provincialism, then, refers to the presence of local traditions that do not allow the values of hierarchy, performance, and individualism to define relations between youth and authority unilaterally. Nowhere in American society is there a community that does not incorporate these values in some fashion. But there is an important difference between a literal adherence to the letter of the law and a free interpretation of its spirit. Glenbar follows the letter of the law, Ribley prefers to capture its spirit.

Thus, Ribley is our most provincial community because the policies of its youth-serving institutions are less responsive to these values, although authority figures certainly recognize their validity. Self-conscious about its marginality vis-à-vis the larger culture, Ribley gives itself an exemption from the full force of the demand for increasingly rigorous standards of performance and individual competition. When authority figures in Ribley make judgments about young people they invoke local considerations that soften, bracket or, simply forget the bearing these values have on the way adults evaluate young people.

We can take another look at authority in light of a community's centrality or marginality vis-à-vis the values of the mainstream society. While these communities cannot be ranked ordered on a unidimensional scale, I will discuss them in view of where they fit with respect to the polar ends of the continuum.

Glenbar comes as close as one can imagine to a situation where there is amity between youth and authority without a feeling of intergenerational solidarity. There is no evidence of an emotionally compelling generational dialogue about what makes a person worthy of respect. But this does not mean that the youth of Glenbar distrust adult representatives of authority. Rather, as we have seen, Glenbar lacks an image of what makes a nonfamilial adult someone who deserves the admiration of young people. Glenbar has moved as close as a human community can to looking at the world without a consistent conception of human virtues and vices.

Young people who peer into this void are distressed by how little they see that is humanly recognizable. Their parents tell them that the world is a place where glittering prizes are to be found. It is the stage upon which one's most profound sense of who one is as a person is given concrete form. Young people try to visualize this realm of self-fulfillment and social distinction. But all they experience is the competitive pressure to reach higher levels of academic excellence. No wonder they turn with relief to the comforts of friendship and intimacy and retreat to a private sphere. There they assure themselves that many of the human qualities that otherwise flow from authority—its capacity for support, guidance, and nurturance—can still be found in relations with their peers.

I would nominate Patusa as my candidate for the community that comes the closest to Glenbar even though one does not normally think of rural towns as cosmopolitan. Patusa has made a systematic attempt to incorporate the values of hierarchy, performance, and individualism into the policies of its youth-serving institutions although it is quite a distance from Glenbar in our hypothetical model of cultural centrality and marginality. The town's dedication to stability and to mainstream values has created a split in its culture. It is pulled between the small-town ethos of goodfellowship and a diffuse desire to be the "best" small-town high school in terms of student deportment and performance in athletic and similar public events. It wants simultaneously to be safe and secure and not give up aspirations to live according to the individualistic ethos of the mainstream culture.

As far as local traditions are concerned, this gives the youth of Patusa very little to hold onto outside of the fact that in a small town adults recognize youth on a personal basis as a matter of course. Thus, it is impossible not to get some feeling for the qualities that make a person worthy of respect, even though that perception is rather washed-out in Patusa. Yet, in the final analysis, the authority of the older generation is best characterized by an empty series of "thou shalt nots." These prohibitions preempt much of the positive content of relations between the generations that would simply emerge over the course of time in this sort of community.

Youth in Cambridge have serious reservations about the worthiness of authority figures. But they draw upon viable traditions of working-class life for clear images of how a person establishes his dignity in the eyes of others and maintains his self-respect. Local traditions are so clearly oriented to compelling images of the desirable qualities associated with sex roles that these youth have little trouble substituting their ideas about what makes a man or woman worthy of respect for the performance values of the larger society. Moreover, local authority figures do not react punitively to youthful demonstrations of excessive individualism. Despite the struggles over hierarchy and performance between the generations, there is considerable underlying solidarity and mutual understanding about the meaning of personal independence and moral autonomy.

As we move into Parsons Park we pass the imaginary line into the provincial sector of our cultural space. Ethnicity and conservative Roman Catholicism moderate the influence of the core values of American culture on the lives of the youth of Parsons Park, though some of the more mobility-oriented youth experience some of the unease that goes with moving into this territory. Yet youth respect authority figures because there is a strong communal image of what makes them virtuous, even though there is a spirited debate between the generations over the proper limits of their authority.

32d Street seems like an anomolous case, but we should remember that the strength of the bond between the generations will gain new meaning as the older generation acquires political power in the wider society. As they become a stable and more prosperous ethnic community, it is possible that 32d Street will be somewhat like Parsons Park, although the issues of personal honor are likely to be more explosive in this community than elsewhere.

I do not think we need to say anything more about Ribley except that it is ironic that the most provincial community is the one in which the relations between the generations are least affected by hierarchy, performance, and individualism. It is the one place where it is possible for an adult to feel confident that the judicious use of his powers will make a positive difference in the lives of those young people who are subject to them. Moreover, it is the one place where an authority figure can experience the full meaning of respect between the generations.

As a final note, we might ask, Does anything we have learned about high school youth help us understand their older contemporaries? I think it is fair to say that the recurrence of demonstrations on the college campuses most closely identified with cosmopolitan youth says something about how they experience authority. In no other institution in American society are youth more prepared to respect their elders and better equipped to measure their stature as moral actors. By confronting their elders with the ostensible contradiction between their ideals and policies, college youth seem to be saying that there is something missing from the way in which they relate to authority.

To put this more concretely, the younger generation is sending a message to its elders about their moral authority. They are saying that the very fact that we hold these demonstrations on the grounds of our community, which is dedicated to the idea of truth and justice, shows that we are not unaware of the self-interest and opportunism that is part of institutional life. And they are sensitive to these moral issues because they are moved by the same impulse to do what is best for oneself. A well-known social scientist was reputed to have said that these students are demonstrating because they feel guilty about all the money they will make after graduation. The students could have replied, "That's true, but it is our inability to transcend that feeling that makes us raise the issue with those who ought to know how to face it with courage and dignity." In other words, students are asking why honorable people overlook much that they personally abhor unless they feel that as authority figures they must make accommodations to the values of hierarchy, performance, and individualism. And since it is precisely those values that so powerfully shape the sensibilites of cosmopolitan youth, they bring this moral dilemma to their elders.

How does one have the courage of one's convictions in a world where tact, compromise, and an ability to get around tough ethical conflicts goes along with success? The students want to know whether they can have their ethical cake and the material rewards that go along with less than noble behavior. It would be presumptuous to answer that question because that is the proper topic for a dialogue between cosmopolitan youth and authority.

Appendix

In view of the increasing methodological self-consciousness of hermeneutic approaches in social science (see Bleicher 1980; Bauman 1978), it seems a little naive to present ethnography as just one of a number of data-gathering techniques. The personal, some would say subjective, element of ethnography raises disquieting questions in the minds of those who think of social science as a method. In their minds, science is defined by measurement, replication, and prediction. Cognitive control over the process of inference and proof is equivalent to the manipulation of theoretically constructed variables on precisely delimited empirical phenomenon which are thought of as iconic representations of social reality. Intersubjective verification protects against ideological distortion and individual prejudice. Science, as method, provides a moment of epistemological transcendence: it elevates the knower above the contingencies of time and place. Human behavior loses its privileged status and becomes part of the natural universe.

It would be a Promethean task to make ethnography conform to this image of science. Interpretations of the meaning of humanly observed situations rely upon the distinction between the intentionality of symbolic life and the mute regularities of natural events. While social science explores the relationship between nature and culture, the historical character of the latter obeys, in large measure, laws mankind imposes upon its experience. The normative cannot be reduced to the material substrata of social existence although much of what we regard as irrational arises, as Ricoeur (1970) says, at the juncture of force (i.e., the biological) and meaning. Yet thought and feeling, action and passion—all of those qualities that identify human agency—are mediated by the symbolic, and, as such, history and culture are inextricably wedded to what people say about themselves. What is ultimately foreign to or cannot be retrieved by consciousness and language lies beyond the boundaries of ethnography.

Ethnography, then, is located in the midst of this on-going conversation about the events, relationships, and experiences that make us social beings. Unlike the democratic ethos of science that any unbiased person will describe the same events in the same way if he accepts the appropriate methodological controls on his observational activities, ethnography substitutes an aristocratic ethic that what the observer sees is dependent upon his powers of moral perception and aesthetic discrimination. An ethnographer who is aware of how he uses his moral imagination to put himself in situations that his own ethical commitments would not otherwise tolerate must have grave doubts that what he does falls under the heading of "value-free" science. It is not that he freely gives in to his personal prejudices. Rather he draws upon his own sense of what is right, proper, or appropriate in order to sensitize himself to the fact that other rational persons do not experience or interpret the world as he does. That he can "identify" with the people he studies without putting aside his own feelings and beliefs about those things that matter to him only proves that most people (outside of methodological discussions in the social sciences) regard the separation between the "ought" and the "is" as a fiction. It is not that the ethnographer merges or confuses the normative and existential aspects of life. Instead, he asks himself how the tensions and contradictions between his values, intentions, and actions can help him understand the connections between what other people say about themselves and how they live their lives.

The ethnographer must, in this sense, become part of the phenomenon he seeks to understand. The theoretical apparatus of social science helps him to avoid being absorbed by the taken-for-granted categories of the social world he is studying. Doing ethnography, then, is a species of self-reflection, a mode of self-consciousness which follows the canons of public scrutiny—of putting one's evidence on the table. The strength and the limitation of ethnography is the ability to make the "otherness" of social experience the basis for understanding its meaning.

This abbreviated justification of ethnography as a mode of self-reflection and social observation does not eliminate the practical realities of fieldwork. Not all ethnographers are equally successful, and some fail outright. This study originally involved eleven communities and twelve ethnographers (two were assigned to a middle-sized industrial city). For reasons of economy, some sites were excluded from this book. Others were either marginally successful or failures. Though we did not keep a diary of the problems we encountered during the period when the actual fieldwork was in the process, it may be worthwhile to look at some of the problems that are involved in this sort of undertaking.

Since we did not keep a record of all the problems we encountered during the period when we sent people out into the field to gather data, our reconstruction of what happened is likely to be faulty with respect to some of the details. We seriously underestimated the logistical problems of locating fieldworkers in different communities in a large state and adequately supervising their work. Even with a division of labor, this task always seemed unmanageable. There is no substitute for constant consultation on a project where one hopes to get wide penetration into the youth world and roughly comparable data on each community.

People were selected as fieldworkers for different reasons. We chose persons who were working on graduate degrees in sociology and anthropology (all three of these fieldworkers received a Ph.D. on the basis of their work on the projects), or who had some professional training (one young woman was working on a Master's degree in community studies, and one young man had a good background in social psychology). We chose others on the basis of their general life experience, or on the basis of recommendations of other researchers, or on what we thought was a good match between personal characteristics and the demands of a particular field site.

Two of the sites failed outright. Both of the fieldworkers were young men in their early twenties and were personable. One of these young men came with high recommendations from a community organizer with whom we had to negotiate to get access to this medium-size city. We had to hire this young man if we wanted to work in many of the neighborhoods of this city. But we felt that he would qualify for the job without this additional incentive. It is hard to say precisely what happened in this site though we visited him on numerous occasions. However, even a cursory glance at his fieldnotes showed that the data was fragmentary and that his contact with young people was, on the whole, superficial and sporadic. He could not find a vantage point either within the youth world or the community at large from which he could systematically pursue the sort of information we were after.

Fieldworkers almost uniformly reported some anxieties about making contact with youth during the initial phases of the fieldwork. No one likes to feel ignored or distrusted by people with whom one hopes to develop a long-term relationship. Some fieldworkers, such as the young man in the middle-size city, could not tolerate this period of uncertainty. Anxious about "when it was going to happen," he dashed around the community bringing back interesting and provocative tidbits of information but never quite following any situation, event, or relationship far enough for us to grasp the outlines of the youth world.

We had lengthy training sessions in which fieldworkers discussed their problems (the major theme was guilt over being a voyeur in the sense of becoming close to young people without taking any responsibility for what they do with their lives) and went over a detailed field guide (which is too lengthy to reproduce here). This document describes in detail the categories of information each fieldworker should get and suggests some of the questions to ask to get it. What we seriously underestimated was the difficulty some people had in conceptualizing a system of social relationships.

In the field sites that failed, the fieldworkers seemed to struggle with the problem of seeing beyond each incident or personality. Everything they saw and heard struck them as equally important, equally disconnected from their previous experiences, and equally suggestive or promising lines of inquiry. It seemed as if they were immersed in a world where everything happened simultaneously and where there were no guideposts for sorting things out. Providing the fieldworkers with our field guide did not compensate for their inability to conceptualize how the things they experienced in the field might form a more coherent picture of how life was organized in that community.

The fieldworker in one site (an industrialized town situated in an agricultural area) that failed could not distance himself from his own adolescence. He could not make contact with the "straight kids" in the community but found himself irresistibly drawn to the "freaks."

The young man in the middle-sized city felt disloyal to his previous sponsor who thought that our project was a way of continuing his protege's community organiztion activities by other means. Moreover, this fieldworker seems to have been trapped by his former role as a community organizer. He was comfortable and successful in that role. But, as a fieldworker, he lacked the direction that made his former role unproblematic for him. We now see that we overlooked what was, in fact, a major role transition because we assumed that the roles were congruent rather than divergent.

The other fieldworker had not settled his personal account with his own adolescence. He could not remove himself enough from the youth scene to avoid taking symbolic sides in the clash of youthful identities and styles. He was, unfortunately for us, part of the data.

Our experience in this instance increased our respect for the power of these youthful symbols to mobilize many of the feelings that comprise the core of a young person's self-image.

We had decided to study an inner-city Mexican-American neighborhood in a very large city and thought that it would be interesting to look at a black community in a middle-sized industrial city that retained many of the social forms and ideologies associated with small-town American life. There have been many fine studies of youth in the ghettos of large cities. In fact, it is not an exaggeration to say that many of the finest accounts of peer group processes in urban communities are contained in this rich and extensive literature on inner-city black youth. It would be a minor bibliographic enterprise just to list the first-rate studies, let alone to cover the entire literature. We decided that it would have been difficult to do substantially more than what already had been done. Instead, we thought we would look at a ghetto-like situation, but one where black youth grow up without all of the pressures, dangers, and excitement of big city street life.

We wondered what we would find if we placed a fieldworker in the white area and a fieldworker in the black neighborhood of the same, middle-sized industrial city. We chose a young man who had an undergraduate degree in sociology and had grown up in a black community. Unfortunately, while he was capable of penetrating the youth network of the black community and made many insightful observations, he was incapable of either writing his observations up or talking them into a tape recorder. During this period, he had many family problems and never really got into the fieldwork.

The data on white youth from this middle-sized city is not included in this report primarily because of the length of the present document. It is written up as a doctoral dissertation, however, and it is interesting as a case where religious groups and institutions play a major role in the organization of the youth world. Another site was a small town in a rural part of the state. It was less affluent than Ribley and provided the data for two Master's dissertations.

A site was located in a socially and economically diverse urban neighborhood. This community is known as a very culturally sophisticated area that has taken on a more affluent character with the return of the upper middle class to the central sections of this city. While the field data in an extremely complex and stratified area such as this cannot be as comprehensive as in a more homogeneous community, the material was more than adequate for a chapter in this book. I decided not to include it, however, largely for reasons of space and format. The logic of paired comparisons meant that either

Glenbar or this community would be an excellent match with 32d Street. I chose Glenbar (although many upper-middle-class families also live in this neighborhood) because it is a pure representation of core American values.

There are differences among fieldwork styles. In anthropology, it is not unusual for a student to go into the field to study one topic only to return with data relevant to an entirely different issue. When asked about the discrepancy between a research proposal and the research report, the student is likely to reply, "Well, I thought I would study land tenure and political factions, but when I got there I discovered that nobody was interested in that subject but that they were all involved in a new messianic cult." There was a considerable tension throughout the project between the research interests of fieldworkers and the desire to have comparable data from each site. The best we could do was to reach a reasonable compromise between the bent of a fieldworker to go off in a given direction and the need to keep the focus on youth groups and their relationships with local institutions. The only point on which there was no compromise was the agreement that each fieldworker would try to spread his contacts in the youth world as widely as possible. The sites reported in this volume were those that came closest to meeting that criterion.

The reader, however, will no doubt pick up differences in presentation of the empirical material in this book. This reflects differences in the relative emphasis fieldworkers gave to observations and interviews. Some fieldworkers rely almost entirely on observations whereas others find interviews more revealing, and some try to keep a balance between the two primary sources of information. On this score, we found that scolding, coaxing, and other attempts at persuasion could not change a fieldworker's basic mode of data collection.

There is some lore among ethnographers with respect to the "fit" between the personal characteristics of the field observer and the social characteristics of the field site. The common assumption is that the closer the match between the two, the easier it will be to enter the community. While this generally holds true, it is far from a firm rule. The young woman who worked in the Mexican-American community had almost no trouble making contact with some of the most violent gangs in the area. She simply went to the park where these youth hung out, sat down on a bench nearby, and announced that she was a graduate student who was studying the area when she was asked what she was doing there. Of course, everything was not smooth sailing from that point on. She had to walk a tenuous line between easy familiarity and professional reserve. If she moved too close to the former pole, it was an indication to some gang members that she was losing the aura of an exotic outsider and was just another girl. If she moved too close to the latter pole, she was suspected of having ulterior motives.

Since the "good kids" in the neighborhood avoided contact with the "bad kids" in the streets, the fieldworker had to make contact with these youth through the schools, agencies, and personal contacts in the community. Good kids spent much of their time in and around their homes, and consequently the fieldworker got to know some of their families extremely well. On the whole, the reverse was true even for some of the gang members with whom she became quite friendly.

As a general rule, the gaps in the information a fieldworker obtains are constrained by the features of the social system in which he or she moves. If there are barriers between peer group involvements and family relationships, and if the fieldworker elects to put primary emphasis on peer groups (as they were mandated to do for this study), then the fieldworker will get comparatively little data on the relations between parents and children. The fieldworker can try to talk to these youth about their relationships with their parents, but that strategy is dependent on the local culture. In Glenbar, the fieldworker spent little time observing parent/child interaction, but as much material as desired could be elicited on this topic. In an inner-city community, the details of a youth's relationships with his or her parents were not easily brought out in ordinary conversation.

Certain individuals in a community are attracted to the fieldworker. Among these are people who have the status, skill, or influence to smooth the fieldworker's movement into the youth world. If the fieldworker is fortunate, some of these people become informants—people who find the fieldworker's project interesting and who consequently spend much time discussing what is happening on the local scene. In light of the norm of reciprocity, the least the fieldworker can do is to return the favor. This means that the fieldworker spends more time with the groups to which the informants belong and gets to know more about them than other groups.

The critical stage after a fieldworker gains entry into the community occurs when one begins to feel locked into a particular group. It sometimes takes considerable pressure to get the fieldworker to make an overture to other youth groups. Once that happens, the fieldworker discovers that the social boundaries in their maps of the youth world are as real as the streets of the community where they live. In Ribley, the fieldworker was more or less adopted initially by some of the more affluent and sophisticated youth. When he made a serious gesture to get to know poor youth he was told, in effect, "We thought you weren't interested in talking to us when we saw you hanging around with those other kids."

A fieldworker cannot be in all places at all times and cannot get the same information about all the youth groups in the community. Uniform coverage is an ideal that is never fully achieved. As a rule, it is the developed identities and styles that capture the attention of the fieldworker.

Many people think that the personal characteristics of the field-worker should blend easily into the milieu. We did not find that was always true. The fieldworker who worked in Parsons Park was as unlikely a person to fit into this community as one could imagine. He was a young man in his thirties who had taught college, had been active in the civil rights movement, had been instrumental in organizing a militant Latino youth group, and had a long, flowing beard.

While his appearance precluded access to the right-wing groups who were stirring up racial antagonism at the time, that is the only segment of the community to which he did not have access. His exotic appearance made him something of a celebrity on the local youth scene. He also was a tolerant, gentle, sensitive, and perceptive person. These qualities bridged the gap between his personal background and the moral outlook of the community. Even if young people did not agree with the things they thought he stood for, they knew that he was genuinely interested in them and that he would not dismiss their feelings and opinions because he did not happen to share them.

A similar though not so extreme case was the person who worked in the working-class suburb of Cambridge. He had done some work for a professor at a local university and came highly recommended, although at the time he was in his late thirties or early forties. After some hesitation we decided, wisely in retrospect, that perhaps age was not a decisive factor in creating rapport with young people. Like our other fieldworker, he had a beard and his previous background and experience was vastly different from the community he studied. But like our other fieldworker, he genuinely liked young people and was very sympathetic to them. He remarked, ironically, that was because he had never decided to become a full-fledged adult. It was because he was a warm, mature, and insightful person but had not lost touch with how it feels to be young that he was so effective in a community where the first response of many young people is to avoid anyone who looks as if they represent adult authority.

As a general rule, fieldworkers who are seen by young people as a "half" generation above them make the most effective fieldworkers. By this we mean that the fieldworkers were seen as older people who had resolved many of the problems they were struggling with but who still understood how it felt to be in their position. Furthermore, such a person is seen as someone who has the social skills and emotional controls of an adult but who has no personal investment in the rules that adults impose on young people.

We will not discuss the multitude of problems that went with entry into each site. They are, by and large, the sort of pedestrian problems that every fieldworker faces, though we made our share of mistakes here too. We hope that these remarks serve as cautionary tales for researchers who may attempt a similar enterprise and as clues for making judgments about the kinds of persons who can function effectively as fieldworkers in the peer group world.

References

Arendt, Hannah. 1958. "What was Authority?" In *Authority*, edited by Carl Friedrich. Cambridge, Mass.: Harvard University Press.

Bauman, Zygmunt. 1978. *Hermeneutics and Social Sciences*. London: Hutchinson.

Becker, Howard. 1963. *Outsiders: Studies in the Sociology of Deviance*. New York: Free Press.

Benne, Kenneth. 1971. *A Conception of Authority*. New York: Russell and Russell.

Bennett, James. 1981. *Oral History and Delinquency*. Chicago: University of Chicago Press.

Berger, Bennett. 1963a. "Adolescence and Beyond." *Social Problems* 10 (Spring): 394–408.

_____. 1963b. "On the Youthfulness of Youth Cultures." *Social Research* 30 (Autumn): 319–342.

Bleicher, Josef. 1980. *Contemporary Hermeneutics*. London: Routledge and Kegan Paul.

Brake, Mike. 1980. *The Sociology of Youth Culture and Youth Subcultures*. London: Routledge and Kegan Paul.

Brown, Michael. 1969. "The Condemnation and Persecution of Hippies." *Trans-Action* 6 (September): 33–46.

Coleman, James. 1961. *The Adolescent Society*. New York: Free Press.

_____. 1971. *Youth: Transition to Adulthood*. Chicago: University of Chicago Press.

Collingwood, R. J. 1972. *Essay on Metaphysics*. Chicago: Henry Regnery.

Cusik, Philip. 1973. *Inside High School: The Student's World*. New York: Holt, Rinehart, and Winston.

Davis, Fred. 1971. *On Youth Subcultures: The Hippie Variant*. New York: General Learning Press.

Eckstein, Harry, and Gurr, Ted. 1975. *Patterns of Authority: A Structural Basis for Political Inquiry*. New York: Wiley.

Eisenstadt, S. N. 1956. *From Generation to Generation*. New York: Free Press.

Erikson, Kai. 1966. *Wayward Puritans*. New York: Wiley.

Flacks, Richard. 1970. "Social and Cultural Meanings of Student Revolt: Some Informal Comparative Observations." *Social Problems* 17 (Winter): 340–357.

Friedrich, Carl. 1958. "Authority, Reason and Discretion." In *Authority*, edited by Carl Friedrich. Cambridge, Mass.: Harvard University Press.

Gadamer, Hans-Georg. 1975. *Truth and Method*. New York: Continum Publishing Corp.

Gans, Herbert. 1969. "Culture and Class in the Study of Poverty." In *On Understanding Poverty*, edited by Daniel Moynihan. New York: Basic Books.

Gillis, John. 1974. *Youth and History*. New York: Academic Press.

Gove, Walter. 1975. *The Labelling of Deviance: Evaluating a Perspective*. New York: Sage.

Gusfield, Joseph. 1975. *Community: A Critical Response*. Oxford: Blackwell.

Hall, Stuart, and Jefferson, Tony. 1976. *Resistance through Rituals: Youth Subcultures in Post-War Britain*. London: Hutchison.

Hegel, G. W. F. 1975. *Philosophy of Right*. Translated by T. M. Knox. London: Oxford University Press.

Hirschi, Travis. 1975. "Labelling Theory and Juvenile Delinquency: An Assessment of the Evidence." In *The Labelling of Deviance*, edited by W. Gove. New York: Sage.

Hollingshead, A. B. 1949. *Elmtown's Youth*. New York: Wiley.

Horkheimer, Max. 1947. *Eclipse of Reason*. New York: Seabury Press.

———. 1972. "Authority and the Family." In *Critical Theory: Selected Essays*. New York: Seabury Press.

Horowitz, Ruth. 1983. *Honor and the American Dream*. New Brunswick, N.J.: Rutgers University Press.

Hunter, Albert. 1974. *Symbolic Communities*. Chicago: University of Chicago Press.

Janowitz, Morris. 1961. *The Community Press*. Chicago: University of Chicago Press.

Keiser, Lincoln. 1969. *The Vice Lords: Warriors of the Streets*. New York: Holt, Rinehart, and Winston.

Kett, Joseph. 1977. *Rites of Passage*. New York: Basic Books.

Kobrin, Solomon, et. al. 1967. "Criteria of Status among Street Groups." *Journal of Research in Crime and Delinquency* (January): 98–118.

König, Rene. 1968. *The Community*. London: Routledge and Kegan Paul.

Laquer, Walter. 1962. *Young Germany*. New York: Basic Books.

Larkin, Ralph. 1979. *Suburban Youth in Cultural Crisis*. New York: Oxford University Press.

Libarle, Marc, and Seligson, Tom. 1970. *The High School Revolutionaries*. New York: Vintage Books.

Lukes, Steven. 1978. "Power and Authority." In *A History of Sociological Analysis*, edited by Tom Bottmore and Robert Nisbet. New York: Basic Books.

Lynd, Helen. 1958. *On Shame and the Search for Identity*. New York: Harcourt Brace.

McCall, George, and Simmons, J. L. 1966. *Identities and Interactions*. New York: Free Press.

MacIntyre, Alasdair. 1981. *After Virtue*. South Bend: University of Notre Dame Press.

Mannheim, Karl. 1952. "The Problem of Generations." In *Essays on the Sociology of Knowledge*. New York: Oxford University Press.

Matza, David. 1961. "Subterranean Traditions of Youth." *Annals of the American Academy of Political and Social Science* 338 (November): 102–136.

———. 1964. *Delinquency and Drift*. New York: Wiley.

———. 1969. *Becoming Deviant*. Englewood Cliffs. N.J.: Prentice-Hall.

Miller, Walter. 1969. "The Elimination of the Lower Class as a National Policy." In *Understanding Poverty*, edited by Daniel Moynihan. New York: Basic Books.

———. 1971. "Subculture, Social Reform and the Culture of Poverty." *Human Organization* 30 (Summer): 111–125.

Musgrove, Frank. 1974. *Ecstasy and Holiness*. London: Methuen.

Parsons, Talcott. 1954. "Age and Sex in the Social Structure of the United States." In *Essays in Sociological Theory*. New York: Free Press.

———. 1961. "The Link between Character and Society." In *Culture and Social Character*, edited by Seymore Lipset. New York: Free Press.

———. 1963. "Youth in the Context of American Society." In *Youth: Change and Challenge*, edited by Erik Erikson. New York: Basic Books.

Parsons, Talcott, and Shils, Edward. 1951. *Toward a General Theory of Action*. New York: Harper.

Partridge, William. 1973. *The Hippie Ghetto*. New York: Holt, Rinehart, and Winston.

Pitts, Jesse. 1971. "The Counter Culture," *Dissent* (June): 216–229.

Rainwater, Lee. 1970. *Behind Ghetto Walls*. Chicago: Aldine.

Ricoeur, Paul. 1970. *Freud and Philosophy*. New Haven: Yale University Press.

Rivera, Ramon, and Short, James, Jr. 1967. "Significant Adults, Caretakers, and Structures of Opportunity: An Exploratory Study." *Journal of Research in Crime and Delinquency* 4:76–97.

Roszak, Theodore. 1968. *The Making of a Counter-Culture: Reflections on the Technocratic Society and its Youthful Opposition*. New York: Doubleday.

Scharr, John. 1970. "Legitimacy in the Modern State." In *Power and Community*, edited by Philip Green and Sandford Levinson. New York: Pantheon.

Schwartz, Gary. 1970. *Sect Ideologies and Social Status*. Chicago: University of Chicago Press.

———. 1972. *Youth Culture: An Anthropological Approach*. McCaleb Module Series. Reading, Mass.: Addison-Wesley.

————. 1981. "Badasses, Freaks, and Working-Class Culture: The Politics of Youth Work in a Suburban Community." In *Children and Their Organizations*, edited by Timothy Sieber and Andrew Gordon. Boston: G. K. Hall.

Schwartz, Gary, and Merten, Don. 1967. "The Language of Adolescence: An Anthropological Approach to the Youth Culture." *American Journal of Sociology* 72:453–468.

————. 1968. "Social Identity and Expressive Symbols: The Meaning of an Initiation Ritual." *American Anthropologist* 70:1117–1131.

————. 1980. *Love and Commitment*. Beverly Hills, Calif.: Sage.

Schwendinger, Herman, and Schwendinger, Julia. 1985. *Adolescent Subcultures and Delinquency*. New York: Prager.

Sennett, Richard. 1980. *Authority*. New York: Knopf.

Sennett, Richard, and Cobb, Jonathan. 1973. *The Hidden Injuries of Class*. New York: Vintage Books.

Short, James, Jr., and Strodtbeck, Fred. 1965. *Group Process and Gang Delinquency*. Chicago: University of Chicago Press.

Simon, Yves. 1980. *A General Theory of Authority*. South Bend: University of Notre Dame Press.

Spender, Stephen. 1969. *The Year of the Young Rebels*. New York: Vintage Books.

Starr, Jerold. 1985. "Cultural Politics in the 1960's." In *Cultural Politics: Radical Movements in Modern History*, edited by Jerold Starr. New York: Prager.

Stinchcombe, Arthur. 1964. *Rebellion in a High School*. Chicago: Quadrangle.

Suttles, Gerald. 1972. *The Social Construction of Communities*. Chicago: University of Chicago Press.

Toch, Hans. 1969. *Violent Men*. Chicago: Aldine.

Vidich, Arthur, and Bensman, Joseph. 1960. *Small Town in Mass Society*. New York: Doubleday.

Von Hoffman, Nicholas. 1968. *We Are the People Our Parents Warned Us Against*. New York: Fawcett Books.

Warren, Roland. 1972. *The Community in America*. Chicago: Rand McNally.

Weber, Max. 1978. *Economy and Society*, vol. 1, edited by Guenther Roth and Claus Wittich, chap. 3. Berkeley: University of California Press.

White, Hayden. 1973. *Metahistory: The Historical Imagination in the Nineteenth Century Europe*. Baltimore: Johns Hopkins University Press.

————. 1978. *Tropics of Discourse: Essays in Cultural Criticism*. Baltimore: Johns Hopkins University Press.

Yinger, Milton. 1960. "Contraculture and subculture." *American Sociological Review* 23 (October): 625–635.

Index